William George Lawes

Grammar and Vocabulary of Language Spoken by Motu Tribe

New Guinea

William George Lawes

Grammar and Vocabulary of Language Spoken by Motu Tribe
New Guinea

ISBN/EAN: 9783337085117

Printed in Europe, USA, Canada, Australia, Japan

Cover: Foto ©Paul-Georg Meister /pixelio.de

More available books at **www.hansebooks.com**

GRAMMAR AND VOCABULARY

OF

NGUAGE SPOKEN BY MOTU TRIBE
(NEW GUINEA),

BY

REV. W. G. LAWES, D.D., F.R.G.S.,

WITH INTRODUCTION BY THE REV. GEORGE PRATT.

THIRD AND ENLARGED EDITION.

SYDNEY: CHARLES POTTER, GOVERNMENT PRINTER, PHILLIP-STREET.

1896.

PREFACE TO FIRST EDITION.

THE following pages represent the first attempt to classify and reduce to a written form the grammar and vocabulary of the language spoken by the Motu tribe of New Guinea. As a first attempt it is necessarily imperfect, but I need make no apology for its publication. The first step towards accuracy and correctness is only taken when the result of observation and study is put into print.

The vocabulary in both parts would have been more full if I had been able, while in New Guinea, fully to prepare it for the Press. When I came to Sydney three months ago, I brought with me in MS. the material for the following pages, but had no intention of printing it. The ready promise of the Hon. A. Stuart, on behalf of the New South Wales Government Press, and the kindly offer of the Rev. G. Pratt to arrange the work and prepare it for the printer, induced me to give to the public that which would have been better for another year's research and preparation.

But for Mr. Pratt's experienced pen and unwearied patience the work would not have been half so good or complete as it is.

My knowledge of the language has been acquired during seven years' residence among the people who speak it.

My colleague, Mr. Chalmers, has contributed largely both to grammar and vocabulary, but must not be held responsible for anything I have published, as there has been no opportunity of submitting the work to him for revision before going to press.

In carrying out the provisions of the Protectorate, which has been proclaimed over part of New Guinea, it will be of the first importance that all who have to do with the natives in an official capacity should be able to speak to the people in their own language. This little work will, I hope, be of some use to those who may be located in the Port Moresby district. From the knowledge we have of the dialects spoken in the Hood Bay and South Cape districts, there is every reason to believe that the grammar of the language of the S.E. Coast, from Maiva to the East Cape, is practically the same, the only difference being in the vocabulary. The consonantal changes in the different dialects are remarkable; consonants of different classes taking the place of each other, as, for instance, *t* being exchanged for *l* or *r*.

In the Motu dialect the sibilant never occurs before an *a*, *o*, or *u*, but at South Cape we meet with the *s* before all vowels, and find the Samoan words—*isu*, nose, and *susu*, breast.

On my return I hope to be able to prepare something like a comparative grammar and specimen vocabulary of the different dialects spoken in the districts where we have mission stations established. I have to ask all using the following pages kindly to supply me with any additions or corrections they may discover, so that the next edition may be a much nearer approach to accuracy and completeness.

W. G. LAWES.

Sydney, 24*th March*, 1885.

PREFACE TO SECOND EDITION.

The present edition has been revised, corrected, and enlarged. A good many new words have been added, and a few pages of phrases likely to be of use to beginners or visitors.

The comparative vocabulary will be of interest to philologists. It comprises 400 words in seven dialects of the South-east Coast, and illustrates the difference which exists, as well as the changes which a word passes through by dropping or changing its consonants.

The New South Wales Government, through the Hon. J. Burns, have kindly consented to print the following pages, and so enabled me to share with others the results of my study and research.

W. G. LAWES.

Sydney, 15th February, 1888.

PREFACE TO THIRD EDITION.

This third edition of Motu grammar and vocabulary has been brought up to present knowledge of the language. More than a thousand words have been added to the vocabulary, and the grammar has been almost entirely rewritten.

In the comparative vocabulary, at the end, the Rev. A. Pearse has kindly revised the Keapara and Galoma lists of words, the Rev. C. W. Abel has done the same for the South Cape dialect, and the Rev. J. H. Holmes has corrected that of Toaripi.

I have again to express my thanks to the New South Wales Government, who, through the courtesy of the Honorable the Premier and Colonial Treasurer, G. H. Reid, Esq., have readily consented to print this new edition. New Guinea and all students of philology are under obligation to them.

W. G. LAWES.

Sydney, 16*th June*, 1896.

INTRODUCTION.

By Rev. G. PRATT.

In the grammar of the Motu dialect of New Guinea one peculiarity is in the use of letters so much alike as to be scarcely distinguishable, e.g., the letters b and p, *keboka* or *kepoka* ; d and t, *bāda* or *bāta* ; g and k, *gadara* or *kadara* ; r and l, *ara* and *ala*.

The pronunciation of t before e and i as ts is also a recent introduction to Niue or Savage Island. When we first went there we found the young people generally using it, whilst the old men, especially on public occasions, pronounced the t. In the same way, the Tahitians have changed b into p, the Sandwich Islanders have changed t into k, and the Samoans are endeavouring to do the same. As these islands had little or no communication with one another, how is it that these changes, as if by common consent, have been made?

The Motuan language seems to be a strange mixture of Papuan and Eastern Polynesian. The grammar is Papuan; the dictionary is Eastern Polynesian. The suffixed pronoun and the method of counting by two threes for six, and two fours for eight, is Papuan. Very peculiar is the declension of the noun by means of pronouns; also, the use of both the separate and the suffix pronoun with the noun, *Lau aegu*, my leg, mine.

Suffix pronoun.	Duke of York Island.
gu, I	g
mu, your	m
na, his	n

These are evidently Papuan roots, made to conform to Eastern Polynesian by adding a vowel to the termination.

Many of the words seem to have Papuan roots, but all take the form of Eastern Polynesian.

The formation of the noun by adding *na* to the verb is like the Samoan *ga*, used in the same way. The use of *a*, in relation to food, *adia* for edia, corresponds with the Samoan lau for lou.

INTRODUCTION.

Some of the numerals are Eastern Polynesian—*ta*, one; *rua*, two; *hitu*, seven. *Hui*, a hair used for ten, resembles the *fulu* hair or feather in Samoan, and seems to indicate the same use of a tally in counting. The singular pronouns, *lau, oi, ia*, are Eastern Polynesian (au, oe, ia). The plural are Papuan.

Having different words for counting different articles is, as far as I know, in use only in the East.

A Tahitian idiom is seen in the word *hanamoa* (lit., to make good), to praise. In Tahitian, haamaitai.

The dearth of particles, and the arrangement of words in a sentence, seem to make the sense obscure. "He Jerusalem journey made, he towns and villages passed through, he them taught went." That is a literal translation of Luke 13, 22.

In arranging and copying out the Dictionary, I was struck with the numerous divergencies from the Eastern Polynesian dialects, and with the very large number of words which have no counterpart there.

Though t is much used, it is often changed to d, as *daudu* for tautu. It is also prefixed to some words beginning with a vowel or h, as *diho* for ifo or hifo, *dae* for ae or hake. In the same way l is prefixed, as lahi for afi, and is often omitted in the beginning or middle of a word, as *tui* for tuli, *ima* for lima.

G being nasal in Eastern Polynesian, is omitted, as *tai* (to cry) for tagi, *taia* (an ear) for taliga, *lao* for lago (a fly). On the contrary g hard is inserted, as *tage* for tae.

M is substituted for g, as *matama* for amataga. Again it is prefixed, as in *miri* (gravel) for ili. N is omitted, as *maino* for manino. Having no f, p or h is substituted for it, as *pata* for fata.

Yet more strange is the alteration of vowels. A long is put for short a, as *māta* (the eye) for măta, *mānu* (a bird) for mănu. O is put for u, as *namo* (a mosquito) for namu, *ramu* (to chew) for lamu.

Some words change their meaning, as *lele* (to swim) means to fly in Eastern Polynesian. *Hanua* (a village) for fanua (land). *Tunua* (to burn Pottery) for tunu (to roast). *Sinavai* (a river) for a waterfall.

INTRODUCTION. xi

The following are from pure Eastern Polynesian roots :—

New Guinea.	Eastern Polynesian.	English.
adorahi	ahiahi	evening
gauaia	gau	to chew
gahu	asuasu	mist, fog
hetuturu	tutulu	to drip
hekalo	tālo	to beckon
huahua	fua	fruit
huru	sulu	torch
kanudi	anu	to spit
kaubebe	pepe	butterfly
kalo	alo	to paddle
sisina	sina	small piece
papapapa	papapapa	flat rock
tamana	tama	father
tupuna	tupuga	ancestors
laoevaeva	evaeva	to go about
laka	laka	step
mavamava	mavava	to yawn
motu	motu	to break
motumotu	motu	an island
mu	gu	dumb
noho	nofo	to sit
nohu	nofu	stinging fish
noinoi	faanoi	to beg
qalahu	ahu	smoke
raroa	vailaloa	flood
rua	rua	two
sinana	tinā	mother
taoatao	taotao	to press down
tari	foe talitali	steer oar
togo	togo	mangrove

The number of compound words and of doubled words is very observable. In the latter case they were not satisfied, as their Eastern brethren are, with doubling part of the word, but repeated the whole, as *hekisehekise*.

From the meanings of the words of the Dictionary many of the customs of the people may be learnt. We find there that, though naked savages, they are fond of adorning themselves with feather head-dresses and chaplets with strings of teeth, shell armlets, and a bone passed through the nose as a "nose-jewel." In addition to these, they paint their bodies, and also tattoo; this is done by making a black paint with burnt resin and water. With this they mark the design on the body of the young man who is to be operated on. Then the skin is punctured by an instrument dipped in the black paint and driven in by a tap with the mallet.

Besides the usual articles of food, consisting of taro, yams, bananas, sugarcane, and cocoanuts, they have sago, which they make into puddings with bananas. They cook their food by boiling in an earthenware pot ; or if an animal, they roast it on a spit. Banana leaves serve for plates. In times of scarcity they eat the stem of the banana.

Fish is grilled on a gridiron of sticks. They also cook with heated stones after the manner of the Eastern Polynesians. The Elema people cook sago in hard cakes, which they sell.

When going to fight they paint their faces red. Their weapons are a spear, bow and arrows, a stone-headed club, and the man-catcher. This last article consists of a loop at the end of a pole, which, being put over the head of the retreating foe on to his neck, held him back. It is armed with a sharp point, so as to pierce the back of the neck. A newly married man is exempt from war.

They make earthenware pots and other vessels for domestic use. In order to shape them, in one hand they hold a stone and insert it inside of the vessel, while with the other hand they fashion the outside with a small piece of flat wood. Their pottery has an ornamental marking on the edge of the bowl, which is equivalent to the trade mark of civilised nations. Dry banana leaves are used for packing when exported.

Besides pottery, they use the cocoanut shell for a drinking cup. To keep oil or fat, they carve a cocoanut shell and make a cover to it.

A kind of ship is made by lashing several canoes together. Caulking is effected with banana leaves and the gum of a tree. On the top of these canoes is erected a platform with a house at either end. In these houses they stow away the crockery, which is taken to be exchanged for sago. The captain has a separate place in which to stow away his crockery. In these ships they make long voyages. Before starting a farewell dance of an indecent character is held.

To assist the steering of these unwieldly structures, large long paddles are let down by the side, and they act as centre-boards.

Like Eastern Polynesians, they beat out the inner bark of the paper-mulberry, with which they make cloth. They also plait mats. Large netted bags are used by the women in which to

INTRODUCTION.

carry their children, and smaller bags of the same kind are used for carrying other articles. They have nets for fishing, and also for catching kangaroos, wild pigs, and dugong. Fish are also speared.

Charms are used, such as a smooth stone to make the yams grow. Also one particular leaf of the banana, that nearest the bunch of fruit (*gōgō*) is thought to make yams fruitful. Coming events are foreshown by sneezing or by quivering of the body. By cracking the fingers they predict the coming home of a ship. During the absence of the men on a voyage, a sacred woman performs certain rites to ensure the safe return of the voyagers. Incantations are used to bring misfortune and death on an obnoxious party. A man in a fit is supposed to be possessed of a demon. The spirits of those killed are believed to appear to survivors in some dreadful form. They believe in spirits who are malevolent; and that certain persons have influence over them, so as to secure their services in executing vengeance on enemies. In sickness the soul leaves the body, and it is the province of the sorcerer to find and bring it back. Passes are made by the sorcerer over the body of the sick man. He receives a payment for his services.

Some of the prevalent diseases are, abscess, ulcers, yaws, rash, rheumatism, whitlow, erysipelas, thrush, vomiting, constipation, fits, palsy, dropsy, and elephantiasis. Sickness is sometimes caused by sleeping on the place where visitors have slept a night or two previously. Villages were sometimes deserted on account of sickness often occurring in it. In drawing blood they use a flint pointed instrument like a small arrow; with this they lanced the forehead by repeatedly discharging it from a small bow. This was the cure for headache. Friends pay visits to their sick friends.

Suicide is committed either by drowning or hanging, or by leaping from a tree or a cliff. Hired assassins are made use of. When grieving for the dead they scratch their faces, so as to draw blood, or else they cut themselves with a flint or shell. A coarse cloth is worn as a mourning garment, or a cane is plaited round the body. The beat of a drum answers to the funeral knell. On the death of a husband, an enclosure of mats is made round the grave; inside of this the widow sits and mourns. They bury their dead.

By way of sports, they have a spinning top. They have a low swing, and also a very high one depending from the top of a high leaning cocoanut palm. They practice throwing the spear, and they run races. A musical instrument is made of reeds and a drum by stretching a green skin over a hollow wooden frame. Native poets compose songs, for which they are paid. The betel nut is chewed.

They marry and are polygamists. Divorce is common. The woman is betrothed to a husband; but breaches of promise are in vogue. Gifts are made in expectation of a return gift. Like civilized people, credit is sometimes given. The stomach is considered to be the seat of the affections; hence, to feel pity is to have the stomach-ache. Cocoanuts are made taboo as in Eastern Polynesia by plaiting a cocoanut leaf round a tree. Fences for their gardens are made by sticks, or split bamboos, placed lengthways, like a hurdle fence. The waterpot is carried either on the head or shoulder. To pass along in front of a chief is regarded as a mark of disrespect.

Hospitality is shown to strangers; but treachery is practised to an enemy. He is invited to partake of food, and then killed, as Amnon was by Absalom.

They have distinguishing terms for the hospitable, kind-hearted, good-tempered, courteous man; and also for the abusive, churlish man. The industrious man, the one who stores up for future use, is praised; while the lazy man and the thief are abused. Thus "they show the law written in their hearts, their conscience bearing witness therewith, and their thoughts one with another accusing or else excusing them."

GEO. PRATT.

GRAMMAR OF MOTU LANGUAGE.

The Motu language is spoken by the Motu tribe living at Port Moresby, Pari, Borebada, Lealea, and Manumanu; also by natives of Delena, Boera, Tatana, Vabukori, Tupuseleia, Gaile, and Kapakapa. There are considerable local differences in pronunciation.

LETTERS.

The Motu alphabet consists of nineteen letters, viz.,—*a, e, i, o, u, b, d, g, h, k, l, m, n, p, q, r, s, t, v.*

A is pronounced,—
    1st. Long, as in "father"; *vāra*, to grow.
    2nd. Short, as in "mat"; *harihari*, to-day; *varavara*, relations.

E, i, o, u, are generally pronounced as in examples below.

There are slight differences in quantity for which no rules can be given.

Usually *e* is sounded as *a* in take.
    i   ,,   *ea* ,, eager.
    o   ,,   *o* ,, no.
    u   ,,   *oe* ,, shoe.

The consonants are for the most part pronounced as in English.

B, native name *bi*. This is generally sounded as *b* in bad; but in some cases it approaches nearly to the *p* sound, and when pronounced quickly is scarcely distinguishable from *p*.

D, native name *di*, as *d* in dip. Like *b*, this has the rougher and softer sound; sometimes it is almost *t*.

G, native name *ga*, as *g* in good. In some words it has a sound between the ordinary *g* and *k*; as *āu ginigini*, a nettle; but *āu ginigini* (almost *k*), a thorny tree.

H, native name *eti* (pronounced *etsi*). (The reason for the name of this letter being at variance with rule is that a large number of natives who speak the Motu language drop the *h*, the name to them would be the same as the vowel *e*.) This is the nearest a native can pronounce to the English name of the letter. It is a characteristic of the Pari and some other natives to drop the *h* entirely; they pronounce *hanua, anua; hahine, aine,* &c.

K, native name *ke*, as *k* in key.

L, native name *la*, as *l* in lady.

M, native name *mo*, as *m* in man.

N, native name *nu*, as *n* in now.

P, native name *pi*, as *p* in pig.

Q, native name *kiu*, as *q* in queen. The *q* in Motuan does not take an *u* after it.

R, native name *ro*, as *r* in robber.

S, native name *sa*, as *s* in sing. *S* never occurs in Motuan before an *a* or *u*, and rarely before *o*.

T, native name *ti*. Before *a, o,* or *u* it is sounded as *t* in take. Before *e* or *i* it becomes *ts*, like the Tsade in Hebrew, *raruoti* pronounced *raruotsi*.

V, native name *vi*, as *v* in victor.

Of diphthongs there are two :—

    ai, pronounced like English *ai* in aisle.

    au   ,,   ,,   *ow* in cow.

No two consonants can ever stand together without a vowel between.

SYLLABLES.

Every syllable must end in a vowel, hence every syllable is an open one, and in introducing foreign names or words this should be remembered. The natives will always so divide a word that each syllable will end in a vowel.

ACCENT.

As a rule the accent is on the penultima; but there are exceptions.

When suffixes are added the accent is shifted forward, as *hahìne, hahinèna, mèro meròna.*

Reduplicated words have the two accents of the simple form, as *kadàra kadàra-kadàra.*

The natives of Tupuseleia, Kapakapa, and Gaile are known by the peculiarity of raising the voice on the last syllable of the sentence.

WORDS.

1. THE ARTICLE.

There does not seem to be any distinctive definite article.

Hari, and adverb of time, now, is often used as a definite article. *Hari kekeni*, the girl.

In the same way, *varani*, yesterday, *vanegai*, the other day, and *idaunegai*, a long time ago, are used, where in other languages an article would be employed. *Varani lakatoi*, the ship, the particular ship which came yesterday, or about which we talked yesterday. *Vanegai ira edeseni?*—Day before yesterday, hatchet, where?

Ta (an abbreviation of *tamona*), one, is used as indefinite article, as, *Lakatoi ta vada emaimu*, a ship is coming.

2. THE NOUN.

Nouns are primitive, as *au*, a tree, *nadi*, a stone. Or they are derivative, as *igui*, a bundle, from *gui*, to tie.

Verbs become nouns by prefixing *i* to the verb root, as *koko*, to nail, *ikoko*, a nail; *lapaia* (root, *lapa*), to smite, *ilapa*, a long knife or sword.

When the noun is the agent performing the action of the verb from which it is derived, *i* is prefixed, *na* is suffixed, and *tauna* or *gauna* added—*Kaha*, to help, *ikahana tauna*, a helper. *Gauna* is used if the instrument is inanimate, as *tore*, to write, *itorena gauna*, a thing to write with.

He is also used instead of *i*, and followed by *tauna*, but the suffix *na* is omitted. *Hekaha tauna* is also a helper, and *hetore tauna* a writer, but a different meaning is introduced. *Ikahana tauna* is one who helps, it may be some one standing by who "lends a hand," but *hekaha tauna* is one whose office it is to help, who perhaps has been appointed and is paid to help. The same applies to the other instance.

There is not much difference between *itorena gauna* and *hetore gauna*; the former, however, may be a stick or anything you write with, while the latter is something made to write with, as a pencil or pen. In the same way *itorena tauna* is the man who writes, but *hetore tauna* one whose profession is to write, a scribe. This distinction may not always be traced, but it is a primary one.

Nouns are also formed from verbs by prefixing *he*, as *dibagani*, to tempt, *hedibagani*, a temptation; *nanadai*, to question, *henanadai*, a questioning.

Similar to the above are the nouns formed from verbs with a causative prefix, as *ahediba tauna*, a teacher; *ahemaoro tauna*, one who makes straight, a judge. *Hediba*, though not used separately, is knowing; *ahediba* for *hahediba*, to cause to know; *ahediba tauna*, a teacher.

Some nouns are formed from verbs by suffixing *na*, as, *doko*, to finish, *dokona*, the end; *bero*, to wound, *berona*, a wound.

In many cases there is no difference whatever between the noun and the verb, as, *bara*, to row, *bara*, an oar; *dogo*, to anchor, *dogo*, an anchor; *kara*, to do, *kara*, conduct.

Abstract nouns are generally formed by adding *na* to the adjective, as, *tau goada*, a strong man, *ia goadana*, his strength; *tau aonega*, a wise man, *ia aonegana*, his wisdom.

GENDER.

Gender can only be expressed by adding *maruane* or *hahine* to the noun, as *boroma maruane*, a boar, *boroma hahine*, a sow.

In a few instances a different word is used for the different sexes.

Tau, a man.   *Hahine*, a woman.
Mero, a boy.   *Kekeni*, a girl.
Dabari, a male wallaby.   *Miara*, a female wallaby.

NUMBER.

A simple noun standing alone has no number, *nadi* is stone or stones, *hisiu*, star or stars, *ruma*, house or houses.

A very few nouns have the first syllable reduplicated for plural, as, *mero*, a boy, *memero*, boys.

When two nouns stand together, one of them in the genitive relation to the other, their number is expressed by the suffix. As, *hanua tauna*, a man of the village, *hanua taudia*, men of the village; *uda auna*, a tree of the forest, *uda audia*, trees of the forest. In these instances, and in many others, *hanua* and *uda* may be considered either singular or plural and so can take either suffix. But a noun that is, and must be, singular cannot take the plural suffix in its genitive, as, *qaragu huina*, the hairs of my head, or a hair of my head, it cannot be *qaragu huidia*. *Lohiabada natuna* may be one or many, but it is incorrect to say, *Lohiabada natudia*, unless they are children of different *lohiabada*.

With a singular pronoun the noun can only take a singular suffix, *lau natugu* may be either my child or my children, but *lau natudia* is inadmissible.

The plural can always be expressed by the addition of a word signifying *some, many, all, &c.* As, *nadi momo*, many stones; *qaragu huina haida*, some hairs of my head; *lau natugu logora*, the company of my children; *manu momo*, many birds.

GRAMMAR.

Any ambiguity of the number of a noun in composition is removed by the suffix of the verb to which it is the object. *Ia natuna e boilidia*, he his children calls. Had it been one child we should say, *ia natuna e boilia*, the verb taking a singular suffix.

CASE.

Case is indicated by the position of noun in sentence by a preposition or by suffixes.

The Nominative is the simple form, and may be known by its position in a sentence, always standing first, *mero vada e heau*, the boy runs; *Lohiabada gunika ai ela*, the chief inland is gone; *sinana natuna e ubudia*, mother her children feeds; *tau hahine e alaia*, the man woman kills, the man kills the woman.

The Genitive relation is expressed by adding the suffix *na* or *dia* of the person to whom the thing belongs. This usage is for parts of the body and personal relations, and for voice, sight, mind, &c., closely connected with a man's own self. When goods, land, weapons, &c., are spoken of the possessive pronoun *ena, edia* is placed after the principal noun, and before that of which it is possessed. *Lohiabada qarana*, chief head his, the chief's head; *mero sinana*, boy mother his, the boy's mother; *hahine imadia*, women's hands; *memero turadia*, boys friends theirs, the boy's friends; *hanua taudia biagudia*, village men master their, the villagers master.

Note, the personal pronoun is often inserted between the two nouns, in the above instances, *memero idia turadia, hanua taudia idia biagudia* would be equally correct.

Property, weapons, land, &c., as follows :—*Tau ena io*, man his spear; *boroma ena ruma*, pig his house; *hahine edia rami*, women their petticoats; *haoda taudia edia rege*, fishermen their nets.

• Food takes *ana* and *adia* instead of *ena* and *edia*. So also does *inai*, enemy, and some others. *Uru*, generation, takes both *ena* and *ana*. *Hahine ana maho*, woman her yam; *memero adia tohu*, boys their sugarcane.

The Dative expressed by *for* in English is only distinguishable from Possessive by the pronoun being put at end of sentence, *dabua, hahine ena*, a dress the woman for. This order is sometimes used in Possessive when there is some emphasis on the particular thing, as in a sentence like this, *Rami be lauegu, dabua hahine ena*, the waist cloth is mine, the dress is the woman's.

Bigu tadigu ana, banana my brother his, the banana is for my brother. The English *to* used with verbs of giving, &c., is expressed in Motuan by the suffix of the verb, as, *lau tadigu ena ira sinada e henia*, my brother his hatchet our mother gave her, i.e., to her.

The Accusative or Objective is known by its position in the sentence, and also by *dekena*, an adverb of proximity. The normal position is after the nominative and before the verb; *Ioane sisia e alaia*, John dog he killed; *kekeni kepere e huridia*, girls the cups washed.

A sentence may be used after the manner of the English passive verb in which case emphasis is laid on the object, and it really becomes the subject of the sentence. In the above instance if both a dog and a cat had been killed, and I had spoken of the cat as killed by a snake, I could say, *sisia Ioane ese e alaia*, (but) the dog by John was killed. Also, *kepere memero ese e huridia, dabua kekeni ese e huridia*, cups boys they washed, (but) clothes girls they washed, *i.e.*, the cups were washed by the boys and the clothes by the girls.

Dekena, dekedia, are used with persons but not with place. *Ioane Tomu dekena ela*, John Tom's side went, John went to Tom. *Memero haroro tauna dekena ela*, boys teacher the side of went, boys went to the teacher. *Kekeni idia sinadia dekedia ela*, girls went to their mothers.

Dekena, dekedia, are often shortened to ena and edia. *Haroro tauna memero gavana ena e hakaudia*, teacher boys Governor side (presence) led, the teacher led the boys to the Governor.

Dekena is not used with place. *Tamagu uma lao, sinagu hanua lao*, my father to the garden is gone, my mother to the village is gone.

The Vocative is indicated by *e*, sometimes *o* following the noun. *Ioane e!* O John. *Lohiabada e!* O Chief.

In invocation *o* is often used. A boy in trouble calls upon his absent father, *Tamagu o!*

Both *e* and *o* sometimes precede as well as follow the noun, *E. Lohiabada e! O tamagu o!*

The relationship of nouns expressed by the above headings, **Nominative, Genitive, Dative, Vocative**, are so classified for the convenience of the English reader and student. They mean that the relationship indicated in English by those cases is expressed in Motuan in such and such a way. Other relationships such as *from, in, by, with*, are expressed by prepositions, as follows :—

From, as, from heaven, by *amo, guba amo ema. Ia tamana ena amo ena*, he has come from his father.

In is expressed by *lalona*, inside, followed by relative *ai Hahine runa lalona ai*, the woman is in the house. Frequently *lalona* is understood and *ai* only used, as, *hahine ruma ai. Dirava guba ai*, God is in heaven.

GRAMMAR. 7

By instrumental, or *with* is generally expressed by *laia* suffixed to the verb, *Ira binai au baine taralaia*, hatchet (is) here wood to adze with. *Ranu binai kepere bae hurilaidia*, here is water to wash the cups with.

Also in the sense of carrying away, *Hari hahine mero e heaulaia*, the woman ran away with the child.

With, in the sense of companionship, by *ida*, as, *sisia boroma ida lao*, dog pig with gone, the dog is gone with the pig. *Memero lohiabada ida lao* boys are gone with (the) chief.

3. THE ADJECTIVE.

The adjective is known by its position in the sentence. The same word may be either a noun, adjective, verb, or adverb; its position in the sentence and the accompanying particles show its character.

The adjective follows its noun, as, *ira namo*, a hatchet good; *maho dika*, a yam bad. Another form is *ira namona, hahine dikana*. This has a definite, emphatic meaning as if the particular hatchet was singled out, this is a good *ira*, or the woman picked out from others, *hahine dikana*, a bad woman that.

Personal qualities are most frequently expressed by two nouns in juxtaposition, the person following the quality, and put in the genitive by *na* suffixed. *Goada tauna*, literally, strength his man; *koikoi tauna*, lying his man, *i.e.*, a liar. The difference in the word taking the *na* may be seen in this example, *mauri auna*, life his tree, *i.e.*, the tree of life, but *au maurina*, tree his life, *i.e.*, sap, or light, or water; *mauri ranuna*, the water of life; *ranu maurina*, water his life, living, not stagnant water.

A kind of compound adjective consists of a noun with an adjective as above. *Hahine udu mauri*, or *udu mauri hahinena*, the woman of the live mouth; *lalo auka tauna*, the man of hard stomach, fearless.

Diminutives are frequently expressed by reduplication, as, *kekeni*, a girl; *kekenikekeni*, little girl; *qarume*, fish; *qarume-qarume*, little fish.

Adjectives of colour are almost all reduplicated, as, *kurokuro*, white; *koremakorema*, black.

By the addition of *ka* the quality is modified, *kurokakuroka*, whitish; *gano*, sharp (edge); *ganokaganoka*, sharpish; *paripari*, wet; *parikaparika*, damp.

Mia placed before the adjective also takes from its quality, as *mia korema*, rather black, *i.e.*, dark-brown; *mia bada*, rather big.

Some adjectives are formed by adding *ka* to verb and reduplicating, as, *dedi*, to slip; *dedikadedika*, slippery; *dala dedikadedika*, a slippery road.

GRAMMAR.

Comparison is effected by using two adjectives in the positive state, as, *inai namo*, this is good; *unai dika*, that is bad.

Also by using the word *herea* to exceed, as, *namo herea*, very good, the best. *Atai*, high, is sometimes used in the same way to express the superlative *inai vada atai, unai idoidiai henuai*, this is above, those are beneath. Also by using *sibona* only, as, *ia sibona namo*, he only is good.

The adjective agrees in personal suffix with pronoun or noun of subject and not with the noun it qualifies, as, *Ai oi natumu dikadia*, we are thy bad children, not *natumu dikana*.

Ibou, idoi all, follow the noun they qualify and takes its suffix, always followed by relative *ai*. *Hanua taudia iboudia ai ema*, all the villagers came; *ai iboumai ai vada a nohomu*, we all are staying.

Idoi is not used in second person *idoimui*, but always *iboumui*. The relative *ai* so invariably follows *ibouna* or *idoina* that it is often written as one word, *ibounai, idoidiai, iboumuiai*, &c.

NUMERALS.

The cardinals are:—

Tamona,	One.
Rua,	Two.
Toi,	Three.
Hani,	Four.
Ima,	Five.
Tauratoi,	Six.
Hitu,	Seven.
Taurahani,	Eight.
Taurahani ta,	Nine.
Qauta,	Ten.
Qauta ta,	Eleven.
Qauta rua,	Twelve.
Rua ahui,	Twenty.
Toi ahui,	Thirty.
Hari ahui,	Forty.
Ima ahui,	Fifty.
Tauratoi ahui,	Sixty.
Hitu ahui,	Seventy.
Taurahani ahui,	Eighty.
Taurahani ta ahui,	Ninety.
Sinahu,	One hundred.
Sinahuta rua,	One hundred and two, &c.
Sinahu rua,	Two hundred.
Daha,	One thousand.
Gerebu,	Ten thousand.
Domaga,	One hundred thousand.

Units are expressed by *dikoana*, as, *qauta mai dikoana ima*, ten and his units five.

A suffix *oti* is added to low units, as, *ruaoti, toioti, hanioti, imaoti*. These are not used in counting but in speaking of them, the two, the three, &c.

Hona is added to small numbers, and is equivalent to *only*, as, *ima hona*, five only.

Persons take a prefix in low numbers, as, *ra, tau rarua*, 2 men; *ta, hahine tatoi*, 3 women; *ha, kekeni hahani*; *la, memero laima*, 5 boys. It does not go beyond 5, but is used with those units with tens, as, *aposetolo quata rarua*, the twelve apostles.

Things of length, such as spears, poles, &c., are counted differently. The numerals have *au* prefixed, as, *auta, aurua*, and so on up to nine, which is *autaurahaniauta*, and ten, *atalata*. After ten they are,—

Rabu rua,	20	*Rabu hitu,*	70
Rabu toi,	30	*Rabu taurahani,*	80
Rabu hani,	40	*Rabu taurahani ta,*	90
Rabu ima,	50	*Sinahu,*	100
Rabu tauratoi,	60		

Of fish, pigs, and wallaby, the ordinary numerals are used up to ten, which is *bala ta*,; 20, *bala rua*; beyond 20, the common numerals are used, as *toi ahui, hari ahui*, up to 100, which is the same as ordinary, *sinahu*.

Cocoanuts are counted by *varo* (strings), as, *varo ta*, 10; *varo rua*, 20, &c.

ORDINALS.

First is *gini gunana*, then, *ia ruana, ia toina, ia hanina*, and so on regularly until the last, which is *gini gabena*.

Numeral adverbs, twice, thrice, &c., are expressed by *ha* prefixed to cardinals, as, *harua*, twice; *hatoi*, thrice, &c.

4. PRONOUNS.

Pronouns have Person and Number, but no Gender or Case.

There are two pronouns for the first person plural, one inclusive (*ita*) which is used when the person addressed is included, the other exclusive (*ai*) which excludes the person addressed.

The dual is formed by adding *raruoti* to the plural, as, *umui raruoti*, you two.

A triad may be formed by changing *raruoti* into *tatoioti*, but it is optional and not often used.

GRAMMAR.

Personal Pronouns.

Lau,	I.
Oi,	Thou.
Ia,	He or she.
Ai,	We (exclusive).
Ita,	We (inclusive).
Umui,	You.
Idia,	They.
Ai raruoti,	We two (exclusive).
Ita raruoti,	We two (inclusive).
Umui raruoti,	You two.
Idia raruoti,	They two.

Possessive Pronouns.

Lauegu,	My.
Oiemu,	Thy.
Iena,	His.
Ai emai,	Ours (exclusive).
Ita eda,	Ours (inclusive).
Umui emui,	Yours.
Idia edia,	Theirs.

The personal pronoun is often omitted, as *emai ruma,* our house.

Ita eda is often contracted into *iseda.*

All kinds of food take *a*, as :—

Lauagu bigu,	My banana.	
Oiamu bigu,	Thy „	
Iana bigu,	His „	
Ai amai bigu,	Our „	(exclusive).
Ita ada bigu,	Our „	(inclusive).
Umui amui bigu,	Your „	
Idia adia bigu,	Their „	

Inai, enemy, and a few others also take *a*. *Uru,* generation, takes either *a* or *e*.

For parts of the body and relations the personal pronoun precedes the noun, and the following terminations are suffixed to it:—

Gu,	1st person singular.
Mu,	2nd ,,
Na,	3rd ,,
Mai,	1st person plural (exclusive).
Da,	,, ,, (inclusive).
Mui,	2nd ,,
Dia,	3rd ,,

As *Lau aegu*,   My leg.
Oi aemu,   Thy leg.
Ia aena,   His leg.
Ai aemai,   Our (exclusive) legs.
Ita aeda,   Our (inclusive) legs.
Umui aemui,   Your legs,
Idia aedia,   Their legs.

In some cases both forms may be used, as, *ena hereva*, *ia herevana*, but there is an important distinction in meaning. *Ena hereva* is his speech, but *ia herevana* is the speech about him. *Dirava ena hereva*, the word of God, *Dirava herevana*, the word about God, His character, will, &c.

In speaking of the parts of the body the personal pronoun is sometimes dropped, as, *qaragu e hisihisimu*, my head aches, instead of *lau qaragu e hisihisimu*. Personal attributes and all near relationships, besides family relations, take the personal suffixes. *Lau turagu* my friend, *lau inaigu* my enemy, *lau biagugu* my master or lord, but *lauegu lohia* my chief.

DISTRIBUTIVE PRONOUNS.

Ta ta, each, as, *idia ta ta e koau*, they each spoke. In sharing or dividing *amo* is added, as *toi toi amo*, three each, *ima ima amo*, five each.

Umui ta one of you, *idia ta* one of them, &c.

DEMONSTRATIVE PRONOUNS.

Ina, ini,   this.
Ena,   that, close to.
Una, unu   that, distant or opposite to.

Ina, ena, una, all take the relative *ai* after them, and are generally written *inai, enai, unai.*

They are also used with *b* prefixed, as, *binai, benai, bunai, bini, bena, bunu.* There is no change for plural.

INDEFINITE PRONOUNS.

Haida	
Hahidaoti	
Hidaoti	Some others.
Ta	Any one.
Idau	
Ma ta	Another.

INTERROGATIVES.

Daika	Who? *daidia* plural.
Dahaka	What?
Edana	Which?
Edana negai	
Aidana negai	When?
Edeseni	Where?

Bedaina also used of persons Where? plural *bedaidia.*

Native idiom is, *Oi ladamu daika?* Who is your name?

5. VERBS.

Verbs are known by certain particles which precede them, and also by suffixes. The verbal particles are of first importance, as by them variations of tense, mood, &c., are expressed. The following are

VERBAL PARTICLES.

Vada, this is unchangeable in all persons and tenses, as, *lau vada diba, oi vada diba,* &c. It is, however, generally accompanied by one of the short particles which change with the different persons, as *lau vada na dibamu,* I know, *oi vada o dibamu,* you (sing.) know, *ia vada e dibamu,* he knows.

Ese is another unchangeable particle. It follows the personal pronoun, but is always followed by the particle of that particular person, as, *lau ese na karaia, ia ese e karaia.* It is never used except with a verb, although in answer to a question no verb need be expressed, as, *daika inai e karaia?* Who did this? to which the answer may be, *ia ese,* he (did understood).

GRAMMAR.

The most important particles, those which distinguish and cling to the verb everywhere, are :—

na, 1st pers. sing.   *a,* 1st pers. plu. exclusive.
o, 2nd „ „   *ta,* 1st „ „ inclusive.
e, 3rd „ „   *o,* 2nd „ „
                        e, 3rd „ „

They have *me* added to them without making any apparent difference in meaning.

name, 1st pers. sing.   *ame,* 1st pers. plu. exclusive.
ome, 2nd „ „   *tame,* 1st „ „ inclusive.
eme, 3rd „ „   *ome,* 2nd „ „
                          eme, 3rd „ „

The above are all used in past or present. Different particles are used for the future. The above characteristic particles reappear compounded with *bai,* as :—

baina, 1st pers. sing.   *baia,* 1st pers. plu. exclusive.
ba, 2nd „ „   *baita,* 1st „ „ inclusive.
baine, 3rd „ „   *ba,* 2nd „ „
                           bae, 3rd „ „

Of these, the 2nd person is irregular, and the 3rd singular has added *n* for euphony (unless the full form was *ne*); the 3rd plural drops *i.*

Note.—*Ba* and *a* in 2nd person become *bava* and *ava* before a verb beginning with *a.*

Do is sometimes put before *baina, ba,* &c., as, *lau do baina torea,* I will write ; *ia do baine karaia,* he will do it. The *do* is probably a contraction of *dohore,* presently, by-and-bye, and implies certainty. *Baina* alone may be, *I will (do),* or, *if I do.* The *do* before *baina* removes this uncertainty. This meaning is more evident in the negative *do se,* which means *not yet,* as, *ia do sema,* he hasn't *yet* come ; that he hasn't come and isn't coming would be, *ia sema.*

Me is also affixed to the future, as, *bainame, bame, baineme,* &c. The shade of meaning is not evident. In the 2nd person it is used in entreaty, but not in command. Sometimes it seems like *to,* or *in order that.*

Besides the prefixes there are

VERBAL SUFFIXES.

Of these, *va* and *mu* are unchangeable. *Va* is used to indicate past time, and *mu* present. *Lau na dibava,* I knew ; *idia e dibamu,* they know.

Mua is sometimes used for *mu*, as, *Oi ai o gimamaimua*.
The pronominal suffixes are used to show the object of all transitive verbs.

Singular.

Ia lau e heni gu,	He gave to me.
Oi ia o heni a,	You gave to him.
Ia oi e heni mu,	He gave to you.

Plural.

Ai umui a heni mui,	We (exc.) gave to you (plu.).
Ita idia ta heni dia,	We (inc.) gave to them.
Umui ai o heni mai,	You gave to us (exc.).
Idia ita e heni da,	They gave to us (inc.).

Koaulaia is added the verb to indicate *about to*, as, *ia e abia koaulaia*, he was going to take it.

There is also a particle post fixed to the verb signifying *about to*, but prevented so that the intention was not carried out. It is formed by adding *to* to the ordinary verbal participles.

nato, 1st pers. sing.		*ato*, 1st per. plu., exclusive.		
oto, 2nd	,,	*tato*, 1st	,,	inclusive.
eto, 3rd	,,	*oto*, 2nd	,,	
		eto, 3rd	,,	

Lau na abia nato ia lau e boiligu, I was about to take it (and or when) he called me.

Directive particles are used after the verb, and are compounded with it, such as *dobi* downwards, *dae* and *isi* upwards, *kau* contact, *oho* away, *tao* which means fixedness, but generally with the idea of restraint, *ahu* around, from *ahu* to close as a circle.

The pronominal suffixes are infixed between the verb and these particles. Examples are :—

Rohamaidobi,	To look down upon us.
Abiadae,	To receive one up (into house).
Gagaisi,	To look up.
Atoakau,	To place on.
Abiaoho,	To take away.
Dabaigutao,	To seize or arrest me.
Koudiaahu,	To enclose them.

In one or two instances the compound verb is so closely compounded that it forms one word, and suffix is added to it; *darahua*, to grope round, not *daraiaahu*.

The suffixes *mu* and *va* are placed at the end of the compound word, as, *abiadaemu*, *atoakauva*, &c.

GRAMMAR. 15

Mani is a word used in present and future, and is placed before the verbal particle, as, *Mani ba mailaia*, just bring it. *Lau mani baina itaia*, just let me see it. The meaning seems to be like the English *just*—"Just try it," "Just look at him," "Just let me see," &c.

Doini, do ini, and *dounu, do unu*, are used before verbs to indicate "still." *Lau doini narimu*, I am still waiting for you. *Ia dounu e nohomu*, he is still dwelling. They can be used with or without the ordinary verbal particles.

PERSON.

There is no change in the verb itself for person. It is expressed by the pronoun and the distinguishing verbal particle, as,

Singular.

1st person	*Lau na dibamu*,	I know.
2nd "	*Oi o dibamu*,	You know.
3rd "	*Ia e dibamu*,	He knows.

Dual.

1st exclusive	*Ai raruoti a dibamu*,	We two (exc.) know.
1st inclusive	*Ita raruoti ta dibamu*,	We two (inc.) know.
2nd person	*Umui raruoti o dibamu*,	You two know.
3rd "	*Idia raruoti e dibamu*,	They two know.

Plural.

1st person exclusive	*Ai a dibamu*,	We (exc.) know.
1st " inclusive	*Ita ta dibamu*,	We (inc.) know.
2nd "	*Umui o dibamu*,	You know.
3rd "	*Idia e dibamu*,	They know.

TENSE.

There are three tenses in Motuan—past, present, and future. These are indicated by the verbal particles, and by the suffixes *va* and *mu*.

Although the tenses are properly only three, they each include many variations, and so complete is the system of particles and suffixes that a native has no difficulty in expressing the exact time of an action. In the following examples I have given the different forms without naming them. The complex arrangement and terminology of grammarians seem quite inapplicable here. Some forms perhaps ought not to be included in the consideration of the verb, but they show how a native expresses the different times and forms of an action. I leave my readers to name tense, mood, &c., as they please. .

Third Person Singular of Helai, to sit.

1. *Ia vada e helai,* He sits.
2. *Ia vada e helaimu,* He is sitting. This is commonly used for the simple present, and *can never* be used of the past. The former example, *ia vada e helai,* may in some instances be used for past.
3. *Ia e helai.*

eme helai, He sat. There is no doubt a different shade of meaning in the *eme,* but I cannot explain it.

4. *Ia e helaiva,* He sat, or, he was sitting. Definitely and certainly past.
5. *Ia e helai vaitani.*

eme he,ai vaitani He has sat, or in narrative it may be, he had sat.

6. *Ia dounu helai,* He is still sitting.
7. *Ia bema helai,* If he had been sitting, or, if he had sat.
8. *Ia baine helai,* He will sit, or, if he sits.

baine me helai.

9. *Ia aine helai,* He will immediately sit.
10. *Ia do baine helai,* He will (certainly) sit.
11. *Ia e helai koaulaia,* He was going to sit.
12. *Ia e helai eto,* He was just going to sit, when something occurred to prevent.
13. *Ia baine helai koaulaia,* If he will be going to sit, or, when he is about to sit down (then do so and so).
14. *Ia baine dounu helai,* If he will be still sitting, *e.g.*, I send a boy and tell him if when you arrive he is still sitting then tell him so and so.

Negative as follows :—

Ia se helaimu,	He is not sitting.
Ia do se helai,	He has not yet sat (but he will).
Ia se helaiva,	He did not sit.
Ia basine helai,	He will not sit, or if he does not sit.
Ia do basine helai,	He will (certainly) not sit.

It will be seen that of the above fourteen forms, Nos. 2, 4, 10 are definite and certain. No. 2 can never be anything but present, now while speaking. No. 4 can never be present or future, and No. 10 is as certainly future. The others are modifications and variations of these. In Nos. 3, 5, and 8 the *me* has a shade of meaning which distinguishes it from the *e* and *baine* but which cannot at present be explained. The *koaulaia* in No. 11 can take the suffix *va* of past and *mu* of present. *Ia e helai koaulaiava*, he was going to sit, and *ia e helai koaulaiamu*, he is now going to sit.

To the above may be added the verb *ura*, to desire, which is compounded with other verbs without being joined to them, as, *ia e helai ura*, he wishes to sit down. *Ia e helai urava*, he was wishing to sit. *Ia baine helai ura*, he will be wishing, or, if he wishes to sit.

Helaina is sitting—*ia helaina neganaai*, the time of his sitting, *i.e.*, while he was sitting.

The Imperative is the same as the future.

Oi ba helai, } sit thou ;
Oi a helai, }

but in entreaty *bame* would be used, as, *oi bame helai*, do you sit down ; or *ame*, for immediate, *oi ame helai*, sit down now.

The Infinitive has no special form. The future is used, *ia baine helai*, to sit ; *me* seems to have something of the infinitive when used after another verb, as, *ia ema baine me itaia*, he came to look. But it cannot always be so used.

The word *totona* is sometimes used when in English we should use the Infinitive, as, *ia itaia totona ema*, he came on purpose to see.

Participles have no form distinct from the above examples. *Ia vada e helaimu*, he is sitting, *Ia vada e helaiva*, he was sitting, are used when in English we should say *he sits, he sat.*

PASSIVE.

Except in two or three instances there is no passive form ; the complete system of suffixes makes it unnecessary. A few instances with what appears to be the Polynesian passive terminations are interesting. *Boilia* from *boi* to call ; *meilia* from *mei* to pass water ; *laqahia* from *laqa* to graze (leg) ; *unahia* to be scaled. These, however, may be the active verbs with the ordinary suffix, and *l* or *h* inserted for euphony—*boilia* for *boiia*, *meilia* for *meiia*, *laqahia* for *laqaia*, *unahia* for *unaia*. The final *a* is only for 3rd person ; *boiligu, meiligu* are used for the 1st. The passive sense can always be expressed by active verb with suffix. *Lau baine alagu*, if I am killed ; *Lau e ura henigu*, I am loved ; *Lau e haberogu*, I am wounded.

B

THE CAUSATIVE.

Ha prefixed to the verb root makes it causative, as, *diba* to know, *hadiba* to cause to know.

Ha does not always make causation, as *hautu* from *utu* to fetch water, does not mean to cause someone to fetch water, *ranu e hautu* is equivalent to *ranu e utua*. *Digu* to bathe, *hadigu* to bathe one's self or another. *Veri* to pull, and also *haveri*.

Ahe is in a few instances used for causation, but when a verb beginning with *he* is made causative the initial *h* is generally omitted, as *ahelaiakau*, instead of *hahelaiakau*, from *helai*; *ahelagaia* from *helaga*; *ahelaloa* from *helalo*. Some natives retain the *h* and say *haheboua* for *aheboua*. There is no doubt but *ha* is the full and complete form.

Ahe is prefixed to make a verbal noun, as *diba* to know, *hadiba* to teach, *ahediba* a teaching, *ahediba tauna* a teaching man, and *ahediba gabuna* a teaching place, or *rumana* house. These never take suffixes. It would be incorrect to say *ahedibaia* or *ahemaorogu*.

THE RECIPROCAL.

The reciprocal relation is expressed by prefixing *he* and suffixing *heheni*; the verb is also generally reduplicated. *Badu*, to be angry, or anger, becomes *hebadubaduheheni*, to be angry with one another. *Heuraheheni* from *ura*, to desire or love one another.

AUXILIARY VERB.

There is an auxiliary verb *henia*, to give, which is used with verbs of speaking, hearing, walking, dwelling, desiring, honoring, &c.

Ia idia e koau henidia,	He spake to them.
Lau ia na kamonai henia,	I gave him hearing, that is obedience.
Lau ia na ura heniamu,	I am desiring, I desire or love him.
Oi lohiabada ba hemataurai henia,	Give you (sing.) respect to the chief. *Anglice*, pay respect to him.

In the second instance above we can also say, *lau ia na kamonaia*, but the meaning would then be, I hear him. In the above example it is, I give him (as a habit) hearing which implies trust, obedience, faith. In the one case it is, I hear him, and in the other, I obey him.

Note.—The verb with *henia* must be treated as one word, and the verbal particle must not be put between them.

Lau baina kamonai henia, never *Lau kamonai baina henia. Davana,* wages, and many others have *henia* in its own signification as a verb to give, and in these cases of course the particle comes between, *davana idia ba henidia,* give them their wages.

Henia takes all the verbal suffixes; *ura henidiava, kamonai henigumu,* &c., in this differing from the directive particles, which always take the pronominal suffixes between them and the verb.

Verb, To Be.

There is no verb *to be.* It is expressed by the pronoun and noun, or adjective, with a verbal particle as copula.

Lau name goada,	I am strong.
Oi vada namo,	You are good.
Ia vada aonega,	He is wise.

And sometimes without the verbal particle, as—

Lau taunimanima,	I am a man (not a pig, &c.)
Oi kekenikekeni,	You are a little girl.
Ia taubada,	He is an old man.

The *mai* of possession is used as a verb *to have,* in this way, *ai mai dika,* we (exc.) have badness, *i.e.,* we are bad. *Oi mai aonega hani,* have you wisdom? *Ita mai vanagi,* we have a canoe. *Umui mai diari,* you have light (are enlightened).

Ma is used before the verb to signify continued or renewed action.

Ma tahua,	Continue seeking, or seek again.
Ma ko au,	Continue speaking, "kept on saying."

PARADIGM OF VERB.

Gini, to stand

Present.

Lau na ginimu,	I am standing or stand.
Oi o ginimu,	Thou standest.
Ia e ginimu,	He stands.
Ai a ginimu,	We (exclusive) stand.
Ita ta ginimu,	We (inclusive) stand.
Umui o ginimu,	You stand.
Idia e ginimu, or	
Lau vada na ginimu,	
Oi vada o ginimu, &c., &c.,	They stand.

GRAMMAR.

Past and also Present.

Lau na (or *name*) *gini*,	I stood or stand.
Oi o (or *ome*) *gini*,	Thou stoodest or standest.
Ia e (or *eme*) *gini*,	He stood or stands.
Ai a (or *ame*) *gini*,	We (exclusive) stood or stand.
Ita ta (or *tame*) *gini*,	We (inclusive) stood or stand.
Umui o (or *ome*) *gini*,	You stood or stand.
Idia e (or *eme*) *gini*,	They stood or stand.

Continuance.

Lau doini gini, or	
Lau doini na ginimu,	I am still standing
Oi doini gini, or	
Oi doini o ginimu,	Thou art still standing
Ia dounu gini, or	
Ia dounu e ginimu,	He is still standing.
Ai doini gini, or	
Ai doini a ginimu,	We (exclusive) are still standing.
Umui doini gini, or	
Umui doini o ginimu,	You are still standing.
Idia dounu gini, or	
Idia dounu e ginimu,	They are still standing.

N.B.—*Doini* is this (place) *dounu* that, the speaker would use *doini* of himself and the place in which he was, *dounu* of those away from him.

Past.

Lau na giniva,	I stood.
Oi o giniva,	Thou stoodest.
Ia e giniva,	He stood.
Ai a giniva,	We (exclusive) stood.
Ita ta giniva,	We (inclusive) stood.
Umui o giniva,	You stood.
Idia e giniva,	They stood
Lau na gini vaitani,	I have or had stood.
Oi o gini vaitani,	Thou hast or hadst stood.
Ia e gini vaitani,	He has or had stood
Ai a gini vaitani,	We (exclusive) have or had stood.
Ita ta gini vaitani,	We (inclusive) have or had stood.
Umui o gini vaitani,	You have or had stood.
Idia e gini vaitani,	They have or had stood.

GRAMMAR.

Conditional.

Lau bama gini,	If I had stood.
Oi boma gini,	If thou hadst stood.
Ia bema gini,	If he had stood.
Ai baiama gini,	If we (exclusive) had stood.
Ita baitama gini,	If we (inclusive) had stood.
Umui boma gini,	If you had stood.
Idia bema gini,	If they stood.

Intentional.

Lau na gini koaulaia,	I was about to stand.
Oi o gini koaulaia,	Thou wast about to stand.
Ia e gini koaulaia,	He was about to stand.
Ai a gini koaulaia,	We (exclusive) were about to stand.
Ita ta gini koaulaia,	We (inclusive) were about to stand.
Umui o gini koaulaia,	You were about to stand.
Idia e gini koaulaia,	They were about to stand.

N.B.—*Koaulaia* may take *va* or *mu*. This form may also be used with future, *Baina ba baine*, &c.

Lau na gini nato,	I was about to stand (but did not).
Oi o gini oto,	Thou wast about to stand (but did not).
Ia e gini eto,	He was about to stand (but did not).
Ai a gini ato,	We (exclusive) were about to stand (but did not).
Ita ta gini tato,	We (inclusive) were about to stand (but did not).
Umui o gini oto,	You were about to stand (but did not).
Idia e gini eto,	They were about to stand (but did not).

GRAMMAR.

Future.

Lau baina gini,	I will stand, or, If I stand.
Oi ba gini,	Thou will stand, or, If thou standest.
Ia baine gini,	He will stand, or, If he stands.
Ai baia gini,	We (exclusive).
Ita baita gini,	We (inclusive) will stand, or, If we stand.
Umui ba gini,	You will stand, or, If you stand.
Idia bae gini,	They will stand, or, If they stand.

Immediate Future.

Lau aina gini,	I will (directly) stand.
Oi a gini,	And so on, regular throughout.

Another form takes *me* after *baina ba*, &c., *baina me bame*, &c. The second person in this form is much used in entreaty and prayer, *Oi bame kahamai,* Do thou help us; *Oi ame kamonaimai,* Do thou (now) hear us.

Future Intentional.

Lau baina gini koaulaia,	I will be about to stand, or, If I am about to stand, &c., &c., &c.

Future Continuance.

Lau dounu (or *doini*) *baina gini.*	If I am still standing, or, I will be still standing,

&c., &c., &c.

The Negative is as follows:—

Lau asina(or *asi name*)*gini,*	I did not stand.
Oi to (or *tome*) *gini,*	Thou didst not stand.
Ia se (or *seme*) *gini,*	He did not stand.
Ai asia (or *asi ame*) *gini,*	We (exclusive) did not stand.
Ita asita (or *asi tame*) *gini,*	We (inclusive) did not stand.
Umui asio (or *asi ome*) *gini,*	You did not stand.
I dia asie(or *asi eme*) *gini,*	They did not stand.

Lau asina ginimu,	I am not standing.
Oi to ginimu,	Thou art not standing.
Ia asie ginimu,	He is not standing.
Ai asia ginimu,	We (exclusive) are not standing.
Ita asita ginimu,	We (inclusive) are not standing.
Umui asio ginimu,	You are not standing.
I dia asie ginimu	They are not standing.

GRAMMAR.

Future.

Lau basina gini,	I will not stand, or, If I do not, &c.
Oi basio gini,	Thou wilt not stand, or, If thou dost not.
Ia basine gini,	He will not stand, or, If he does not stand.
Ai basia gini,	We (exclusive) will not stand, or, If we do not, &c.
Ita basita gini,	We (inclusive) will not stand, or, If we do not, &c.
Umui basio gini,	You will not stand, or, If you do not, &c.,
Idia basie gini,	They will not stand, or, If they do not, &c.

So also the imperative.

VERB *ita*, TO LOOK.

The verb *gini* above is intransitive, but to look implies something to look at. The root *ita* is not used without a suffix, except in the imperative, *A ita !* look thou. The termination *ia* is the suffix of the 3rd person singular. If the object be changed, as, look at me, the suffix of 1st person *gu* must be added to the root *ita* instead of *ia*, *Oi lau o itagu*, or *itagumu*, or *itaguva*, and so with each person, remembering that the root is *ita*, and not *itaia*.

PRESENT.

Lau na itaiamu,   I am looking.
Oi o itaiamu,
&c., &c.

Another form :—
Lau vada na itaiamu,
Oi vada o itaiamu,
&c., &c.

The 1st person singular object would be :—
Oi lau o itagumu,   Thou art looking at me

The 2nd person singular of object.
Lau oi na itamumu,   I am looking at you.

Continuance.

Lau doini itaia, or
Lau doini na itaiamu,   I am still looking.
Oi dounu itaia, or
Oi dounu o itaiamu,   Thou are still looking.
&c., &c.

Past and also Present.

Lau na (or *name*) *itaia,*	I looked or look.
Oi o (or *ome*) *itaia,*	Thou lookedst.
&c., &c.	

Past.

Lau na itaiava,	I looked.
Oi o itaiava,	Thou lookedst.
&c., &c.	
Lau na itaia vaitaniva,	I have or had looked.
Oi o itaia vaitaniva,	Thou hast or hadst looked.
&c., &c.	

Conditional.

Lau bama itaia,	If I had looked.
Lau boma itaia,	If thou hadst looked.
&c., &c.	

Intentional the same as *gini* above.

Future.

Lau baina itaia,	I will look, or If I look.
Oi ba itaia,	Thou wilt look, or If thou lookest.
&c., &c.	

Immediate Future.

Lau aina itaia,	I will (immediately) look
Oi a itaia,	Thou wilt (immediately) look.
&c., &c.	

Other forms are same as *gini* above.

The verbs, *mai* to come, and *lao* to go, are irregular in past and future as:—

Lau nama,	I came.
Oi oma,	Thou camest.
Ia ema,	He came.
Ita tama,	We (inclusive) came.
Ai ama,	We (exclusive) came
Umui oma,	You came.
Idia ema,	They came.
Lau bainama,	I will come.
Oi baoma,	Thou wilt come
Ia bainema,	He will come.
Ita baitama,	We (inclusive) come.
Ai baiama,	We (exclusive) come
Umui baoma,	You come.
Idia baema,	They come.

GRAMMAR.

Lao to go is the same substituting *l* for *m*, thus :—

Lau nala,
Oi ola,
Ia ela, &c., &c.

The negative is :—

Lau asi nama,	I come not, or did not come.
Oi toma,	Thou comest not, or didst not.
Ia sema,	He comes not, or came not.
Ai asiama,	We come not, or came not.
Ita asitama,	We (inclusive) come not, or came not.
Umui asioma,	You come not, or came not.
Idia asicma,	They come not, or came not.

And so with *lao* to go.

Mai and *lao* are also used in all persons with *vada*, as, *Lau vada mai, Ia vada lao, Idia vada mai,* &c., &c. *Mai* and *lao* also take the *va* and *mu* suffixes. *Lau na maimu, Oi o maiva, Ai a laomu,* &c.

6. ADVERBS.

There is nothing in the form of adverbs to distinguish them from adjectives. Almost every adjective can be used as an adverb. They are frequently reduplicated, as *namo, namonamo, dika, dikadika.*

iniseni,	here.	*iniheto,*	thus.	
unuseni,	there.	*ela.*		
hari,	now.	*ela bona,*	until (future).	
io, oibe,	yes.	*ema.*		
lasi	no.	*ema bona,*	until (to present time).	
edana negai,	when.			
edeseni,	where ?	*vaia.*		
dohore,	presently.	*vavaia,*	habitually.	
haragaharaga.	quickly.	*lasi,*	out of.	
edeheto,	how ?	*vareai,*	into.	
initomaia,	thus.	&c., &c., &c.		

*Adverbial particles have already been treated of under *verbal particles.*

7. PREPOSITIONS.

amo,	from.	*vareai,*	in.
lalo,	within.	*unukaha*	beyond.
muri,	without.	*inikaha,*	on this side.
atai,	above.	*vaira,*	in front.
henu,	below.	*daina ai,*	
ida,	with.	*daigu ai, &c.,*	on account of,
dekena,	to, by side of.		for sake of.
lasi,	out.		&c., &c.

8. CONJUNCTIONS.

mai,	and.	*ena be,*	notwithstanding.
ā,	but.	*bona,*	and, especially with proper names.
danu,	also.		
garina,	lest.		
ida,	together with.	*madi be,*	because.
			&c., &c.

9. INTERJECTIONS.

ināi,	Oh ! exclamation of wonder.
inā,	Oh ! exclamation of dissent or reproof.
lau dahakai nado,	exclamation of indignation.
hī,	pish ! get out !
iā,	dissent.
	&c., &c.

SYNTAX.

Much that belongs properly to the syntax has been already stated under the different parts of speech. The following notes on the order of words in a sentence, some idioms, and particles, will complete it.

The noun or pronoun in the nominative case usually precedes the verb, as, *Mero vada heau*, The boy runs. *Ia bainema*, He will come. With verbs active, the agent is always put first, and the subject acted upon next, followed by the verb, as *Lau ia na dadabaia*, I he beat him, that is, I beat him. *Ia natuna lau e hadikagu*, His child I abused me.

Observe the suffix agreeing with the object is always added to the verb as in the above examples, *Lau ia na dadabaia*, I he beat him. *Ia natuna*, his child, *lau*, I, *hadika gu*, abused me. The suffix to a noun requires its corresponding pronoun to precede it, as, *Lau imagu*, I hand my, my hand. *Idia matadia vada e hapapadia*, their eyes them were opened them. Also in such sentences as these, *Hanua taudia idia rumadia*, Village men their houses them.

In these instances the *lau*, *idia*, seem redundant. In similar languages the suffix only would be used, *imagu* not *lau imagu*, but in Motuan the noun takes the personal pronoun before it and corresponding suffix after it. As a colloquialism *imagu*, *uegu*, *qaragu* may be used alone, and one may hear *imagu e hisihisimu*, my arm is sore, but the full grammatical form is *lau imagu*, &c.

The genitive of material is made by putting the nouns in apposition, and suffixing *na* to the qualified noun, as *biri rumana*, palm leaf house his, a palm leaf house. The plural takes *dia*, as *nara vanagidia*, cedar canoes theirs, cedar canoes. Also nouns signifying the use to which a thing is applied, as, *Kohu rumana*, goods house his, a store-house. *Ira segea gauna*, hatchet sharpen thing, a hatchet sharpener.

The personal pronoun and its noun must agree in person. A pronoun of the singular number cannot take a noun with a plural suffix. When in English we should say "my eyes," in Motuan it is "my eye" only, two must be added to make it dual, as *Lau matagu ruaoti.* "My children" will be *Lau natugu.* If plural has to be expressed particularly, a noun of multitude will be added, as *oreana* the company, or *logora* all.

Hani the sign of a question is always put last in the sentence. *Mero vada gorere hani?* The boy ill is? It is like the English, Eh? A pause is made before *hani.* A question is often indicated by tone of the voice solely.

Interrogative adverbs come last in sentence, as *Ia be daika?* Who is he? *Id'a edeseni ai?* Where are they? &c.

Verbs compounded with directive particles take the suffix between the root verb and its particle, *butugutao* I am seized— *butu* is the root, *tao* signifies restraint, fixedness, *butuatao* is to be seized, but when the speaker is the one seized he says, *butugutao.* The suffixes *va* and *mu* of time are, however, put at the end of such compound words, *butugutaomu, abimudae, abimudaeva,* to receive up (into house), *koudiāhu,* from *kou* to enclose and *ahu* around, *dia* the 3rd pers. plu. suffix comes between the two, *kou dia ahu,* but *koudiāhumu.*

In addition to what has already been said about the verbal particles it is well to remember that the particles distinctive of the three persons are, *na, o, e,* in plural the *na* loses the *n,* and the inclusive takes *t* instead, so that the plural is *a, ta, o, e.* The future changes the *o* into *a,* except in a few cases where *bo* survives. The *ba* again of 2nd pers. before verbs in *a* is lengthened into *bava, bava abia, bava alaia,* &c.

Vada is capable of many shades of meaning undefinable. It is always used of past or present, except occasionally in an imperative, which has the future form, as *vada ba kara.* When there has been indecision, as a man who purposed going but was asked to stay, when he has decided to stay, *ia vada noho.* Of state and condition it is always used, *ia vada e gorere, ia vada e mate.*

The exact force of *me* as in *eme, bame,* &c., has yet to be defined.

The suffix *mu* is sometimes changed into *mua,* as, *gimamaimua* for *gimamaimu* protecting us. Besides the suffixes and particles already noticed, *lasi* and *vareai* are much used in composition with verbs. *Lasi* is to extract, withdraw, and may generally be translated by *out,* while *vareai* is its opposite and may be rendered *in. Veria lasi* to pull out, *toia vareai* to insert, *laka lasi* to go out (of a house), *laka vareai* to enter (a house). The *lasi* and *vareai* take the suffixes *mu* and *va*, as *toia vareaiva, laka lasiva, veria lasimu.*

Natives differ considerably in their use of *va* the verbal suffix of time. Some use it with almost every verb in a narrative of past occurrence, while others are more sparing in the use, reserving it to save ambiguity in time. Speakers generally put themselves in the time of the event they are narrating, and use the suffixes accordingly. No rules can be given for the use of *va*, but for events of recent occurrence, and to ensure definiteness, it can always be safely used. A boy sent to another village on some commission and two or three days absent, would on his return relate his experiences, putting *va* to almost every verb, but an historical event of a year or two back would be told with only a *va* occasionally to make the events clear in their relation to each other.

Sibo na only, and *ibou, idoi* all, take suffixes of person. They immediately follow their *noun* or *pronoun* and agree with it in person, as, *lau sibogu na koaumu* I only say it, *ai iboumaiai idia iboudiai a hamaorodia,* we all make it known (told) to them all.

A peculiar idiom is, *ia urana e uramu, ia garina na garimu,* &c. He desiring desires, *i.e.,* he desires; his fear I am fearing, *i.e.,* I am afraid of him. *Idia nao garidia e garimu* they the foreigners fear are fearing, *i.e.,* they are afraid of the foreigners. It may sometimes be translated, because of, on account of, as, *Ia bigu baduna e badu,* the bananas' anger (anger about bananas), he is angry. *Mero hitolo taina e taimu,* the boy hunger cry is crying, *i.e.,* is crying on account of hunger.

Lau dabua hemaraina na hemaraimu I shame of clothes am ashamed, *i.e.,* I am ashamed because of my clothes. It is a very common idiom and to learners a difficult and obscure one.

The *mai* of possession is an important particle, *ia mai kohu hani?* has he any goods? *hodu mai anina,* the water pot has contents—is not empty; *bema mai asi bama lao,* if I had had a canoe I should have gone; *ai mai dika,* we have badness, *i.e.,* we are bad. The complete form would be, *ai mai dikamai ida, we have badness with us, oi mai aonegamu ida* thou wisdom with thee. *Lau mai goadagu ida* I have strength with me. If the question is asked, have you all pencils, the answer from one will be, *mai egu* I have mine, from another, *asi egu,* not mine, I haven't one.

Banava, an impersonal verb, to think, or suppose, erroneously, is used without usual particles, *lau banava,* &c.

A good many colloquialisms are not correct grammatically, but are sanctioned by usage. The verbal particles are often dropped, as, *ia koau* for *ia e koau*, *lau itaia*, for *lau e itaia*, *mailaia* for *ba* or *bame mailaia*. A very common usage of *lasi*, the adverb, is quite incorrect; *diba lasi*, *kamonai lasi*, *itaia lasi*, are common enough, and while natives use them in speaking to foreigners, they would never do so among themselves. They are instances of "pidgin" Motuan that are much to be regretted. *Lau asina dibagu*, not *lau diba lasi*, is correct Motuan; *oi tome kamonai*, not *oi kamonai lasi*; *ia se itaia*, not *ia itaia lasi*. The negative, *lasi*, is an answer to a question *no*, but is rarely used as a negative following a verb.

A negative is repeated before each member of a sentence, as, *Lau asina toreisi*, *oi basina henimu*, I will not rise, will not give thee.

An emphatic negative of common use is, *lasi*, *lasi*, *vaitani*, no, no, never. It closes a sentence and may be preceded by ordinary negative, *basina henimu*, *lasi*, *lasi*, *vaitani*, I will not give thee, no, no, never.

ENGLISH MOTU VOCABULARY.

A

A or An, Ta.
Abandon, Negea. Lakatania.
Abandoned, Vada negea.
Abase, Hamanaua.
Abash, Ahemaraia.
Abate, Hamaragia.
Abbreviate, Haqadogia.
Abdomen, Boka.
Abet, Durua.
Abhor, Lalo dika henia.
Abhorrence, Lalo dika.
Abide, Noho.
Ability, Diba. Aonega.
Abject, Dika rohoroho.
Able (to do, &c.), Karaia diba.
Ablution, Digu. Hadigua.
Abode, Noho gabuna. Ruma.
Abolish, Haorea.
Abominable, Dika rohoroho.
Abominate, Lalo dika henia. Ihihiraia.
Abortion, Mara dika.
Above, Atai.
Abound, Diagan. Hoho. Momo.
About, adv. Hegege (round about).
Lao evaeva (to go about).
Abreast (to walk), Laka bou. Laka aheveri.
Abridge, Haqadogia.
Abrogate, Ruhaia. Koauatao.
Abscess, Veto.
Abscond, Heau.
Absent, Noho lasi. Lasihia.
Absolve, Koauatao.
Absorb, Dodo.
Abstract, Abialasi. Verialasi.
Absnrd, Kavakava.
Abundance, Momo. Diagau.
Abuse, Hadikaia.
Accede, Ura henia. Gadudae.
Accept, Abia.
Access, Mai dalana.
Accompany, Bamoa. Ida lao (preceded by person accompanied.)
Accomplice, Bamona.
Accomplish, Karaia vaitani.
According, Hahegeregere. Bamona (following thing or speech with which it accords.)
Account, Hereva. Sivarai.
Account, (on account of) Daina ai.
Accumulate, Haboua.
Accurate, Maoromaoro.
Accurse, Uduguilai.
Accuse, Habade. Loduhenia.
Accustom, Hamanadaia.
Ache, Hisihisi.
Acid, Iseuri.
Acknowledge, Koau. Hegore lasi.
Acquiesce, Kamonai. Ere tamona.
Acquire, Abia.
Acrid, Hegara.
Across (to go), Hanai.
Act, Kara.
Active, Goada. Mauri.
Adage, Idaunegai hereva.
Adapt, Halaoa. Hahegeregere.
Add, Haboua.
Adhere, Kamoa.
Adjacent, Badibadina.
Adjoin (of houses, &c.), Gini hetabila.
Adjourn, Ununega koaulaia.
Adjudge, Ahemaoro henia.
Adjure, Ominuo (adopted from the Greek.) Koau henia.
Adjust, Hagoevaia. Gabunai atoa.
Admirable, Namo herea.
Admire, Hanamoa.
Admit, Iduara kehoa.
Admonish, Sisiba henia.
Adopt, Butuaoho.
Adore, Hanamoa.
Adorn, Hera karaia. Hagoevaia.
Adrift, Hure.
Adult, Sinana. Tamana. Tauna vada e lo.
Adulterer, Heudahanai tauna.
Adultery, Henaohenao. Heudahanai.
Adversary, Inai.
Adverse, Nega didadika.

Adversity, Nega dika.
Advise, Sisiba henia. Lalo c ania.
Advocate, Ahcmarumaru tauna.
Adze, Ira. Oinu (*introduced.*)
Afar, Daudau.
Affable, Gado naino tauna.
Affection, Lalokau henia. Urahenia.
Affirm, Koau.
Afflict, Hahisia.
Affright, Hagaria.
Affront, Hadikaia.
Afloat, Heilu.
Afoot, Tanoa mo lao.
Afraid, Gari.
After, Gabea. Murina.
Afterbirth, Momo.
Afternoou, Dina ɡ elona.
Afterpains, Mariva.
Again, Lou (*following verb*) ; Ma, (*preceding.*)
Against (*opposite*), Hegagaheheni.
Age, Lagani (*followed by number of years.*)
Aged, Tau or Hahine bada, Gauka.
Agent, Boloa tauna *and* Ibodohi tauna.
Aggravate, Habadaia.
Aggressor, Ima guna tauna.
Agitate (*as water in a bottle*), Qada-qadaia.
Ago (*long ago*), Idaunegai.
Agony, Hisihisi bada.
Agree, Koau bou. Lalo tamona.
Agreement, Taravatu.
Aground, Guihohoa.
Aha ! Hi ! Hinā !
Ahead, Vairanai. (*to go*) Laka guna.
Aid, Durua. Kahaia.
Aim, Diu.
Air, Lāi (lit. wind).
Alarm, Hagaria.
Alas ! Ināi. Inaio !
Albino, Gahukagahuka tauna. Huro-kahuroka tauna.
Alien, Idau tauna.
Alike, Hegeregere. (*of persons*) Hei-daida.
Alive, Mauri.
All, Idoinai. Ibounai. Logora.
Alleviate, Hisihisi hamaragia.
Allot, Haria. Karoa.
Allotment, Ahuna.
Allow, Mia. Haduaia.
Allure (*by deceit*), Koia.
Ally, Durua tauna. Hekaha tauna.
Almost, Moko (*before the verb.*)
Aloft, Ataiai.

Alone, Sibona.
Also, Danu.
Altar. Ihaboulaina pata.
Alter, Haidau.
Alternate, Hadava. Doga, doga.
Although, Enabe.
Altogether (*to do*), Karaia hebou. (*to stay*) Nohobou.
Always, Nega idoinai.
Amass, Haboua.
Amazed, Hōa. Laumadaure.
Amazing, Hahoaia gauna.
Ambassador, Isiaina tauna.
Ambiguous. Hereva se inaoro.
Ambition, Heagi tahua.
Ambush, Banitao.
Amend, Kara hamaoromaoro.
Amends, Davana. Qara henia.
Amidst, Bokaragina.
Amiss, Kererekerere.
Amongst, Bokaragina.
Ample, Bada.
Amuse, Hamoalea.
Anchor, Dogo.
Anchorage, Hedogo gabuna. Hegogo gabuna.
Ancient, Gunana. Idaunegai gauna *or* tauna.
Ancle, Ae komukomu.
And, Mai.
Angel, Aneru. (*Introduced.*)
Anger, Badu.
Animal, Boroma (*literally pig*).
Annoy, Gādegāde. Dāuahuahu.
Annul, Negea. Haorea.
Anoint (*head*), Horo. (*body*) Hetahu.
Another, Ma ta. Idau.
Answer, Haere.
Ant, Bilailo. Dimaili (*very small*) ; Mudumu (*white*).
Ant hill. Tano dubu.
Anxious, Lalo haguhi.
Any, Haida. Taina.
Apart, Idauhai.
Apartment, Daeutu. Daehudu.
Apologize, Maino noinoi. Hama-rumarua.
Apparel, Dabua.
Apparition, Lauma. Vatavata.
Appeal, Noinoi henia.
Appear (*as a spirit*), Hanihia. Hahedina.
Appease, Hamarumarua.
Applaud, Hanauoa.
Apply (*ask*), Henanadai.
Appoint, Koaulaia.
Approach, Laka kahila.

Approve, Namo koaulaia.
Arbitrate, Ahemaoro karaia.
Architect, Ruma iseuna tauna.
Arduous, Metau. .Malakamalaka.
Areca (*tree and also nut*), Buatau.
Argue, Hepapahuahu.
Arise, Toreisi.
Arm, Ima.
Arm v., Ima gauna abia.
Armpit, Kadidia.
Arms, Ima gaudia.
Army, Tuari.
Around, Hegege.
Arouse, Haoa.
Arrange (*things*), Kokosi. Atoa namonamo.
Arrest, Rosia. Dabaiatao.
Arrive, Lasi. Ginidae. *By sailing*, Heaukau.
Arrogance, Hekokorogu.
Arrow, Diba.
Arrowroot, Rabia.
Artery, Varovaro.
Artifice, Hedibagani.
As, Bamona.
Ascend, Daradae, (*mountain*). Daekau.
Ashamed, Hemarai..
Ashes, Rahurahu. Gahu.
Ashore, Tano ai.
Ask, Henanadai.
Aslant, Sehe..
Asleep, Mahuta.
Assault, Hadikaia.
Assemble, Haboua.
Assent, Namo koaulaia. Gadudae.
Assiduous, Goada.
Assist, Durua. Kahaia.
Associate *s*., Bamona. *v*. Bamoa.
Asthma, Roë.
Astonish, Hahöa. Lauma hadaurea.
Astray, Laka kerere; (*of pig, &c.*) Dōbi.
Astride, Helai dagadaga.
Asunder, Idau hai atoa. Parara.
Asylum, Magu.
At (*place*), Unuseni ai.
Atoll, Motumotu dava lalona ai.
Atone, Davana henia.
Atonement, Davaria.
Attack, Alala henia.
Attain, Abia. Davaria.
Attempt, Karaia toho.
Attend (*to listen*), Kamonai; (*to attend to a person*) Isiai laoheni..
Attest, Hamomokanilaia.
Attracted, Veria. Tao.

C

Audience, Kamonai.taudia.
Austere, Koautora tauna.
Authority, Siahu.
Avarice, Kohu hekisehekise bada.
Avenge, Davana karaia.
Avert, Helaoahu.
Avoid (*spear, &c.*), Dekea.
Avoid (*to shun*), Heirilaia.
Await, Naria, Helaro.
Awake, Noga.
Away, Idauhai.
Axe, Ira.

B

Babe, Natuna karukaru.
Back, Doru.
Backbite, Murina hadikaia.
Backbone, Turia mava.
Backside, Kunu.
Backslide, Dedi dobi.
Backwards (*to walk*), Laka muri. Lakatua.
Bad, Dika.
Bag (*small netted*), Vaina; (*large*) Kiapa; (*canvas*) Nulu; Moda.
Bait, Guma. Idoa.
Bake, Hamudoa. Gula.
Bald, Boha; "qara boha," Lama boha.
Bale, *v*. (*if thrown without dipping*) Petaia; (*dipped and then poured over the side*) Ranu seia.
Bale, *s*. (*of cloth, &c.*), Ikumi.
Ballad, Ane.
Bamboo, Bāu.
Banana (*fruit*), Bigu; (*tree*) Dui.
Bananas, different kinds of. See Appendix.
Band, Igui gauna.
Bandage, Hilia dabuana.
Bang, Regena bada. Poudagu.
Banish, Lulua.
Banishment, Idauhai lulua.
Bank (*of river*), Popoto.
Banner, Pepe.
Banter, Hevaseha.
Bar (*of wood*), Au.
Barb, Igara.
Bard, Ane. sisibaia tauna.
Bargain, *v*. Taravatu. Henega.
Bark, *s*. Au kopina.
Bark, *v*. Qaru.
Barren, Gabani (*of animals*).
Barricade, Dara kouahu gauna.
Barter, Hoihoi.

Base *the*, Badina.
Bashful, Hemurai. Igodiho.
Basket, Bosea.
Bason, Oburo. Biobio. Kibokibo, *introduced word*, Besini.
Bastard, Ariara natuua.
Bat, Mariboi.
Bathe, Digu.
Battle, Alala karaia.
Bay, Dogudogu. Tabero.
Beach, Kone.
Beads, Akeva.
Beak, Udu.
Beam, Mukolo.
Bear, *v.* (*as fruit*) Dobi ; (*give birth*) Mara ; (*to endure*) Aheauka ; (*to carry*) Huaia ; (*do on, as in labour*) Lado.
Beard, *s.* Aukihuina.
Bearer, Huaia tauna.
Beast, Boroma.
Beat, Dadaba Bota.
Beat, (*as a ship*) Heaudae heaudiho.
Beat out (*as native cloth*), Tadaia.
Beautiful, Namo herea (*of men*), Raho namo.
Becalmed, Vea (*if by day*) ; Gaima (*if by night*).
Because, Madi be.
Beckon, Hekalo.
Become, Halaoa.
Becoming, Namo herea.
Bed, Mahuta gauna.
Bedridden, Ruma noho.
Beetle, Manumanu.
Before, Vairanai.
Beg, Noi hegame.
Beget, Havaraia.
Beggar, Hegame tauna.
Begin, Matama.
Beginning, Matamana.
Begone, Baola. Lao.
Beguile, Koia.
Behaviour, Kara.
Behead, Qara utua.
Behind, Murina.
Behold, Ba itaia. *Interj.* Inäi.
Belch, Gado lohilohi.
Believe, Kamonai.
Bell, Gaba.
Bellow, Lolo. Tai lolololo.
Belly, Boka.
Bellyfull, Boka kunu.
Belong (*to him*) Iena.
Beloved, Lalokau tauna. Ura henia tanna.
Below, Henuai.

Belt, Gaba torana (*wide over hips*), Koekoe torana.
Bench, Pata.
Bend, Hagagevaia.
Beneath. Henuai.
Beneficial, Namo.
Benevolence, Harihari bada.
Benight, Hanua eme boi.
Beseech, Noinoi.
Beside, Badibadinai.
Besiege, Tuari hegegedae.
Besmear, Hedahu.
Bespeak, Nanaia.
Best, Namo herea.
Bestow, Henia.
Betray, Taotore.
Betroth, Maoheni.
Better, Inai namo (*thing compared with*), Unai dika.
Between, Ihuanai.
Bewail, Tāi.
Beware, Itaia namonamo.
Beyond, Unuka.
Bible, Buka helaga.
Bid (*command*), Hahedua. Hagania.
Bier, Mate tauna patana.
Big, Bada.
Bigamy, Hodara.
Billow, Sinaia.
Bind, Guia.
Bird, Mānu. For names of different kinds, see Appendix.
Birth, Vafa.
Birth premature, Kercnai e vara.
Bit (*a piece*), Sisina. (*horse's*) Hosi udu iatona gauna.
Bite, Koria.
Bitter, Idita.
Black, Koremakorema. (*very black*), Dubaduba.
Bladder, Posi.
Bladebone, Larolaro turiana.
Blame, Koau henia. Hadikaia.
Blaspheme, Dirava hadikaia.
Blaze, Hururu. Paitapaita.
Blaze, *v.* (*trees*) Daroa. (*fire*) Lahi huruhuru. Baitabaita.
Bleed, Rara diho. Budiabudia. (*from the nose*), Udu makohi.
Blemish, Dika. Bebekabebeka.
Bless, Hanamoa.
Blessed, Namo.
Blind, Matakepulu.
Blink, Varirivariri.
Blister, Goua.
Blood, Rara.
Bloody, Rorakararaka.

Blossom, Au huahua.
Blossom, v. Burea.
Blow, v. (as wind), Tōa. (with the mouth) Hihiria. (nose) Iluhai.
Blue, Gadogagadoga, and also green.
Blunder, Kererekerere.
Blunderbuss, Ipidi.
Blunt, Gāno lasi. Buru.
Boar, Boroma maruane.
Board, Leilei.
Boast, v. Heagi.
Boat, Boti. (Introduced).
Body, Tāu. Anitarana.
Bog, Kopakopu.
Boil, v. n. Daidai.
Boil to, Nadna.
Boil, s. Iholulu. (blind) Atuahu.
Bold, Goada.
Bold-faced, Kopi hemarai lasi.
Bone, Turia.
Bonnet, Qara gauna.
Bony, Vidigara.
Book, Buka. (Introduced.)
Booty, Dadidadi gaudia or Kohudia.
Border, Isena.
Bore, v. (a hole) Budua.
Borrow, Koautorehai.
Bosom, Geme.
Both, Rua davana.
Bother, Haraivaia.
Bottle (native), Ahu. (Foreign) Kavapu.
Bottom (of sea), Qari.
Bough, Rigi.
Boundary, Hetoa.
Bow, s. Peva.
Bow (to string), Rohea.
Bow and Arrow (for bleeding) Ibasi.
Bow down, v. Tomadiho.
Bowels, Bokalau.
Bower, (of bower-bird) Sinoleke rumana.
Bower-bird, Sinoleke.
Bowl (wooden), Dihu. (Earthenware) Nāu.
Bows (of canoe) Itama. (Sharp bows) Robonarobona.
Bowstring, Maora.
Box, Māua.
Boy, Mero.
Boyish, Mero bamona.
Brackish, Māga.
Brag, Heagi herevana.
Brain, Hara. " Qara harana."
Branch, Rigi.
Brandish, Hare.

Brass, Vco. auri raborarabora. (Introduced.)
Brave, Goada. Asi bokana.
Brawl, Lolo.
Bread, Palaoa, Areto. (Introduced.)
Breadfruit, Unu.
Breadth, Lababana.
Break (string), Motu. (Spear, &c.), Qaidu. (Pottery, &c.), Huaria.
Breaker (in sea), Sinaia.
Breast, Geme.
Breastbone (of bird), Abagoro. (Of mammal) Gemegeme.
Breath, Laga.
Breath (short), Lagatuna.
Breath (deep), Hahodi.
Breathe, Laga.
Breathless, Lagatuna.
Breeches, Biribou. (Introduced.)
Breed, Mara (act of bringing forth).
Breeze, Lāi.
Bridge, Nese hanai pātana.
Bright, Hururuhururu. Kiamakiama.
Brimful, Honuhonudae.
Bring, Mailaia.
Bring forth, Mara.
Brink, Isena.
Brisk, Lega haraga tauna.
Bristle, Boroma huina.
Brittle, Makohi haraga.
Broad, Lababana bada. Gamoga bada.
Broil, Nonoa. Gabua.
Brood, s. Serina.
Brood, v. Hadetari. Laloa.
Brother, Tadikāka. (younger), Tadina. (elder), Kakana.
Brother-in-law, Ihana.
Brown, Korema. Uriuri, mia koremakorema.
Browse, Rei ania.
Bruise, Rara arukubou.
Brush, n. Iareva. Hedaro gauna.
Brushwood. Āu maragimaragi.
Bubble, Lohilohia.
Bud, Komukau.
Buffet, Tutua.
Build (a house), Ruma karaia. (a wall), Nadi larebaia.
Builder, Ruma ikarana tauna.
Bullet, Ipidi nadina.
Bully, Dagedage tauna.
Bunch (tied together), Igui. (of fruit), Takona. (of cocoa-nuts), Rovae.
Bundle. Ikumi.
Buoy, Uto.

Burden, Maduna (*if carried on a stick.*)
Burn, *v.*, (*food*) Halaka. (*grass*), Doua. (*house*), Alaia.
Burn, *n.*, Lahi alaia.
Burnish, Hahururuhururua.
Burrow, Tahia.
Burst, Pāpa. Pou.
Bury, Guria.
Bush, Uda. (*fallow ground*), Vahu.
Business, Gau karaia. Totona.
Busy, Heqarahi.
But, A.
Butterfly, Kaubebe.
Buttock, Kunu.
Button, Pitopito (*intr xluced word.*)
Buy, Hoihoi.
By (*instrument*),—laia (*suffixed to verb.*)
By (*near*), Badibadina. Dekena.
By-and-bye, Dohore.

C

Cable, Matáboi. Gadea.
Cackle, Tāi.
Cadaverous, Raborarabora.
Cage, Ruma.
Cajole, Hauamoa koikoi. Koau laloa..
Cake, Mone. Palaoa ataka.
Calamity, Dika.
Calculate, Duahia.
Caldron, Uro bada.
Calf (*of leg*), Doku.
Calk, Demaia.
Call, *v.*, Boiboi.
Call, *n.*, Boiboi.
Calm (*in the day*), Vea ; (*at night*), Gaima.
Calm, *v.* Hamarumarua.
Calumniate, Hadikaia.
Camp, Taruha hebou.
Camp, *v.* Taruha.
Camp to strike. Ladaia.
Can, Karaia diba.
Cancel, Rohoa.
Cane, Oro. Vagoda.
Cannibal, Taunimanima ania tauna. Hiluae ani tauna.
Cannon, Ipidi bada.
Cannot, Karaia diba lasi.
Canoe (*small*), Vanagi ; (*large*), Asi.
Canoe maker, Ikede tauna.

Cap, Qara gauna.
Capable, Karaia diba. Aonega.
Capacious, Gabana bada ; (*of house*) Lababana bada.
Cape, Iduka.
Capsicum, Urehegini, Oboro (*introduced name.*)
Captain (*of ship*), Lakatoi tauna.
Captive, Abi mauri tauna.
Care, Lalo haguhi (*to take care of*), Dōsi. Naria.
Careful, Namonamo. Abia balaheni.
Careless, Kererckerere. Matalahui.
Carpenter, Kamuta (*introduced*).
Carpenter wasp. Dina matana.
Carry (*on the shoulder*), Huaia ; (*pick-a-back*), Geia ; (*on a pole between two*), Huaia boroma ; (*as water pot*), Ehea ; (*on the head*), Oraia ; (*astride on neck*), Udua.
Carve (*a joint*), Ivaia ; (*wood, &c.*) Koroa.
Cast, Tohoa.
Cast away, Tohoa daure.
Cast down, Tahoa dobi.
Castigate, Dadabaia.
Castle, Magu.
Castrate, Abona abia.
Cat, Pose (*introduced*).
Catch, Butuatao.
Catch (*by contagion*), Kara ; (*with suffix*) karagu, &c.
Catch (*of thing thrown*), Gobea.
Catch hold, Abia. Kahua.
Catechize, Henanadai.
Caterpillar, Bulelamo.
Cat's cradle (*the game*). Harigau.
Cause, *s.*, Koauna. Badina.
Cause, *v.*, Havaraia.
Causeway, Dala.
Caustic, Hegara.
Cautious, Metailametailn.
Cave, Kohua.
Cavil, Koauatubu.
Cease, Doko. Vadaeni.
Cedar, Besele.
Cede, Henia.
Celebrate, Hanamoa. Ahelaloa.
Cemetery, Mate guria gabuna.
Censure, Koau henia. Sisiba henia.
Census, Taunimanima duahia.
Centipede, Aiha.
Centre, Bokaragi.
Certain, Momokani etomamu.
Certify, Koaulaia.
Chain, Gadea.
Chair, Helai gauna.

CHA (37) COL

Challenge, Boi gagadae. Hare henia.
Chamber, Daehudu.
Change, Boloa.
Channel, Mātu.
Chant, Ane.
Character, Kara.
Charcoal, Gida.
Charge v., Hetamanu.
Charge (a gun), Ipidi anina.
Charity, Hebokahisi.
Charm (cocoa nut), Biobio.
Chaste, Igodiho haniulato. Se mata dikana.
Chat, Hereva.
Chatterer, Udu mauri.
Chase, v., Hāvaia.
Chasm, Koupa.
Chastise, Dadaba.
Cheap, Hoihoi davana maragi.
Cheat, Koia.
Check, Dokoatao. Laoahu.
Cheek, Vaha.
Cheer, Tauhalō.
Cheerful, Lalo namo tauna.
Cherish, Ubua. Naria.
Cherisher, Iubuna tauna.
Chest, Geme. (a box), Māua.
Chestnut, Omada.
Chew, Gauaia. (the pandanus), Oria.
Chicken, Kokorogu natuna.
Chide, Koaukoau. Sisiba henia.
Chief (thing), Herea gauna.
Chief, s., Lohiabada.
Child, Natuna.
Childbirth, Mara, natuna abia.
Childish, Meromero bamona.
Chill, v. Hakerumaia.
Chin, Hade.
Chip, Memeuse.
Chip, v., (wood), Siria ; (as edge of shell), Hepede.
Chirp (as lizard), Tanatana.
Chisel, Vadu.
Chisel (small) Pako.
Choice, adj. Namo herea.
Choke, Gādo ai hetera. (by another), Gado gigia.
Choose, Abia hidi. (by inspection), Ita hidi.
Chop, Talai.
Churlish, Koautora tauna.
Circular, Kubolukubolu.
Clammy, Parikaparika.
Clamour, Helogohelogo.
Clang, Hataia.
Clasp (hands), Ima patapata.
Clash, Huaria.

Clasp (in arms), Rosia.
Class, Verina. Oreana.
Clatter, Regeregena.
Claw, Ima.
Clay, Raro.
Clean, Goevagoeva.
Cleanse, Hagoevaia.
Clear, Nega.
Clear (away), Abiaoho. Laohaia.
Cleave to, Badinaia.
Cleave (to split), Hapai araia.
Clever, Aonega.
Cliff, Hagahaga.
Climb (tree), Urua.
Cling, Hekamokau.
Clip, Haqadogia.
Close (near), Kahilakahila.
Close, v., Ahu. Kouahu.
Cloth, Dabua.
Clothe, Dabua hadokilaia.
Clothes, Dabua.
Clothes, to put on, Ahedokia.
Clothes, to take off, Dokia.
Clothing, Dabua.
Cloud, Dagadaga. Ori.
Cloudy, Dagahu.
Cloven, Parara.
Clownish, Guni tauna bamona.
Cloy, Laloalu.
Club stone (flat round), Gahi. (egg-shaped), Tanala. (star-shaped), Iorimuni. (knobbed), Kikitaka.
Club wooden, Kaleva.
Cluck, Tāi.
Clump (of trees), Uda motu.
Clumsy, Ima maniano.
Cluster (of fruit), Takona.
Clutch, Hekamotao.
Coagulate, Hetari. Hemani.
Coarse (cloth), Nulu.
Coarse (rough), Butubutu.
Coast, Tano isena.
Coat, Pereue (adopted from the Tahitian).
Coax, Noinoi.
Cobweb, Valavala.
Cock, Kokorogu maruane.
Cockcrowing, Kokorogu tāi.
Cockfight, Kokorogn heatu.
Cocoanut, Niu. (young fruit) Gāru.
Coequal, Hegeregere.
Cogitate, Lalo. Lalo haguhi.
Coil (in hand), Tāia ; (on deck) Kekea.
Cold, Keru ; (of food), Keruma-keruma.
Colic, Boka hisihisi.

Collar-bone, Dōa.
Collect, Haboua.
Collection (*of things*), Senuscnu. Hegigibou.
Collision, Tatakau.
Colors :—
　Black, Koremakorema, also dark brown, &c. Very black, Duba-duba.
　Blue and Green, Gadogagadoga.
　Blue Dark, also Violet, Dahulu-dahulu.
　Bright (*very dark*). Ogoaogoa from Ogoa, plumbago.
　Brown (*color of Motuans*), Uriuri.
　Brown light, Gagvre.
　Brown (*as chesnut horse*), Mia koremakorema.
　Pink, Pailapaila.
　Red, Kakakaka.
　Red brown (*as Raggiana feathers*), Kasilikasili.
　Green pale, Manahuromanahuro.
　White, Kurokuro.
　Yellow white, Mia kurokuro.
　Yellow, Raborarabora.
　Yellow (*deep orange*), Magemage.
Comb, Iduari.
Combat, Heatu.
Combine, Haheboua.
Combustible, Lahi haragaharaga.
Come, Mai. Aoma.
Come (*in sight*), Vada diua. Ginidae.
Comet, Hido.
Comfort v. Tauhalō.
Command, Hagania. Haduaia.
Commandment, Ahegani herevana.
Commemorate, Ahelaloa.
Commence, Matamaia.
Commend, Hanamoa.
Commerce, Hoihoi karaia.
Commit, Henia.
Common (*to make*), Petapetalaia.
Commotion, Herouherou.
Compact, Taravatu. Henega.
Companion, Bamona.
Company, Hutuma. (*visitors*) Vadi-vadi.
Compare, Hahetoho. Hahegeregerc.
Compassion, Hebokahisi.
Compel, Hahedua.
Compensate, Davana henia.
Compete, Goada helulu daika herea.
Competent, Karaia diba.
Complain, Maumau.
Complete, Idoinai. v. Hagugurua.
Completely, Guguru.

Compliment v., Hanamoa henia.
Comply, Gadudae. Oi be koaulaia.
Compose (*a song*), Ane sisibaia.
Comprehend, Diba.
Compute, Duahia.
Comrade, Ibamona.
Conceal, Ehuni.
Conceited, Heagi tauna. Hekokorogu tauna.
Conceive, Rogorogo.
Conch, Kibi.
Conciliate, Hamarumarua.
Concise, Qadogi.
Conclude, Hadokoa.
Conclusion, Dokona.
Concourse, Hegogo bada.
Concur, Koaubou.
Condemn (*to death*), Revaia. Rataia.
Condescend, Hamanaua.
Conduct, s., Kara.
Conduct, v., Hakaua.
Confer, Herevahereva.
Confess, Koaulaia. Ahedinarai.
Confide, Hamaoroa.
Confirm, Hamomokania.
Conflict, Heatu. Alala.
Confounded, Laumadaure.
Congregate, Haheboua.
Conjecture, Lalo koau.
Conquer, Qalimu.
Conscience, Lalona.
Consecrate, Ahelagaia.
Consent, Gadudae. Namo koaulaia.
Consider, Laloa.
Cousign, Henia.
Console, Tauhalō.
Consort, s., Adavana.
Conspire, Hereva ehuni.
Constantly, Nega idoinai.
Consternation, Kudou hetaha.
Constipation, Tubuahu.
Constrain, Hahealo.
Construct, Karaia.
Consult, Ida hereva (*preceded by the person consulted*).
Consume (*by fire*), Lahi e alaia ore. Goleaoho ; (*to eat*), Ania ore.
Contagious, Dāi hanai hisina.
Contemn, Hadikaia.
Contemplate, Laloa.
Contend, Heatu. Hepapahuahu.
Content, Boka kunu.
Contents, s., Anina.
Contention, Hepapahuahu.
Contest, Heatu. Alala.
Contiguous, Badibadina.
Continual, Nega idoinai.

Continue, Mia hanaihanai. (*to do, to sit, &c.*), doini, dounu.
Contract, *s.*, Henega, Koauhamata.
Contract, *v.*, (*from cold*), Hegogo.
Contradictory, Hegeregere lasi.
Contribute, Henia.
Contribution, Gau vada henia.
Control, Hakaua. Dokoatao.
Controversy, Hepapahuahu.
Contumacy, Ura dika.
Convalescent, Mauri maraginmaragi. Tau dainamo.
Convene, Haheboua.
Conversant, Vata diba.
Conversation, Herevahereva.
Convert, Haloua.
Convey, Laohaia.
Coo, Mu.
Cook, *s.*, Nanadu tauna.
Cook, *v.*, (*boil*), Nanadu.
Cookhouse, Nanadu ruma : (*roast on fire*) Gabua ; (*bake*) Hamudo, Gula ; (*in English oven*) Nadua, an introduced use ; (*fry*) Paraipani ; (*toast*) Nanaia.
Cool, Kerumakeruma.
Coop (*for fowls*), Kokorogu ruma.
Copious, Gaubadabada.
Copper, Veo (*introduced*).
Copulation, Gagaia.
Copy, *s.*, Oromana. Itohona revareva.
Coquette, Hegera.
Coral, Irigi. Nadi kuro. Lade.
Cord, Qanau.
Core (*of boil*), Komutu.
Cork, Iqadobe.
Corn, Koani (*introduced*).
Corner, Daeguni.
Corner-stone, Nadi daegunina.
Corpse, Tau mate.
Corpulent, Nuana bada.
Correct, Maoromaoro.
Corrupt, *v.*, Hadikaia.
Corrupt, *adj.*, Dika.
Cost, Davana. (*What ?*), dahaka davana ?
Costive, Boka tubuahu.
Costly, Hoihoi bada.
Cottage, Ruma maragi.
Cotton (*introduced word*), Vavae ; (*sewing*), Varo.
Couch, Hekure gauna.
Cough, Hūa.
Council, Taubadadia hegogo.
Counsel, *v.*, Sisiba henia.
Count, Duahia. Hagaua.
Countenance, Vaira.

Counteract, Koauatubu. Laoahu.
Counterfeit, *v.*, Koia.
Countermand, Koauatao.
Countless, Duahia lasi.
Country, Tano.
Countryman, Tano tauna.
Couple, Ruaoti.
Courage, Goada.
Courteous, Gādo namo.
Courtezan, Ariara hahine.
Cousin (*younger*), Tadina ; (*elder*), Kakana. Vara bamona, Mauri bou, Mauri dudu.
Cove, Dogudogu.
Covenant, Taravatu.
Cover, Kaluhia. Bubuni. (*As box*), Vava.
Covet, Hekisehekise henia.
Covetous, Mata ganigani. Kokosina.
Coward, Mai bokana tauna. Gari tauna.
Cower, Rāki karaia.
Coy, Hemarai.
Crab, Kokoba. Bava.
Crack (*in boards, &c.*), Māka ; (*in pot, &c.*), Roro.
Crackle, Hepoupouahu.
Craft, Dagi.
Crafty, Hedibagani tauna.
Crag, Haga.
Cramp, Hegagiudae.
Crash, Makohi.
Crave, Noinoi.
Crawfish, Ura. Depuru.
Crawl, Rāu. (*as a snake*), Vero.
Creak, Koke.
Crease, Magugu.
Create, Karaia.
Creep, Laka helada.
Creeper, Āu hilia.
Creepy, Hemaihemai.
Crevice, Maka.
Crew (*of ship*), Lakatoi memero. Neseriki memero.
Crime, Kara dika. Taravatu tataiautu.
Crimson, Kakakaka.
Cringe, Raki karaia.
Crinkle, Magugu.
Cripple (*lame*), Ae dairiki.
Crockery, Uro. Hodu, &c.
Crocodile, Uala.
Crook, *v.*, Hagagevaia.
Crookback, Doruqagugu. Doru laobo.
Cross, Āu hiri baribara. Satauro. (*Introduced*).

Crossway, Dala katakata.
Crouch, Rāki karaia.
Crow, v., Kokorogu tai.
Crowbar, Isiva.
Crowd, Hutuma.
Crown, Qara gegea gauna.
Crown (of head), Qara tupua.
Cruel, Dagedage.
Crumb, Momoruna.
Crumple, Magugu kainekaine.
Crush (under foot), Aemoia.
Cry, Tai.
Cubit, Kubita (introduced).
Cuff, Huaria.
Cultivate, Uma ladoa.
Cunning, Aonega
Cup, Kchere. (Shell), Bio. (Teacup), Kaputi.
Cure, Hamauria.
Curly, Hui tuma.
Current (of river, &c.), Aru.
Curse, Hadikaia. Uduguilai.
Curtain, Sescahu.
Curve, n., Gagevagageva.
Custom, Kara.
Cut (up), Ivaia ; (off), Utua.
Cutlass, Ilapa.
Cuttlefish, Urita.

D

Daily, Daba daba idoinai.
Damage, Hadikaia.
Damp, Parikaparika.
Dance, Mavaru.
Dandle, Harohoa.
Dare, Goada.
Dare (to defy), Hare.
Dark, Dibura.
Darling, Lalokau tauna (man), or natuna (child).
Dart, v., Qanua.
Dash (on ground), Tahoa dobi.
Daub, Hetahu. Tabaiahu.
Daughter, Kekeni. Natuna hahine.
Daunt, Hagaria.
Dawn, Daba e kinia.
Day, Dina.
Dazzle, Mata paia.
Dead, Mate.
Deaf, Taia kudima.
Deaf (to make), Hakudimaia.
Deal, Hoihoi karaia.
Deal out, Hagaua.

Dear (in price), Hoihoi davana bada.
Dear (beloved), Lalokau.
Dearth (of food), Doe.
Death, Mate.
Debate, Herevahereva. Hepapahuahu.
Debauch, Hadikaia.
Debilitate, Hamanokaia.
Debility, Manakamanoka.
Debt, Abitorehai davana. Dodi.
Debtor, Abitorehai tauna.
Decapitate, Qara utua.
Decay (fruit), Pouka ; (wood), Houkahouka.
Decease, Mate.
Deceit, Koikoi.
Deceive, Koia.
December, Biriabada.
Decent, Namo.
Decide, Koaulaia.
Deck, v., Ilaha karaia. (With ornaments) Hera karaia.
Deck, s., Ilaha.
Declare, Koaulaia. Hedinarai.
Decline, Dadaraia.
Decorate, Hera karaia. Hāiraina karaia.
Decorous, Kara namo.
Decoy, Koia.
Decrease, Hamaragia.
Decree, Lohiabada ena hereva. Ahe gani hereva.
Dedicate, Ahelagaia.
Deep, Dobu.
Defaced, Hadikaia.
Defame, Eredika koaulaia.
Defeat, Darere.
Defect, Dika.
Defend, Naria. Gimaia.
Defer, Dohore koaulaia.
Deference, Hematalaurai.
Defiance, Hare.
Deficient, Idoinai lasi. Diahoho.
Defile, Hamiroa. Hadikaia.
Define, Koaulaia maoromaoro.
Deformed, Tāu dika.
Defraud, Koia.
Defy, Heqada karaia. Hare henia.
Degrade, Hadikaia.
Delay, Halahe. Haraga lasi.
Deliberate, Herevahereva.
Deliberately, Metailametaila.
Delicious, Namo herea.
Delight, Moale.
Delirium, Lalona e boio. Koau kava.
Deliver, Hamauria.
Delude, Koia. Hagagevaia.

Deluge, Ututu bada.
Delusion, Koikoi.
Demand, Noinoi.
Demolish, Haorea. Buatari (as town, &c.)
Demon, Demoni. (Introduced.)
Demonstrate, Ahedinarai.
Denial, Hegore.
Denounce, Loduheheni.
Depart, Idauhai lao.
Depend, Abidadama henia.
Depopulate, Taunimanima haorea.
Depose, Doria dobi. Abiaoho.
Deprave, Hadikaia.
Deprive (take away), Idauhai laohaia.
Depth, Dobu.
Deputy, Boloa tauna.
Deride, Gonagonalaia.
Decend, Diho. (Mountain) Hekei.
Decendant, Tubuna.
Decent, Hekei darann.
Describe, Hamaoroa.
Desecrate, Hadikaia.
Desert, v., Lakatania.
Desert, s., Tano gagaena or dekedekenarahu.
Design, Lalokoau.
Desire, Hekischekise, Urana ura.
Desist, Doko.
Desolate, Dekedekenarahu:
Despatch, v., Siaia.
Despicable, Dika rohoroho.
Despite, Hadikaia.
Despised (adj.) Pekara. Ihihiraia.
Despond, Lalo dika.
Destination, Totona gabuna.
Destitute, Asi gauna. Ogogame.
Destroy, Haorea. Buatari.
Detach, Kahuanege.
Detail, Koaulaia hegege.
Detain, Rūa.
Detect, Abia. Davaria.
Determine, Lalona ura e hamaoroa.
Detest, Inai henia.
Devastate, Hadikaia rohoroho.
Deviate, Idauhai lao.
Devoid (of sense) Asi aonega.
Devote, Ahelagaia.
Devour, Ania.
Dew, Hunu.
Diadem, Qara gegea gauna.
Dialect, Gādo.
Dialogue, Herevahereva heheni.
Diarrhœa, Boka hekukuri.
Dictate, Ahegani hereva.
Did, Karaia.
Die, Mate.

Die (red colour), Hakakakakaia; (black), Hakoremakoremaia.
Differ, Idau.
Difficult (to do, open, &c.), Auka.
Diffident, Hemarai.
Diffuse, Buloa.
Dig, Geia.
Dilapidate, Hamakobia.
Dilatory, Haraga lasi. Nohorinohori.
Diligent, Goadagoada.
Dilute, Ranu buloa.
Dim, Valahuvalahu.
Diminish, Hamaragia.
Dip, Uruadiho.
Dip up, Kadoa.
Dire, Dika bada.
Direct, v., Hadibaia. Hamaoroa.
Direction (towards) Hagerea.
Directly, Haragaharaga. Harihari.
Dirge, Ehona kurea lao kurea laomu.
Dirt, Miro.
Dirty, Miro.
Disagree, Hereva tamoua lasi.
Disappear, Boio. Lasihia.
Disapprove, Hanamoa lasi.
Disaster, Dika butuatao.
Disband, Karoho.
Disbelieve, Hedalo kepokepoa.
Discern, Diba.
Discharge, v., Lulua. Siaia lao.
Disciple, Hadibaia mero.
Disclose, Hamaoroa. Koaulaia.
Discompose, Haraivaia. Turiariki.
Discord, Helogohelogo.
Discourage, Lalona hamanokaia.
Discourse, Haroro.
Discourteous, Eredika.
Discover, Ahedinarai.
Discreet, Aonega.
Discriminate, Hasinadoa.
Disdain, Badu henia. Ihihiraia.
Disease, Gorere.
Disembowel, Bokaia.
Disfigure, Hadikaia.
Disgrace, Ahemaraia.
Disgraceful, Hemaraia kara.
Disgust, Lalo dika.
Dish Nāu. Dihu. (deep), Dihu dobuna; (shallow), Dihu posena.
Dishearten, Hagaria, Hamanokaia.
Dishevelled, Hui hepanihepani, Hemogebemoge.
Disinter, Guria tauna abiaisi.
Disjoin, Ruhaia nege.
Dislike, Lalo dika henia.
Dislocated, Heladaoho. Helide.

Dismiss, Siaia lao.
Dismount, v. a. Abiadobi.
Dismount, v. n. Diho.
Disobedient, Koauedeede.
Disown, Dadaraia.
Disperse, Karoho.
Dispirit, Hamanokaia.
Display, Hedinarai.
Displease, Habadua.
Dispossess, Dadidadi. Abiaoho.
Dispute, Koauatubu.
Disregard, Asi e ita. Asi e kamonai.
Disreputable, Harina dika.
Disrespect, Lagāua.
Dissatisfy, Lalo namo lasi.
Dissemble, Hedi'agani karaia.
Dissent, Heirihe. ri.
Dissever, Utua nege.
Dissimilar, Hegeregere lasi.
Dissolve, Veve.
Distant, Daudau.
Distemper. Gorere.
Distend, Kuroro.
Distinguish, Toana diba.
Distress, Nega dikadika.
Distribute, Henia hagauhagau.
District, Kahana.
Disturb, Hahoaia.
Disturbance, Heai karaia.
Ditch, Koupa.
Dive, Hedai.
Diverse, Idau.
Divide, Karoa. Haria.
Division, Karoa ahuna.
Divorce, v. Hadihoa.
Divulge, Koaulaia.
Dizzy, Kakala. Mata madaimadai.
Do, Karaia.
Docile, Manada.
Doctor, Muramura tauna.
Doctor, v. Muramura henia. (by native sorcerer), Daroa.
Dodge, v. Dekea.
Dog, Sisia.
Dolt, Kavakava.
Dominion, Basileia. (Introduced.)
Doom (to death), Rataia.
Door, Mu. Iduara ikouna.
Doorway, Iduara.
Dot, Toutou.
Dotage, Garugaru bamona.
Double, Ere rua.
Double-minded, Lalo rua.
Double-up, Lokua.
Doubt, Daradara.
Dove, Pune.
Down, Diho. Dobi.

Downward, Henuai.
Doze, Mahuta.
Drag, Veria. Dabuia (as anchor), Dadaroha.
Drake, Mokora maruane. (Introduced.)
Draught (fluid drank), Gurita.
Draw, Veria.
Draw (entice, allure), tao, iena ai e taomu.
Draw near, Laka kahila.
Draw-rope (of well), Itudobina varona.
Dread, Gari.
Dream, Nihi.
Dregs, Nurina.
Dress, Dabua.
Drift, v. Hure.
Drift, s. Keri.
Drill, s. Ibudu gauna.
Drink, Inua.
Drip, Hetuturu.
Drive, Ahavaia.
Drivel, Tāba.
Drizzle, Sisimo.
Droop, Marai.
Drollery, Hevaseha kara.
Drop, Hetuturu.
Dropsy, Rara dika e dae.
Drown, Maloa.
Drowsy, Mata e gara.
Drum, Gaba. (bamboo) Sede.
Drunk, Muramura heala. Kekero.
Dry, Kaukau.
Dry (to, in the sun), Raraia.
Duck (tame), Mokora. (Introduced.)
Duck (wild), Ohuka. Bala.
Dull (of tools), Gano lasi. Buru.
Dumb, Mu.
Dunce, Kavakava.
Dung, Tage.
Durable, Auka bada.
Dusk, Mairumairu
Dusk, Gahu
Dwell, Noho
Dwelling, Noho gabuna. Ruma.
Dwindle, Hamaragia. Hagadoia.
Dyspnœa, Laga tuna.

E

Each, Ta ta, Hagauhagau.
Eager, Ura bada
Ear, Taia. (of corn), Bogo.
Early (in the morning), Daba matana.

Earn, Gau kara davana.
Earnest, Momokani.
Earth, Tano.
Earthquake, Laga karaia.
Earthworm, Biruka.
Ease, v. (*to be at*) Noho namonamo.
East, Mairiveina.
Eastward, Mairiveina kahana.
East-wind, Lai mairiveina.
Easy, Haragaharaga.
Eat, Ania.
Eat together, Anibou.
Eat up, Aniore.
Eatable, Aniani gauna,
Eaves, Seasea.
Ebb, Gui.
Ebulition, Lohilohia.
Echo, Hetohotoho.
Eclipse (*sun*), Dina gobaiahu.
  (*moon*), Hua gobaiahu.
Eddy, Aru. Kavabulobulo.
Edge, Isena.
Edible, Aniani gauna.
Edict, Ahegani herevana.
Edge, Matana.
Educate, Hadibaia.
Eel, Daqala.
Efface, Hamatea. Rohoa.
Effigy, Laulau.
Effort, Karaia toho.
Effulgent, Huruluhururu.
Egg, Katoi.
Eight, Taurahani.
Eighteen, Quata taurahani.
Eighty, Taurahani ahui.
Either, Iava, as, *namo e iava dika*.
Eject (*from the mouth*), Pururua.
  (*from the house*) Doria lāsi.
Elate, Hamoalea.
Elbow, Diu.
Elders, Taubadadia.
Eldest, Vara guna.
Elect, Koaulaia hidi.
Elegy, Sesera.
Elephantiasis, Badau (*preceded by the member*), as, *ae badau*.
Elevate (*as a pole from the ground*), Piuaisi.
Eleven, Qauta ta.
Elongate, Halataia.
Elude, Heau.
Emaciate, Tau gadili.
Emasculate, Abona e abia.
Embalm, Muramura hetahu.
Embark, Lakatoi gui.
Embassy, Hesiai taudia. Koaukauna memero.

Embellish, Hanamoa.
Embers, Gida.
Embrace, Rosia.
Embrocation, Hetahu muramura.
Emerge (*from diving*), Sesedaeroha.
Emetic, Hamumutaia.
Eminence, Ataina.
Emissary, Isiaina tauna.
Emmet, Dimaili.
Employ, *v. a.* Siaia.
Employment, Gau karaia.
Empty, Asi anina.
Encamp, Taruha karaia.
Enclose, Gegea. Hegege madai.
Enclosure, Ara. Ikou.
Encompass, Hegege.
Encounter, *s.* Alala.
  v. Toia hedavari.
Encourage, Hahealo.
Encumber, Hametaua.
End, Dokona.
Endeavour, Karaia toho
Endless, Asi dokona.
Endure, Aheauka.
Enemy, Inai.
Energetically, Turiaturia.
Energy, Goada. Lega gada.
Enfeeble, Hamanokaia.
Enforce (*to instigate*), Havaraia.
Engage (*to work*), Gau kara bae karaia.
Engagement, Henegahenega.
Engrave (*wood*), Koloa.
Enjoin, Hetamanu.
Enjoy, Moale. Lalo namo.
Enkindle, Haraia.
Enlarge, Habadaia.
Enlighten, Hadiaria. (*With torch*), Hakedea.
Enmity, Inai henia.
Enough, Davana.
Enough! Vadaeni.
Enquire, Nanadai.
Enrage, Habadua.
Ensign, Pepe.
Ensnare, Idoa.
Entangle, Hiria. Mogea.
Enter, Vareai.
Entertain, Hagerea. Heabidae.
Entice, Hedibagani.
Entire, Idoinai.
Entrails, Bokalau.
Entrance, Iduara.
Entrap, Doa.
Entreat, Noinoi.
Entwine, Hiria.
Enumerate, Duahia. Koaulaia hegege.

Envelope, v. Kumia.
Envelope, s. Ikumi gauna. (of a letter) Leta iudana gauna.
Envious, Hebore karaia.
Envoy, Hesiai.
Envy, Vagege. Hebore.
Epidemic, Hisi karaia.
Epilepsy, Tororotororo.
Equal, Hegeregere.
Equivalent, Davana.
Erect, Gini.
Err, Kererekerere.
Errand, Koaukau.
Eruption (on skin), Lari. Kuhikuhi.
Escape, Heau. Roho mauri.
Escort, Iatona taudia.
Essay, v. Karaia toho.
Establish, Badinaia.
Eternal, Hanaihanai.
Evasive, Hedibagani hereva.
Even, Manada. Hegeregere.
Evening, Adorahi. See also under "Time."
Ever, Hanaihanai.
Every, Idoidiai.
Evident, Dina.
Evil, Dika.
Evil speaking, Koau dika.
Eulogy, Hanamoa herevana.
Exact (to be), Maoromaoro.
Exaggerate, Hemusemuselaia. Habadaia.
Exalt, Abiaisi.
Examine, Nanadaia. Tahua.
Example, Oromana kara. Hagoina.
Exasperate, Hadagedagea.
Exceed, Herea.
Excel, Sibona namo. Asi idaina.
Excellent, Namo herea.
Exchange, Davana.
Excite, Haloa. Aherouheroua.
Exclaim, Koau. Lolo dagu.
Excoriated, Hekopa.
Excrement, Tage.
Excuse, v. Ahekora.
Execrate, Hadikaia.
Execute, Karaia.
Execute (a criminal), Alaia.
Exempt, Tabu.
Exert, Hagoadalaia.
Exhibit, Ahedinarai.
Exhort, Hahealo.
Exile, s. Iluluoho tauna.
Exorbitant (in price), Davana bada.
Expand, Habadaia.
Expect, Naria. Laroa.
Expectorate, Kanudi.

Expedient, Namo baine karaia.
Expedite, Haragaia.
Expel, Luluaoho.
Expert, Lega haraga.
Expiate, Davana henia.
Expire, Mate.
Explain, Hamaoroa.
Explode, Hapoua. Poudagu.
Expose, Ahedinaraia.
Expound, Hadibaia. Hamaoroa.
Extend, Habadaia.
Exterior, Murina kopina.
Exterminate, Haorea. Alaia ore.
Extinct (as fire), Bodo.
Extinguish, Habodoa.
Extirpate, Alaia ore.
Extol, Heatolaia. Hanamoa.
Extraordinary, Hoa gauna.
Extremity, Dokona.
Extricate, Ruhaia. Hamauria.
Exuberant, Vara rohoroho.
Exult, Heagi.
Eye, Mata.
Eyeball, Mata anina.
Eyebrow, Ibuni mata.
Eyelid, Mata kopina.

F

Fable, Hereva hegeregere.
Face, Vaira.
Face, v. Vaira henia.
Fade, Marai.
Faint, Matelea. (from fatigue), Manori.
Fair (wind), Lai namo.
Faith, Kamonai. Abidadama henia.
Faithful, Kamonai bada. Momokani.
Faithless, Se kamonai.
Fall, Keto. (from height), Moru. (of tree, &c.), Gari.
Fallow, Vahu.
False, Koikoi.
Falsehood, Hereva koikoi.
Falter, Manokamanoka.
Famed, Harina bada.
Family, Iduhu. Veve.
Famine, Doe.
Famish, Hitolo mate.
Fan, Itapo gauna.
Fan, v. Tapoa.
Far, Daudau.
Farewell, Ba mahuta!
Farewell (to bid), Ahetoni.

Farthest, Dokona gauna (*thing*), tauna (*man*).
Fashion, Oromana. Seuseuna.
Fast, *v.* Anivāga.
Fast (*to make*) Ahunua. Qadua.
Fast, Koua kunukakunuka, (*as boat on reef*), Tatakunu.
Fasten, Koua. (*As string*), Qadua.
Fastening, Koua gauna. Iqadu gauna.
Fasthanded, Lega haraga.
Fastness, Magu.
Fat, *adj.* Digara.
Fat, *s.* Digara.
Father, Tamana.
Fathom, Roha.
Fatigue, Manori. Tau e boera.
Fatigue, *v.* Aheboera. Aheqarahia.
Fault, Kererekerere.
Favour, Harihari.
Favourite, Lalokau natuna (*child*).
Fear, Gari.
Feast, Aria. (*Of cooked food*), Anibou.
Feather, Hui.
Feeble, Manokamanoka.
Feed, Ubua. (*to feed him*), Ana henia.
Feel (*to grope*), Darahu. (*to feel a thing whether hard or soft*), Dauatoho.
Feign, Hedibagani.
Felicity, Moalena. Lalo namo.
Fell, Hagaria.
Fellow, Ibamona.
Female, Hahine.
Fence (*of upright sticks*), Ara. (*lengthwise*), Kahi. (*wire, &c.*), Magu.
Ferment, Tubu.
Ferocious, Dagedage.
Fertile, Tano namo.
Fetch, Mailaia. (*A person*) Maihenia, Laohenia.
Fetid, Bodaga.
Feud, Heai.
Fever, Gorere siahu. (*Intermittent*) Tau harihari.
Few, Gadoi.
Fibre (*coconut*), Buru.
Fickle, Hereva momo.
Fierce, Dagedage.
Fifteen, Quata ima.
Fifth, Ia imana.
Fiftieth, Ia ima ahuina.
Fifty, Ima ahui.
Fig, Suke (*Introduced*).

Fight, Heatu. Alala karaia.
File, Iliili.
Fill, Ahonua.
Fillip, Pidia.
Filth, Miro.
Fin, Taiana.
Final, Dokona.
Find, Davaria.
Fine (*weather*) Dina namo.
Finger, Ima qagiqagi.
Fingernail, Ima qagiqagi kahauna.
Finish, Hadokoa. Vadaeni.
Fire, *s.* Lahi.
Fire, *v.* Doua.
Fire (*a gun*), Ipidi karaia.
Firefly, Kobo. Kobokobo.
Fireplace, Rahurahu.
Fireshovel, Rahurahu ikadona gaga.
Firewood, Au. Lakulaku audia. (*a woman's burden of*), Au kodana.
Firm (*not loose*), Auka. Tutukatutuka.
First, Gunaguna. Gini gunana.
Firstborn, Natuna roboa.
Firstfruits, Uma anina roboa.
Fish, *s.* Qarume. Different kinds of, see Appendix.
Fish, *v.* Haoda. Alatore.
Fisherman, Haoda tauna.
Fishhook, Kimai.
Fissure, Maka.
Fist, Ima kahua kubolukubolu.
Fit, *adj.* Namo.
Five, Ima.
Fix, Atoa goevagoeva.
Flabby, Moruta. Se aukamu.
Flame, Lahi hururuhururu.
Flame, *v.* (*to cause*), Ahururua.
Flannel, Dabua mamoe. (*Introduced*).
Flash (*as lightning*), Kevaruaisi.
Flat, Palakapalaka.
Flatter, Hanamoa hedibagani.
Flavour, Mamina.
Flay, Ivaia.
Flea, Sei.
Flee, Heau.
Fleet, *adj.* Ae haraga.
Fleet (*of fishing canoes*), Haoda bada, (*Of large trading canoes*), Hiri badabada.
Flesh, Anina.
Flexible, Perukaperuka.
Fling, Tahoa.
Flint, Vasika.
Flirt, Hekela or Hegera.
Float, *s.* Uto.
Float, *v.* Hure. Keni.

Flock, *v.* Arua mai..
Flock, *s.* Serina.
Flog, Dadaba.
Flood, Ututu.
Flour, Palaoa (*Introduced*).
Flow *v.* Veve.
Flow (*tide*), Hagaru.
Flower, Au huahua.
Fluent, E hereva namo. Mala haraga.
Fluid, Ranu.
Flute, Ivirikou.
Fly, Roho.
Fly, *s.* Lao.
Foam, Qaraqı ra.
Foe, Inai.
Fog, Ninoa, Gahu.
Foil, Laoahu.
Fold, *v.* Lokua.
Follow, Murina laka. Heuduri. Gava.
Follower, Imurina tauna.
Folly, Kavakava.
Fond, Lalokau henia.
Food, Malamala. Aniani gauna.
Food (*cold*), Malamala bahuna.
Food (*for voyage or journey*), Laqa.
Fool, Kāva. Bobo.
Foot, Ae palapala.
Footpath, Dara.
Footprint, Ae gabu.
For, Egu and Agu. Emu and Amu, &c.
Forage, *v.* Aniani tahua.
Forbear, Aheauka.
Forbid, Koauahu. Koauatao.
Ford, *v.* Turu hanai.
Forefinger, Qagiqagi dodori.
Forego, Koauatao.
Forehead, Bagu.
Foreign, Idau.
Foreland, Iduka.
Foremost, Gunalaia.
Forenoon, Daba.
Forest, Uda.
Foretell, Koaulaia dose vara negana
Forget, Reaia. Lalo boio.
Forgive, Koauatao.
Fork, Dinika.
Forked, Gada.
Forlorn, Ihareha.
Form, Oromana.
Former, Gunana.
Formerly, Gunaguna.
Fornication, Rahea. Eno. Hendahanai.

Forsake, Lakatania.
Fort, Magu.
Fortitude, Lalo auka.
Fortunate, Nega namonamo.
Forty, Hari ahui.
Forward, *adv.* Vairanai.
Foul, Dika.
Found, Davaria.
Foundation, Badina.
Founder, Maloa.
Four, Hani.
Fourfold, Ere hani.
Fourfooted, Ae hani.
Fourteen, Qauta hani.
Fowl, Kokorogu.
Fowlingpiece, Ipidi (*Introduced*).
Fragile, Makohi haraga.
Fragrant, Bonana namo.
Frail, Manokamanoka.
Frantic, Kāva bamona.
Fraud, Koikoi. Hineri.
Free, Ura qalimu tauna.
Freight, Lakatoi anina.
Frequent, Loulou.
Fresh, Matamata.
Freshwater, Ranu.
Fretful, Tai momo.
Friend, Turana.
Fright, Gari.
Frighten, Hagaria.
Fringe, Rimuna.
Frisk, Rohoroho.
Frivolous, Kiri tauna.
Frizzy, Hui tuma.
Frog, Parapara.
From, Amo.
Front, Vaira.
Front, *v.* Vaira henia.
Froth, Qaraqara.
Frown, Vaira hūa.
Frugal (*to be*), Abia uamonamo.
Fruit, Au huahua.
Fruitlessly, Abia lasi.
Frustrate, Koauatubu.
Fry, *v.* Hadedea. Parai pani (*Introduced*).
Fuel, Lahi āuna.
Fulfil, Hamomokanilaia. Haginilaiadae.
Fulgent, Hururuhururu.
Full, Honu.
Full grown, Daia kunu. Tauna e lo.
Fumble, Lega metau.
Fun, Kadara. Hevaseha.
Furious, Dagedage bada.

FUR (47) GRO

Furniture, Ruma gaudia.
Further, Unukaha.
Futile, Se abimu.
Future, Ununega.
Fy! Ina!

G

Gad, Loa.
Gale, Guba. Orc.
Gall, s. Aotuna.
Gambol, Kadara.
Gaol, Ruma koua. Dibura ruma.
Gape, Udu hagaia.
Gardening, Biru.
Gargle, Hegomogomo.
Garment, Dabua.
Garrulous, Udu mauri.
Gash, Bero.
Gasp, Lagadae lagadae.
Gate, Ikokou.
Gateway, Ikokou.
Gather (as fruit), Bitua. Bulukia. (as cloud), Kamo.
Gaze, Raraia.
Geld, Apo ivaia.
Generation, Uru.
Gentle, Manada.
Gentleman, Lohiabada.
Genuine, Korikori.
Germinate, Havaraia.
Get, Abia.
Ghost, Vatavata.
Giddy, Mata madaimadai. Lagaga.
Gift, Harihari gauna. Herahia gauna.
Gill, Lāda.
Gimlet, Ibudu gauna.
Ginger, Agi. Sioha.
Gird, Rioa. Gegea.
Girl, Kekeni. Haniulato.
Give, Henia.
Glad, Moale.
Glare (of sun), Dina tara.
Glass, Varivari.
Glisten, Hururuhururu.
Globular, Kubolukubolu.
Gloom, Dagahu.
Glorify, Heatolaia.
Glow, Kiamakiama.
Glutton, Aniani bada tauna.
Gnash, Ise hahedai.
Gnaw, Koria.
Go, Leo.
Go about, Loa.

God, Dirava.
Godliness, Dirava urana ura kara.
Gold, Auro. (Introduced.)
Good, Namo.
Goodbye, Bamahuta.
Good looking (of men), Raho namo. Ginibo kanabo. (of women), Hane namo.
Goodnight, Bamahuta.
Goods, Kohu.
Gorge, Koupa.
Gossip, Herevahereva.
Gourd, Ahu.
Govern, Siahu karaia. Ahegani.
Government, Siahu karaia taudia.
Grace, Harihari.
Gradually, Metailametaila.
Grain (of wood), Idiho.
Grandchild, Tubu.
Grandfather, Tubu.
Grandmother, Tubu hahine.
Grant, Henia.
Grapple, Rosia.
Grasp, Kahua.
Grass, Rei. (On bottom of boat, &c.) Mava.
Grass (different kinds of)—
Honehone, Short.
Dibagadi, Long.
Kudekude, Long.
Kurukuru, Long (used for thatch).
Grashopper, Qadi.
Grate, v. Lilia. (Coacoanut), Oria. (As boat on reef), Tatakau.
Grave, Guri.
Gravel, Miri boroko.
Graze, Halaqahia.
Greasy, Dedidedi.
Great, Bada.
Great grandchild, Sene.
Great grandfather, Sene.
Great grandmother, Seno hahine.
Greedy, Aniani dika. Mata ganigani.
Green, Gadogagadoga.
Green (unripe), Karukaru.
Greet, Hanamoa.
Greyhair, Hui buruka.
Grieve, Tāi. Boka hisihisi.
Grind (axe, &c.), Segea.
Grindstone, Uro.
Gripe, v.n. Pudipudi.
Groan, Ganagana.
Groin, Dagadaga.
Grope, Darahu.
Ground, Tano.
Ground plate, Itari āu.

GRO (48) HEA

Grounded, Tatakuuu.
Groundless, Asi badina. Koauna lasi.
Grove (of cultivated trees), Imea.
Grow, Vara. (Of children), Badahobadaho.
Growl, Koaukoau.
Grumble, Maumau.
Grunt, Ruku.
Guard, Gima. Naria. Kito.
Guess, Koau kava, koau kava.
Guest, Vadivadi.
Guide, Hakaua.
Guide, s., Ihakuua tauna.
Guilt, Dika.
Guilty, Dika tauna.
Gullet, Gado baubau.
Gulp, Hatono.
Gum, Tode, "āu todena."
Gums, Mao.
Gun, Ipidi. (Introduced.)
Gunpowder, Pauda. (Introduced.)
Gunwale, Iseise.
Gush, Larilaria.
Gush out (as blood), Budia lasi.
Gut, s., Bokaran.
Gut, v., Bokaia.

H

Habit, Kara.
Habitation, Ruma.
Habitual, Diua idoinai. Vaia.
Habituate, Hamanadaia.
Hack, Tarai hepatapata.
Haft, Halala.
Hair, Hui.
Hairy (man), Dera tauna.
Hale, Tāu namo.
Half, Karoa rua.
Half-full, Hekābi.
Half-moon, Hua lokaloka.
Half-way, Dala e haruaia heidaheida.
Hallow, Ahelagaia.
Halt, Lagaani.
Halve, Haruaia heidaheida. To cut in half, Bokaraginai ivaia.
Hammer, v., Hodoa.
Hammer, s., Hamara. (Introduced.)
Hammock, Ivitoto.
Hamper, v., Dokoatao.
Hand, Ima palapala.
Handful, Ima-honu.

Handkerchief, Muko.
Handle, v., Halalana karaia.
Handle, s., Auauna. (Of hatchet), Halala.
Handsaw, Iri.
Handsome, Ginibo kanabo. Raho namo (of men), Hanc namo (of women).
Handwriting, Revareva.
Hang, Tauadac.
Hanker, Hekisehekisc.
Happy, Lalo namo. Moale.
Harangue, Haroro. Koau heuia.
Harbour, Dogo gabuna. Madavamadavana.
Hard, Auka.
Harden, Aheauka.
Hardly (enter), Heloge.
Hark, Kamonai.
Harlot, Ariara hahine.
Harm, Dika.
Harpoon, Karaudi.
Harsh, Koautora. Koaudika.
Haste, Haragaharaga.
Hasty, Badu kava.
Hat, Qara gauna.
Hatch (eggs), Pāpa.
Hatchet, Ira. (American axe), Qara qaitu.
Hatchet-head, Ira.
Hate, Badu henia.
Haughty, Hekokorogu.
Haul, Veria. Haroro.
Have, Abia. (particle of possession) Mai.
Haven, Metai gabnna.
Havoc, Haorea.
Hawk, Bogibada. Bivai.
Haze, Gahu. Nino.
He, Ia.
Head, Qara.
Head, adj., Biaguna.
Headland, Iduka.
Headlong, Moru hedaqa.
Headstrong, Ura dika.
Heal, Homauria.
Health, Gorore lasi.
Heap, Senusenu.
Hear, Kamonai.
Heart, Kudou (physical). Uto (of wood).
Hearth, Rahurahu.
Heat, Siahu.
Heated, Hasiahua.
Heathen, Etene. (Introduced.)
Heave, v.a., Tahoa.

Heave, v.n., Heudeheude.
Heaven, Guba.
Heavy, Metau.
Heel, Ae gedu.
Height, Gau lata. (house), Arana latana.
Heir, Dihina.
Helm, Tari gauna.
Help, Kahaia. Durua.
Helve, Auauna.
Hem, Isena.
Hen, Kokorogu hahine.
Henceforth, Harihari ela.
Her, Ia.
Herb, Aniani avana.
Herd, Serina.
Here, Iniseni. Inai.
Hereafter, Gabea.
Hero, Goada tauna.
Heron, Nogo.
Hesitate, Daradara.
Hew, Tarai. Utua.
Hiccough, Baturo.
Hide, Kopina.
Hide, v., Hunia. (crime or fault), Vagoaia.
High, Gaulatalata.
Highminded, Hekokorogu.
High-water, Davara bada. (rising), Hagaru. (very high tide), Davara hadaka e dihomu, Dodō.
Highway, Dala korikori.
Hill, Orooro komuta.
Hillock, Orooro maragi.
Him, Ia.
Hinder, Laoahu.
Hindermost, Maurina tauna. Gabea tauna.
Hinge, Hinere. (Introduced.) Garugaru.
Hip, Koekoe.
His, Ena. (Of food), Ana.
History, Idaunegai herevana.
Hit, Huaria. Tutua. Pataia. (not miss), Tubu.
Hither and Thither, Ini mai unu lao.
Hoard, Haboua.
Hoarse, Gado dika.
Hobble, v., Ae guia.
Hog, Boroma.
Hoist, Daralaia ; (sail of canoe), Diua ; (of ship), Hekida.
Hold, Abia. . Kahua.
Hold ! Vadaeni.
Hold (of ship), Tua.
Hole, Matu.

Hollow, Asi anina.
Home, Noho gabuna korikori.
Homesick, Hanua tāi.
Honest, Henao lasi.
Honour, v., Hematauraia. Qahia. Nuai.
Honey, Labolabo bata ranuna.
Hoof, Ae kahauna.
Hook, Kimai.
Hooked, Igāu.
Hoop, Ava keikei.
Hoop, v., Lolo.
Hope, Laroa.
Hopeless, Baia.
Horizon, Guba dokona.
Horn, Doa.
Hornbill, Bobolo.
Hornet, Ubama.
Horrible, Dikabada.
Horse, Hosi. (Introduced.)
Hospitable, Gaiho namo. Heabidae tauna.
Hot, Siahu.
Hotheaded, Tagutagu tauna.
House, Ruma.
Household, Ruma taudia.
Householder, Ruma biaguna.
How? Ede heto.
Howl, Tāi.
How many? Hida.
Hubbub, Helogohelogo.
Hug, Gugubaia. Posia.
Huge, Gaubadabada.
Hum, Hu.
Humane, Hebokahisi.
Humble, adj., Manau.
Humorous, Hevaseha tauna.
Humpback, Doru qagugu.
Hundred, Sinahu.
Hunger, Hitolo. (for meat), Gādo.
Hunt, Labana.
Hurl, Tahoa.
Hurricane, Ore.
Hurry, v., Haragaia.
Hurt, Hahisia.
Husband, Adavana.
Hush ! Asi regeregena.
Hush, a child, v., Hadoloa.
Husk, Kopina.
Husk, v. (cocoanuts), Isia ; (with teeth), Daria.
Hut, Ruma.
Hymn, Ane.
Hypocrisy, Kara koikoi. Hedibagani.
Hypocrite, Koikoi tauna.

D

I

I, Lau.
Idiot, Kūva tauna.
Idle, Lahedo. Bokamate.
If (*past*), Bema ; (*fut.*), Baino.
Ignite, Haraia.
Ignorant, Kavakava.
Iguana, Ariha ; (*small*), Tāutāu.
Ill, Gorere.
Ill-treat, Hadikaia.
Ill-nature, Dagedage.
Illumine, Ha liaria.
Image, Laula ı.
Imagine, Lalo koau.
Imitate, Hagoia.
Immature, Garugaru.
Immediately, Harihari.
Immerse, Bulubulu.
Immorality, Kara dika.
Immortal, Mate basine diba
Immovable, Auka bada. Tutuka-tutuka.
Immutable, Lalo lou lasi.
Impatient, Aheauka lasi. Noho iroiro.
Impede, Laoahu.
Impenitent, Asi helalo.
Imperfect, Idoinai lasi.
Imperious, Hekokorogu.
Impertinent, Koau dika.
Impetuous, Ura dika. Tagutagu tauna.
Implicate, Habadelaia.
Implore, Noinoi.
Impolite, Lagāua.
Importune, Noinoi.
Impose (cheat), Koia.
Impossible, Karaia diba lasi.
Improper, Namo lasi.
Improve, Hanamoa.
Impudent, Ere dagedage.
Impure, Miro.
In, Lalonoi.
Inaccessible, Asi dalana.
Inactive, Lahedo.
Inarticulate, Logologo.
Incapable, Karaia diba lasi.
Incessant, Nega idoinai.
Incision, Ivaia.
Incite, Hāloa.
Incivility, Ere dika.
Inclined, Lalona ura.
Incomparable, Asi idaina.
Incomplete, Idoinai lasi.
Incomprehensible, Diba lasi.
Inconsolable, Tauna se halōa.

Incorrect, Dia maoromaoro.
Incorrigible, Matana se ganimu.
Increase, Habadaia.
Incumber, Hametaua.
Indecent, Hemarai kara.
Indecision, Daradara mo.
Indeed, Etomamu.
Indefatigable, Goada bada.
Indelible, Rohoa lasi.
Indemnify, Qara henia.
Indicate, Hamaoroa.
Indifferent, Ura lasi.
Indigent, Ogogami.
Indignant, Badu.
Indignity, Hidikaia.
Indiscreet, Aonega lasi.
Indiscriminate, Kererekerere.
Indistinct, (*speech*) Logologo.
Indolent, Lahedo.
Industrious, Hulo tauna.
Inexhaustible, Ia basine ore.
Inexpedient, Namo lasi.
Inexperienced, Manada lasi.
Infamous, Harina dika.
Infant, Karukaru.
Infect, Hisi dāi hanai.
Infirm, Manokamanoka.
Influenza, Kulu karaia.
Inform, Hadibaia. Koau henia.
Ingratitude, Hanamoa lasi.
Inhabit, Noho.
Inhale, Hohoa.
Inhospitable, Gaiho dika.
Inhuman, Hebokahisi lasi.
Iniquity, Kara dika.
Injunction, Ahegani herevana.
Injure, Hadikaia.
Injustice, Maoromaora lasi.
Ink, Inika. (*Introduced.*)
Inland, Guni.
Inlander, Guni tauna.
Innocent, Dia dika.
Innumerable, Duahia lasi.
Inquire, Nanadai.
Inquiry, Henanadai.
Insane, Kāva.
Insatiable, Boka kunu lasi.
Insecure, Auka lasi.
Inseparable, Kahuanege lasi.
Inside, Lalonai.
Insignificant, Maragimaragi.
Insincere, Momokani lasi.
Insipid, Mamina lasi.
Insist, Koaulaia loulou.
Insnare, Idoa.
Insolent, Ere dagedage.
Inspect, Itaia tarikatarika.

INS (51) KIS

Instantly, Harihari.
Instead, Boloa.
Instep, Ae ganagana.
Instigate, Havaraia.
Instruct, Hadibaia.
Instrument, laia or raia *post-fixed to the verb*.
Insufficient, Davana lasi. Seme davana.
Insult, Hadikaia.
Inter, Guria.
Intercede, Herohemaino. Noinoi.
Intercept, Laoahu, Vaira lao.
Interdict, Koauahu.
Interior, Lalonai.
Intermediate, Bokaraginai.
Interminable, Asi dokona.
Internal, Lalona.
Interpret, Gado hahegeregerea.
Interrogate, Henanadai.
Interrupt, Hereva tataiautu.
Interval, Ihuanai.
Interview, Ia ida hereva.
Intestine, Bokalau.
Intimate to, Hamaoroa.
Intimidate, Hagaria.
Into, Vareai.
Intoxication, Muramura heala. Kekero.
Intrepid, Goada.
Intrust, Henia baine legua.
Inundation, Ututu.
Inure, Hamanadaia.
Invalid, *n.*, Gorere tauna.
Invert, Hurea.
Investigate, Tahua. Henanadai.
Invisible, Itaia lasi.
Invite, Koaulaia.
Invoke, Hahane. Noinoi.
Inward, Lalona.
Ire, Badu.
Iron, Auri. (*Introduced*.)
Iron, *v.*, Dabua hamanadaia.
Irreconcilable, Maino lasi.
Irresistible, Goada bada.
Irresolute, Daradara.
Irreverent, Boka toto tauna.
Irritable, Badu kava badu kava.
Irritate, Hadagedagea.
Island, Motumotu.
Itch, *v.*, Hemaihemai.

J

Jabber, Hereva momo.
Jaded, Tau e boera. Manori.
Jail, Ruma koua.
Jaw (*the lower*), Auki.
Jealous, Vagege. (*sexual*) Mama.
Jeer, Kirikirilaia.
Jerk, Veria dagu.
Jest, Hevaseha.
Jester, Havaseha tauna.
Jog, Doria.
Join (*as two pieces of wood*), Hiriakau.
Joint, Garugaru.
Joint (*of meat*), Regena. (*of wood*) Isiriu.
Joist. Lava.
Joke, Hevaseha.
Jostle, Hesede matemate.
Journey, Laolao.
Joy, Moale.
Judge, *s.*, Ahemaoro tauna.
Judge, *v.*, Ahemaoro karaia.
Judgment, Henanadai ikarana. Ahemaoro karaia.
Judicious, Aonega.
Jug, Siagi. (*Introduced*.)
Juice, Ranuna.
Jump (*up*), Rohoisi. (*Down*) Rohodobi.
Junction (*of roads*), Dala katakata.
Jurisdiction, Siahu.
Just, Kara maoromaoro.
Justice, Kara maoromaoro.
Justify, Hamaoromaoroa.

K

Kangaroo, Magani. (*Male*) Tapari. (*Female*) Miara.
Keen (*edge*), Gano.
Keep, Abia.
Keeper, Gima tauna. Ileguna tauna.
Kernel, Anina.
Kettle, Tikata. (*Introduced*.)
Key, Ki. (*Introduced*.)
Kick, Helaha.
Kid, Goti natuna. (*Introduced*.)
Kidney, Nadinadi.
Kill, Alaia.
Kin, Varavara.
Kind, Harihari bada. Hebokahisi.
Kindle, Haraia. Bania.
King, Gaubada. (*preceded by hanua*) Parapavana.
Kingdom, Basileia. (*Introduced*.)
Kinsman, Varavara.
Kiss, Aherahu.

Kitten, Pose natuna. (*Introduced.*)
Knee, Tui.
Knead, Kuia.
Kneel, Tuihadaia. (*on one knee*) Hetoisi.
Knife, Kaia. (*Introduced.*)
Knock, Pidipidi. (*together as knees*) Tabubutabubu.
Knot, Qadua.
Knotted, Qaduaqadua.
Know, Diba.
Knuckle, Ima garugaru.

L

Labour, Heqarahi.
Labourer, Gau kara tauna.
Lack, Dabu.
Lad, Mero.
Ladder, Vatavata.
Lade, Atoakau.
Lady, Lohiabada hahinc.
Lagoon, Gohu.
Lame, Ae sike. Ae dairiki.
Lament, Tāi.
Land, Tano.
Land, *v.*, Hedoa. Tano ai diho.
Landing-place, Doa gabuna.
Landslip, Hevarure.
Language, Gādo.
Languish, Manokamanoka.
Languor, Tau manokamanoka.
Lap, Kopa.
Larboard, Dalima kabana.
Lard, Digara.
Large, Bada. (*Of thread, &c.*) Baroko.
Larynx, Gado baubau.
Lascivious, Mata dika. Mata bodaga.
Lash, *v.*, Dadaba. Qadia.
Lash (*to fasten*), Mataia. Qadua.
Lass, Kekeni.
Last, Dokona. Gini gabena.
Last, *v.*, Mia hanaihanai.
Lasting, Mia hanaihanai.
Last night, Varani hanuaboi.
Late (*of expected ship, &c.*), Vanovano.
Late in the day, Dina diho.
Laud, Heatolaia. Heagilaia.
Laugh, Kiri.
Launch, Davea dae.
Laundress, Dabua ihurina hahinc.

Law, Taravatu. Doha. (*Introduced meaning.*)
Lawful, Koauahu lasi.
Lawless, Bokatoto.
Lazy, Lahedo.
Lead, *v.*, Hakaua.
Leader, Ihakauna tauna. Igunalaina tauna.
Leaf, Rau.
League, Taravatu.
Leak (*in a canoe*), Dudi.
Lean, *v.* (*on a stick*), Hetotao. (*On a table, &c.*), Gorukau. (*Against*), Dabikau.
Lean, *adj.*, Hidiho. (*Person*), Tau varotavarota.
Leap, Roho.
Learn, Hadibaia.
Least, Maragina.
Leather, Boroma kopina.
Leave, *v.*, Lakatania.
Leave off, Vadaeni! Mia!
Leaven, Hatubua gauna. Obue. (*Introduced.*)
Leavings, Aniani orena.
Lecherous, Mata dika.
Left (*side*), Lauri.
Left behind, Hetavauhe. (*Persons*), Lakatani.
Left-handed, Ima lauri tauna
Leg, Ae (*entire leg and foot*)
Legend, Gori.
Leisure, Noho kava negana
Leisurely, Metailametaila.
Lend, Henitorehai.
Length, Lata. (*of house* Roha maorona. (*of land*) Oromana latana.
Lengthen, Halataia.
Lenity. Hebokahisi.
Less, Unai bada (*that is big*); inai maragi (*this is small*).
Lessen, Hamaragia.
Lest, Garina.
Let (*allow*), Gadudae. Haduaia.
Let (*hinder*), Laoahu.
Letter, Leta. (*Introduced*), Revareva.
Level, Manadamanada.
Level, *v.*, Hataoraia.
Levity, Kiri momo.
Lewd, Mata dika.
Liar, Koikoi tauna.
Liberal, Harihari bada.
Liberty, Haduaia lasi, ia sibona.
Lick, Demari.
Lid, Kaluhia gauna. Itoreahu.
Lie, *s.*, Koikoi.

Lie, v. (down), Hekure. (On the side),
Enodele. (On the back), Hekuregaga.
Lie (in wait), Banitao.
Life, Mauri.
Lift, Abiaisi.
Light, s., Diari.
Light, v., Rohokau. (A fire), Haraia.
Light, adj., Haraga.
Lightheaded, Koaukava.
Lightning, Kevaru.
Like, Bamona.
Like, v., Ura henia. Hekisehekise.
Likeness (portrait), Laulau.
Lily (large white), Repati.
Lime, Ahu.
Limit, Toana.
Limp, Ae sike.
Limpid, Nēka.
Line fishing, Varo.
Linger, Halahe.
Liniment, Hedahu muramura.
Lip, Udu bibina.
Liquefy, Haveve.
Liquid, Ranu.
Liquor amnii. Aru.
Listen, Kamonai.
Litter, s., Momo.
Little, Maragi.
Live, Mauri.
Liver, Ase or ate.
Lizard, Vaboha.
Lo! Ināi!
Load, s., Maduna.
Load, v. (on shoulder), Paga ai atoakau.
Loaf, Palaoa.
Loathe, Lalo dika henia.
Lock, v., Ki karaia. (Introduced.)
Lofty, Latalata.
Log, Au.
Loins, Koekoe.
Loiter, Halahe.
Lonely, Sibona noho. Dara doko.
Long, Lata.
Long, v., Ura henia. Hekisehekise.
Look, Itaia. (up), Gagaisi. Rohadae. (down), Igodiho. (about), Roharoha.
Look! A itaia!
Looking-glass, Varivari.
Loop, Budia.
Loose, Heladohelado.
Loosen, Ruhaia.
Looseness (diarrhœa), Hekukuri.

Lop, Utua.
Loquacious, Hereva momo. Udu mauri.
Lord, Biaguna. Lohiabada.
Lose, Reaia. Haboioa.
Lost, Boio.
Loud, Regena bada. Gado bada.
Lounge, Hekure.
Louse, Utu.
Love, Hebokahisi. Lalokau henia.
Low, Qadogi.
Low, r., Gou.
Lower, v., Abia dobi.
Lowly, Manau tauna.
Low-water, Komata gui. Davara maragi.
Lucky, Dirava namo.
Luff, v., Hagoria.
Lug, Veria.
Lukewarm, Siahusiahu.
Lull (in wind), Lai gavena.
Luminous, Diaridiari.
Lump (as of clay), Tabata.
Lunatic, Kāva tauna.
Lungs, Baraki.
Lure, Hedibagani.
Lurk, Banitao.
Lust, Mata dika.
Luxuriant, Vara bada. Mauri bada.

M

Mad, Kāva. Dagedage.
Maggot, Uloulo.
Magistrate, Gima tauna. Ahemaoro tauna.
Magnify, Habadaia.
Magnitude, Badana.
Maid, Kekeni. Haniulato.
Maidservant, Hesiai hahine.
Maimed, Doko (preceded by the member, as "ima doko").
Maintain, Abia tarikatarika.
Majority, Hutuma.
Make, Karaia.
Malady, Gorere.
Male, Maruane.
Malediction, Uduguilai.
Malice, Lalo dika.
Mallet, Lavu. (for beating out native cloth), Itadara.

Man, Tannimanima. Tau.
Mangle (*to tear*), Hedarc.
Mangrove (*general name*), Aqa. The *different kinds are*, Aniani, Arara, Buagi, Kavera (*edible*), Kirima, Laubada, Roda.
Manifest, Dina.
Manifold, Eremomo.
Mankind, Taunimanima.
Manner, Kara.
Mansion, Ruma bada.
Manslaught'r, Taunimanima ïalana.
Many, Hutɩma. Diagau. Momo.
Mar, Hadikaia.
Mare, Hosi hahine.
Margin, Isena.
Mark, Toana.
Marriage, Headava.
Married, to be, Adavaia.
Marrow, Turia harana.
Marry, Headava.
Marsh, Kopukopu.
Marvel, Hoa.
Massacre, Alala.
Mast, Autubua.
Master, Biaguna.
Masticate, Gauaia.
Mat, Geda.
Match, *v.*, Hahegeregerea.
Match, *s.*, Masisi. (*Introduced.*)
Matchless, Sibona herea. Asi idaina.
Mate, Ibamona. (*of ship*), Lakatoi dori duduna tau.
Materials, Karalaia gaudia.
Matron, Sinana. Hahine bada.
Matter (*pus*), Hula.
Mature (*of animals*), Tamana, Sinana. (*Of fruit, &c.*), Lō. Lokaloka.
Mean, Gaiho dika.
Meaning, Anina.
Meanness, Gaiho dika kara.
Measure, Hahetoho gauna.
Measure, *v.*, Hahetoho karaia.
Mediate, Herohemaino.
Mediator, Herohemaino tauna.
Medicine, Muramura.
Meditate, Lalo haguhi.
Meek, Manada tauna.
Meet, *v.*, Hedavari. (*To go to meet*), Vaira lao. (*On the road*), Toia hedavari.
Meeting (*an assembly*) Hegogo.
Melancholy, Vaira huaia.
Melt, Haveve.
Melt, *s.*, Baraka.
Menace, Heqata káraia.

Mend (*nets*), Laumea. (*Mats, &c.*), Bania.
Mention, Koaulaia.
Merchant, Hoihoi tauna.
Merciful, Hebokahisi tauna.
Merciless, Hebokahisi lasi.
Merry, Lebulebu.
Mesh, Māta.
Message, Koaukau.
Metal, Nadi.
Metaphor, Hereva hegeregero.
Methought, Lau lalogu e tomamu.
Metropolis, Hanua bada.
Midday, Dina tupua.
Middle, Ihuana baine raka.
Middle-aged, Eregabe.
Middling, Namo sisina.
Midnight, Malokihi.
Midrib (*of sago frond*), Kipa.
Midriff, Valavala.
Midst, Bokaragina.
Midway, Dala harunia heidaheida.
Midwife, Heqaroto hahine.
Might, Goada.
Mild, Manada.
Mildew, Valavala.
Milk, Rata.
Mimic, Hetohotoho.
Mind, *s.*, Lalona. Aonega. Dara.
Mind, *v.*, Kamonai. (*Take care of*), Naria.
Mine, Lauegu.
Mingle, Buloa.
Minister, *v.*, Isiai laoheni. Legua.
Minute, Minuta. (*Introduced.*)
Mire, Kopukopu.
Mirror, Varivari.
Mirth, Lebulebu.
Misapprehend, Kamonai kerere.
Misbehave, Kara kererekerere.
Miscarriage, *s.*, Natuna inegena.
Miscarry (*in birth*), Natuna e negea.
Mischievous, Ima mauri.
Miscount, Duahia kerere.
Misdemeanour, Kara dika.
Miserable, Lalo dika. Se moalemu.
Misfortune, Nega dika.
Misgive, Daradara.
Misguide, Hakaua kerere.
Misinform, Hadibaia kerere.
Mislead, Koia.
Miss, *v.*, Daradoko.
Missionary, Haroro tauna.
Mist, Ninoa. (*At sea*), Gahu.
Mistake, Reaia. Kererekerere.
Mistrust, Daradara.
Misunderstanding, Diba lasi.

Mitigate, Hamaragia.
Mix, Buloa.
Moan, Ganagana.
Mock, Gonagonalaia. Hetohotoho.
Moderate. Bada lasi. (*Of sun or wind*), Gavena.
Modest (*woman*), Igodiho hahine.
Moist, Parikaparika.
Moisten, Hapariparia.
Mole, Toutou.
Mollify, Hamarumaru.
Monarch, Gaubada.
Monday, Monidei. (*Introduced.*)
Money, Moni. (*Introduced.*)
Month, Hūa.
Monument (*of stone*), Nadi gini.
Moon, Hua.
Moon new, Hua dogagi.
More, Haida.
Morning, Daba.
Morning star, Hisiu bada.
Morrow, Kerukeru.
Morsel, Taina. Sisina.
Mosquito. Namo.
Moth, Gaubebe.
Mother, Sinana.
Mother of Pearl, Mairi.
Motherly, Sinana bamona.
Mouldy, Valavala.
Moult, Helata.
Mound, Orooro beruta.
Mountain, Orooro.
Mountainous, Orooro mo.
Mourn, Tāi.
Mouth, Udu.
Mouthful, Udu honu.
Move, Raivaraiva.
Much, Bada.
Mud, Kopukopu.
Muddy, Kopukopu.
Mulberry (*paper*), Sihi.
Multiply, Habadaia.
Multitude, Hutuma. Aru.
Mumble, Maumau.
Munificent, Harihari bada.
Murder, Roromaia.
Murderous, Alala tauna.
Murmur, Maumau.
Musket, Ipidi. (*Introduced.*)
Musty, Valavala.
Mute, Mu.
Mutilate, Ivaia.
Mutter, Manmau. Hereva henugu.
Mutual, He prefixed, and hehcni suffixed.
My, Lauegu.
Myself, Lau.

N

Nail, Ikoko. (*finger or toe*), Kahau.
Naked, Sihi lasi.
Name, Ladana.
Name, *v.*, Ladana hatoa; (*to name after some one*), Nemaia.
Nape, Lokoru.
Narrate, Koaulaia.
Narrative, Sivarai.
Narrow, Hekahihekahi. Rotona.
Nasty, Dika.
Nation, Bese.
Nationality, Besedia ; (*Beretani besedia*), of British nationality.
Native, Hanua taudia korikori.
Native custom, Hanua kara.
Naughty, Kara dika.
Nausea, Gado lohilohi.
Nauseate, Gado lohilohi mo karaia.
Navel, Udo.
Nay, Lasi.
Near, Kahilakahila.
Nearly, Moko na.
Neck (*of animals or man*), Aio.
Necklace (*shell*), Taotao. Aio gauna.
Needle, Kobi. Nila. (*Introduced.*)
Needy, Ogogami.
Neglect, Itaia lasi.
Neighbour, Dekena tauna.
Nephew (*man's sister's children*), Vava ; (*brother's children*) Natu.
Nephew and niece (*woman's brother's children*), Lala ; (*sister's children*) Natu.
Nest, Manu rumana.
Net (*fine, fishing*), Reke ; (*larger*) Ole ; (*very large for dugong, &c.*) Varo ; (*kangaroo*) Huo ; (*pig*) Koda ; (*bag*) Daqai.
New, Matamata.
Next, Murinai. Gabenai.
Niece (*man's sister's daughter*), Vava ; (*man's brother's daughter*) Natu.
Niggard, Harihari lasi.
Nigh, Kahilakahila.
Night, Hanuaboi.
Nimble (*in work*) Lega haraga. Gada.
Nine, Taurahani ta.
Ninefold, Ere taurahani ta.
Nineteen, Qauta taurahani ta.
Ninety, Taurahani ta ahui.
Nip, Hegigi.
Nipple, Rata matana.
No, lasi.

Noble, Namo herca.
Nobody, Asi tauna.
Nod, Aio mareremarere; (*with sleep*) Ladorāi.
Noise, Regena.
Nominate, Ladana hatoa.
None, Lasi vaitani.
Noon, Dina tupua.
Noose, Idoa.
North, Mirigini.
North-east wind, Totōdae.
Nose, Udɪ; (*thin as European's*) Udu nesenese; (*wide*) Udu lahalaha; (*flat*) Udu koba.
Nostril, Udu maduna.
Not, Asi (*before the verb*); Lasi (*after v.*).
Notch, Koroa (*in edge of knife, &c.*), Hamakaia.
Noted, Harina bada.
Nothing, Asi anina.
Notify, Koaulaia.
Notorious, Harina bada.
Notwithstanding, Ena be.
Nought, Lasi vaitani.
Nourish, Ubua.
Nourishment, Aniani gauna.
Novel, Matamata.
November, Biriakei. Novema.
Novice, Matamata tauna.
Now, Harihari.
Nowadays, Inai negana.
Noxious, Dika.
Nudity, Sihi lasi.
Nuisance, Taia goegoc gauna. Dika.
Numb, Tamoru.
Number to, Hagaua, Duahia.
Numberless, Momo bamona.
Numerous, Hutuma bada.
Nurse, Rosia.
Nut, Huahua mai koukouna.
Nutriment, Aniani gauna.
Nutshell, Ikoukouna.

O

Oar, Bara.
Oath, Ominuo. (*Introduced.*)
Obdurate, Ura dika.
Obese, Boka bada.
Obey, Kamonai.
Object to, Koauedeede.
Obscure, Valahuvalahu.
Observe, Itaia.

Obstacle, Helaoahu gauna.
Obstinate, Ura dika.
Obstruct, Helaoahu.
Obtain, Abia. Davaria.
Occasion, Badina.
Occupation, Dagi. Kara.
Occupy, Noho.
Ocean, Gādo bada.
Octopus, Urita.
Odious, Dika bada.
Odour, Bouana.
Offence, Hadikaia.
Offer, Henia koaulaia.
Offering, Herahia; (*to God*) Ihaboulaina gau.
Office, Dagina.
Offspring, Natuna.
Often, Nega hoho. Loulou.
Oh! Inā!
Oil, Diaranu.
Old, Gunana; (*men or women*) Tau or hahine bada. Gauka.
Omen, Toana.
On, Dorinai. Latanai.
Once, Tamona.
One, Tamona.
Onerous, Metau.
Only, Sibona. Mo.
Open, Kehoa. (*the mouth*) Ahagaia.
Openhanded, Harihari bada.
Opening, Mātu.
Openly, Hedinarai.
Ophthalmia, Mata hisihisi.
Opinion, Koau.
Opponent, Inai.
Opportune, Nega namo.
Oppose, Koauatubu.
Opposite, Hegagaheheni.
Oppress, Dagedage henia.
Opulence, Kohu diagau.
Or, E. Iava.
Orange (*wild*), Vauto. Anani. (*Introduced*).
Oration, Haroro.
Orator, Haroro tauna.
Ordain, Siaia. Haduaia.
Order, *v.*, Ahegani. Haduaia.
Ordure, Tage.
Orifice, Matuna.
Origin, Badina.
Ornament, Hera gauna.
Orphan, Ihareha.
Other, Idau.
Our, Ita eda (*inclusive*). Ai emai (*exclusive*).
Ourselves, Ita.

Oust, Lulua.
Out, in composition Lasi, as, Laka lasi.
Out of, Halasia.
Outcast, Ihareha tauna.
Outcry, Lolo dagu.
Outer, Murina.
Outlet, Dala.
Outrun (to be), Heautania.
Outside, Murimuri.
Outward, Murimuri kahana.
Oven, Amu. Gula.
Over, adv., Atai ai.
Overcast, Dagahu.
Overcome, Qalimu.
Overdone (in cooking), Halaka ; (of yams) Hepata.
Overflow, Hepulai dobi.
Overhang, Hereaherea.
Overhead, Atai ai.
Overlay, Enoatao.
Overpower, Qalimu.
Overrun, Heautania.
Overshade, Goruahu.
Oversleep, Mahuta bada.
Overspread, Latanai lahaia.
Overtake, Lasiatao.
Overthrow, Uheahebubu.
Overturn, Uheahebubu.
Owe, Dodi. Abitorehai davana.
Owl, Baimumu.
Own, Korikori (following noun).
Owner, Biaguna.
Oyster, Silo.

P

Pacify, Hamarumarua.
Pack, s., Maduna.
Pack up, Haboua kahinaikahinai.
Packing, s., Dogoro.
Paddle, v., Kalo.
Paddle, s., Hode.
Pagan, Dibura tauna.
Page, Buka rauna.
Pain, Hisi.
Paint, s., Muramura ; v. (the face), Umua.
Pair, Ruaoti.
Palace, Lohiabada na ruma.
Pale, Kurokakuroka.
Paling, Ara.
Palliate, Hamaragia.
Palm (areca), Buatau ; (cocoanut), Niu.
Palm (of hand), Ima palapala.

Palpable, Hedinarai.
Palpitate, Rohodae rohodae.
Palsy, Pāda.
Paltry, Maragimaragi.
Pang, Hisihisi.
Pant, Lagadae lagadae.
Papaw, Nita. Loku. (Introduced).
Paper, Pepa. (Introduced).
Parable, Parabole. (Introduced.) Hereva hegeregere.
Paralytic, Pāda tauna.
Paramount, Hereaherea.
Parcel, Ikumi.
Parch, Marai (by the sun).
Pardon, Dika ikoautaona.
Pare, Duhia.
Parents, Tamana, sinana.
Parley, Herevahereva.
Paroquet, Kiloki.
Parrot (green), Kāikāi ; (red) Odubora.
Parsimonious, Harihari lasi.
Part, Kahana. Sisina.
Part, v., (from) Tūa. Ahetonia.
Partake, Taina ania.
Participate, Taina abia.
Partner, Bamona.
Party, Orea.
Pass, v., Hanaia lao.
Passage (boat), Boti dalana. Kadaha.
Passenger, Guikau tauna.
Passing, Hanaia lao.
Passion, Badu bada.
Past (time), Idaunegai.
Pastime, Kadara.
Pat, Pataia.
Patch, Bania.
Path, Dara.
Patience, Aheauka.
Pattern, Revareva. Oromana. Seuseuna.
Paucity, Hoholasi.
Paunch, Boka.
Pavement, Veve hanaihanai.
Payment, Davana. (for blood), Heatotao gauna. Qara henia. (of doctor), Idume.
Paw, Ima.
Pay, Davana.
Peace, Maino.
Peaceably (to live), Hedalo boubou.
Peak, Orooro komoge.
Pearl, Kavabukavabu.
Pebble, Nadi kubolukubolu.
Peace, int., Maino.
Peck, Koria.

PEC (58) POL

Peculiar, Idau.
Peel, v., Duhia.
Peep, Haigo.
Peerless, Sibona hcrea.
Pelt, Nadi hodoa.
Pen, Revareva itorelaina gauna. Puri.
Penalty, Davana.
Pencil, Puri. Penitala. (*Introduced*.)
Pendant, Pepe.
Penetrate, Laloua lno.
Penitet.ce, Helalo karaia.
Pensive, Hade tari.
People, Taunimanima.
Peopled, Mai taunimanima.
Perceive, Itaia.
Perch, v., Rohokan.
Perfect, Namo idoinai.
Perfidious, Koikoi.
Perforate, Budua auru.
Perform, Karaia.
Perfume, Muramura bonana.
Perish, Mate.
Permanent (*durable*), Auka bada.
Permission (*to give*), Tubukau henia.
Permit, Haduaia.
Perpetual, Nega idoinai.
Perpetuate, Hanaihanai.
Persecute, Dagedage henia.
Persevere (*continue*), Malakamalaka.
Persist, Uradika.
Person, Tauna.
Perspicuous, Dina. Ehuni lasi.
Perspire, Varahu.
Persuade, Noinoi. Lalona e ania.
Perturbation, Kudou vada hetaha.
Peruse, Duahia.
Perverse, Ura dika.
Pervert, Hagagevaia. Hereva e mogea.
Pestilence, Hisi karaia.
Phosphorus (*on sea*), Gaova. Hadidi.
Physic, Muramura.
Physician, Muramuru tauna.
Piece, Taina. Sisina. (*Of string, wood, &c.*) Tua.
Pierce, Qadaia.
Pig, Boroma.
Pigeon, Pune. (*Goura*), Tulumu or Tumulu.
Pile, Senusenu.
Piles (*of house*), Du.
Pilfer, Henao.
Pillage, Dadidadi.
Pillow, Iqina.
Pillow, v., Aheqinaia.
Pimple, Usiusi.

Pinch, Hegigi, Hekinitari.
Pineapple, Painapo. (*Introduced*.)
Pink, Pailapaila.
Pipe (*bamboo*), Baubau.
Pish, Hi!
Pit, Guri.
Pitch, s., Muramura koremakorema.
Pitch, v., Tahoa.
Pith, Houkahouka.
Pitiful, Hebokahisi havaraia.
Pitsaw, Iri bada. (*Introduced*.)
Pitted, Budubudu.
Pity, Hebokahisi.
Placable, Manada.
Place, n., Gabuna.
Place, v., Atoa.
Placid (*as a lake*), Ven.
Plague, s. (*of sickness*), Hisi.
Plague, v., Hadagedagea, Hadikaia.
Plain, n., Taora.
Plaint, Tāi. Ganagana.
Plait, Bania.
Plane, Nana gauna.
Plank, Leilei.
Plant, Au.
Planting-stick, Isiva.
Plaintain (*plant*), Dui; (*fruit*) Bigu.
Plantation, Uma.
Plaster, Gabaia muramura.
Plat or Plot, Tano kahana.
Plate, Kepere posekaposeka, abbre viated to posena. Mereki. (*Introduced*.)
Plate soup, Kepere dobukadobuka, abbreviated to dobuna.
Play, Kadara.
Plead, Noinoi.
Pleasant (*to taste*), Mamina namo.
Please, v., Hamoalea.
Plenty, Momo. Diagau.
Pliant, Lorckaloreka.
Pluck, Gari lasi.
Pluck, v. (*fruit*), Bulukia. (*By pulling down branch*) Dabaia qaidu. (*Birds*) Hui budua.
Plug, Iqadobe.
Plumage, Mānu huina.
Plumbago, Ogoa.
Plump, Tāu namo.
Plunder, Dadidadi gauna.
Plunge, Paudobi. Edai dobi.
Point, Matana.
Point, v., Duduia.
Poison, Mate muramurana.
Pole, v., Doaia.
Pole, (*for poling a canoe*), Aivara.
Policeman, Idagahuna tauna.

Policeman, village, Hanua idagahuna tauna.
Polish, Dahua kimorekimore
Polite, Kara namo.
Polute, Hadikaia.
Polygamy, Hodala.
Pomp, Hairaina bada.
Pond, Gohu.
Ponder, Laloa. Hedaraune.
Ponderous, Gaubadabada.
Poor, Ogogame.
Pop, Poudagu.
Populace, Hanua taudia.
Popular, Harina namo.
Populous, Taunimanima momo.
Pork, Boroma anina.
Porpoise, Kidului.
Port, Hedoko gabuna.
Portent, Toana. Qare.
Portion, Ahuna.
Possess, Abia.
Possessed (demoniacally), Boloa.
Possible, Karaia diba. Abia diba.
Post, Autubua ; (side), Ihuaihu.
Posteriors, Kunu.
Posterity, Tubudia.
Postpone, Dohore.
Potent, Goada.
Potsherd, Ataga.
Pouch, Vaina ; (marsupial), Mapau.
Pound, Pauna. (Introduced.)
Pound (money), Pauni.
Pound, v., Qadaia. Pataia.
Pour, Seia,.(into) Vedaia.
Poverty, Ogogame. Asi gauna.
Powder (dust), Gahu. (Gunpowder) Pauda. (Introduced.)
Power, Goada. Siahu.
Powerful, Goada tauna. Siahu tauna.
Practice, Kara.
Praise, v., Hanamoa. Heatolaia.
Prate, Hereva kava hereva kava.
Pray, Guri. Guriguri koaulaia.
Prayer, Guriguri.
Preach, Haroro.
Precarious, Moru garina.
Precede, Gunalaia.
Precept, Ahegani herevana.
Precious (of affection), Lalokau ; (in value) Davana bada.
Precipice, Hagahaga.
Predict, Dose vara negana ai e koaulaia
Pre-eminent, Hereaherea.
Prefer, Abia hidi.
Pregnant, Rogorogo.
Prepare, Haguevaia

Prepay, Davana henia guna.
Preposterous, Kavakava.
Presence, Vairana.
Present, v., Henia.
Present (at), Harihari.
Present, s., Herahia gauna. Harihari gauna.
Presently, Dohore.
Preserve (to keep), Abia tarika-tarika.
Press (in crowd), Hesede matemate ; (down) Kapuatao.
Pretend, Hedibagani karaia.
Pretty, Namo.
Prevail, Qalimu.
Prevaricate, Koikoi.
Prevent, Laoahu.
Previous, Gunana. Gunaguna.
Price, Davana.
Prick, Qadaia.
Prickly, Ginigini.
Pride, Hekokorugu.
Priest, Kohena. (Introduced.)
Prince, Lohia natuna.
Principal (thing), Herea gauna ; (person) Herea tauna.
Print, v., Revareva karaia.
Print (of foot), Aegabu.
Prior, Gunana.
Prison, Ruma koua. (Introduced meaning.)
Private, Hamaoroa lasi.
Privately, Ehuniehuni.
Probity, Kara maoromaoro.
Proceed (imp.), Aola.
Proclaim, Haroro.
Procrastinate, Dohore koaulaia.
Procure, Abia.
Prodigal, Petapetalaia.
Prodigious, Gaubadabada.
Produce (of garden), Uma anina.
Productive, Anina bada.
Profane, Koau dika.
Proffer, Henia toho.
Proficient, Diba bada.
Profit, Kohu e abilaia.
Progeny, Natudia.
Prognosticate, Dose vara negana ai e koaulaia.
Prohibit, Koauatao. Doha.
Project, v., Herea.
Prolific, Natuna momo.
Prolong, Habadaia. Halataia.
Promiscuous, Idauidau.
Promise, Koauhamata.
Promontory, Iduka.
Prompt, v., Haragaharaga.

Promptly, Haragaharaga.
Promulgate, Haroro.
Prone, Gorudiho.
Pronounce, Koaulaia.
Proof, Hamomokanilaia.
Prop, Imuta. Itotohi. Tō.
Propagate, Havaraia.
Propel (*by poling*), Doaia.
Proper, Namo. Maoromaoro.
Property, Kohu.
Prophesy, Dose vara negana ai e kcaulaia.
Propitiate, Hamarumarua.
Propitious (*time*), Nega namo.
Proposal, Koaulaia.
Propose, Koau.
Proprietor, Biaguna.
Prosperous, Nega namo.
Prostitute, Ariara hahine.
Prostrate, Gorudiho.
Protect, Gima.
Protract, Halataia.
Protrude, Herea.
Proud, Hekokorogu.
Prove, Hamomokanilaia.
Proverb, Hereva hegeregere.
Provide, Abia.
Provision (*food*), Malamala; (*for journey or voyage*), Laqa.
Provoke, Habadua.
Proximity, Kahilakahila. Dia daudau.
Proxy, Boloa.
Prudent, Aonega.
Prune, Rigi utua.
Pshaw! Hi!
Public, Hedinarai.
Publish, Haroro.
Pucker, Magugu.
Pudding (*sago*), Dia.
Puerile, Meromero bamona.
Pugnacious, Heatu tauna.
Pull, veria. (*up grass*), Butua.
Pumpkin, Mausini (*Introduced*).
Pungent, Hegara.
Punish, Davana henia. Matana e hagania.
Punishment, Davana korikori. Matana ihaganina.
Puny, Maragimaragi. Misikamisika.
Pup, Sisia natuna.
Pupil, Hadibaia tauna.
Puppy, Sisia natuna.
Purchase, Hoihoi.
Pure, Goevagoeva.
Purge, Boka hekukuri.
Purloin, Henao.

Purple, Kakakaka.
Purport, Hereva auina.
Purpose (*in coming or going*), Totona.
Pursue, Gavaia.
Purulent, Hula bamona.
Push, Doria.
Pustule, Sihaurisihauri.
Put, Atoa; (*down*) Atoa diho; (*on clothes*), Ahedokia.
Put off (*on another*), Ahekora.
Putrefy, E pata.

Q

Quail, *s.* Kibi.
Quake, Gari. Dagu.
Quarrel, Heai.
Queen, Gaubada hahine. Hanua pavapavana hahinena.
Quell, Hatui.
Quench, Habodoa.
Querulous, Daradara mo.
Query, Henanadai.
Quest, Tahua.
Question, Henanadai.
Quick, Haragaharaga. (*be quick*), Kara haraga. Mate mauri!
Quickly, Lega haraga.
Quicklime, Ahu hegara. Ahu siahu.
Quiet, Asi regeregena.
Quill, Manu huina.
Quit, Lao. Lakatania.
Quite, Vadaeni. Idoinai.
Quiver, Diba baubauna.
Quotation, Ini koautoma.

R

Rabid, Dagedage bada.
Race (*to run*) Valāu. Heauhelulu.
Radiant, Hururuhururu.
Raft, Pata. (*of logs*), Krave.
Raft, *v.* Ravea.
Rafter, Tuidae.
Rag, Dabua sisina.
Rage, Badu.
Ragged, Hedarehedare.
Rail, *s.* Tabikau āuna.
Rail, *v.* Hadikaia.
Raillery, Gonagonalaia. Kirikirilaia.
Rain, Medu.
Rainbow, Kevau.
Raise, Abiaisi. Hatoreaisi.
Ram, *v.* (*as earth*) Hadaia kunu.
Ramble, Loa.

Rancour, Lalo dika.
Random, Kererekerere. Matalahui.
Rank (growth), Vara rohoroho.
  (Smell) Bodaga.
Rankle, Laloatao.
Ransom, Davana. Qara henia.
Rap, Pidipidi.
Rapid, Haragaharaga.
Rare, Tamotamona.
Rascal, Dika tauna.
Rash, adj. Aonega lasi.
Rash, s. Lari.
Rat, Bita.
Ratify, Hamomokanilaia.
Rattan, Oro ; (larger) Vakoda.
Rattle, Hataia.
Rave, Koau kava koau kava.
Ravish, Henaohenoa.
Raw, Nadu lasi. Kasili.
Raze, Rohoa. Buatari.
Razor, Vasika.
Reach, v. Eme kau ; (a place) Lasi.
Read, Revareva duahia.
Ready, get (lakatoi) Laia.
Real, Korikori. Momokani.
Rear, s. Murina.
Rear, v. Havaraia.
Reason, Badina. Koauna.
Reassemble, Haboua lou.
Rebuke, Sisiba henia. Koauatao.
  Bagu koau.
Recede, Lou. Laka muri.
Receive, Abia.
Recent, Matamata.
Recite, Koaulaia.
Reckless, Kererekerere.
Reckon (count), Duahia.
Recline, Hekure ; (on the side)
  Egediho.
Recognise, Toana diba.
Recollect, Hedaraune.
Recompense, Davana.
Reconcile, Herohemaino karaia.
Recover, Abia lou ; (from sickness)
  Tauna dainamo. Mauri.
Recount, Koaulaia hegege.
Recriminate, Hepapahuahu.
Rectify, Hamaoromaoroa.
Red, Kakakaka.
Redeem (a person), Davalaia.
Reduce, Hamaragia.
Redundant, Gaubadabada.
Reed, Siriho.
Reef, Moemoe.
Reel, v. Raraga.
Reflect, Laloa. Helalo karaia.
Reform, Hamaoromaoroa.

Refractory, Koauedeode.
Refrain, Lagaani.
Refuge, Magu.
Refuse, s. Momo.
Refuse, v. Kamonai lasi.
Regard, v. Hagerea.
Region, Kahana.
Regret, Helalo karaia.
Rehearse, Koaulaia.
Rein, Ihakauna varona.
Reject, Dadaraia. Hihihiraia.
  Negea.
Rejoice, Moale.
Rejoinder, Haere.
Relapse, Dika lou.
Relate, Koaulaia.
Relative, Varavara. Mauri duduna.
Relax, Tūa.
Release, Ruhaia nege. Haheaua.
Relent, Lalona lou.
Reliance, Abidadama henia.
Religion, Dirava kara.
Relinquish, Negea.
Rely, Abidadama henia.
Remain, Noho.
Remainder, Orena.
Remedy, Hanamolaia gauna.
Remember, Hedaraune. Helalounc.
Remind, Ahelaloa.
Remission, Koauatao.
Remnant, Orena.
Remorse, Helalo.
Remote, Daudau.
Remove, Abiaoho.
Remunerate, Davana henia.
Rend, Hedare.
Rendezvous, Haboua gabuna.
Renounce, Negea.
Renowned, Harina bada.
Repair, v. Hamatamataia ; (a rent)
  Bania.
Repast, Aniani ania.
Repeal, Koauatao.
Repeatedly, Loulou.
Repeat, Koaulaia lou.
Repel, Lulua.
Repent, Helalo.
Repine, Tāi.
Reply, Haere.
Report, Hari.
Repose, v. Hekure.
Represent, Koaulaia.
Repress, Koauatao.
Reprimand, Sisiba henia. Koau henia.
Reproach, v. Lodu henia.
Reproof, Koau henia. Sisiba henia.
Reptile, Gaigai bamona.

Repudiate, Dadaraia.
Repulse, Lulua.
Repute, Harina bada.
Request, s. Henanadai. Noinoi.
Require, Henanadai. Tahua.
Requite, Davana henia.
Rescue, Hamauria.
Research, Tahua malakamalaka.
Resemble (a person), Heidāida; (things) Bamona.
R 'sent, Davana karaia.
Reside, Noho.
Residence, Ruma.
Residue, Orena.
Resin, Domena. Lamanu.
Resist, Koauatubu.
Resolve, Lalo koau.
Respect, v. Matauraia. Qahia.
Respire, Hahoho.
Respond, Haere henia. Ere hadavaia.
Rest, v. Lagaani.
Rest, Lagaani gabuna.
Restore, Loulaia.
Restless, Tau mauri.
Restrain, Rūa.
Resurrection, Itoreisina.
Retain, Rūa. Koauatao.
Retaliate, Davana karaia.
Retard, Laoahu.
Retch, Mumuta.
Retire, Lao.
Retreat, v. Lou.
Return, v. Lou. (after estrangement), Darodac.
Reveal, Ahedinarai.
Revenge, Davana karaia.
Revere, Hanamoa. Hemataurai.
Reverse (end for end), Sivaia.
Revile, Hadikaia.
Revive, Mauri lou.
Revolve, Hegilohegilo.
Reward, v. Davana henia.
Rheumatism, Lōki.
Rheumatic, Lōki karaia.
Rib, Turiarudu.
Rich, Tāga tauna.
Rid, Abiaoho.
Ride, Gui.
Ridge, Nese.
Ridgecap, Bisiva.
Ridgepole, Magani bada.
Ridicule, Kirikirilaia.
Rifle, v. Henaoa.
Right, Maoromaoro; (hand), Idiba.
Rigid, Tororotororo.
Rim, Isena.
Rind, Kopina.

Ring, v. Gaba doua.
Ring (finger), Ima qagiqagi vagivagina.
Ringworm, Huni.
Rinse, Huria. Dairia.
Rip, Bolaia.
Ripe, Mage. Lō.
Ripen (on the tree), Hamagea; (off the tree, as bananas) Ikou karaia.
Rise, Toreisi.
Rival, Inai.
River, Sinavai.
Road, Dara.
Roam, Loa.
Roar, Tāi bada. Gou.
Roast, Gabua.
Rob, Dadidadi.
Robust, Tau namo.
Rock (flat), Papapapa; (high), Haga.
Rock, v. Aheudeheudea.
Roe, Bila.
Roll, Lokua.
Roof, Guhi; (of verandah), Bakubaku.
Room, Daehutu.
Roost, Mahuta.
Root, Ramuna.
Root up, Ragaia.
Rope, Qanau.
Rose (Chinese), Vahuvahu.
Rot (of wood), Houkahouka; (frui Pouka.
Rotten (as mats, nets, &c.), Mot kamotuka, Minagaminaga.
Rough, Butubutu; (road), Nadi momo.
Round, Kubolukubolu.
Round (to go), Hegegedai.
Rouse, Haoa.
Routed, Aheaua rohoroho.
Rove, Toia vareai.
Row, Ere.
Row, v. (a boat), Baraia.
Rub, Dahua.
Rubbish, Momo.
Rudder, Tari gauna.
Rude, Guni tauna bamona. Se hematurai.
Ruffian, Dagedage tauna.
Rule, s. Hahetoho gauna.
Ruler, Lohiabada.
Rumble, Regena.
Rumour, Harina.
Rumple, Magugu.
Run, Heau.
Rush, Heau helulu.
Rust, Hogohogo.

S

Sabbath, Sabati. (*Introduced.*)
Sable, Koremakoreina.
Sabre, Ilapa. Dare.
Sack, *v.* Dadidadi.
Sack, Nulu. Moda. Puse. (*Introduced.*)
Sacred, Helaga.
Sacrifice (*to God*), Ihaboulaina boroma.
Sad, Boka hisihisi.
Saddle, Hosi helai gauna.
Safe, Vada mauri.
Sago, Rabia (*small package of*), Kokoara (*large package*), Gorugoru.
Sail, *s.*, Lara. Geda.
Sail, Heau.
Sake, Bagu.
Salary, Gau karaia davana.
Sale, Hoihoi.
Saline, Damena bamona.
Saliva, Kanudi.
Sallow, Raboraraborn.
Salt, Damena.
Salt, *v.* Damena karaia.
Saltpans, Laguta.
Salt water, Tadi.
Salvation, Ahemauri badina
Salute, Hanamoa henia.
Same, Bamona. Tamona.
Sanctify, Ahelagaia.
Sand, Raria.
Sandalwood, Bado, also Boto.
Sandbank, Boe.
Sap, Au ranuna.
Sapient, Aonega.
Sapling, Au maragi.
Satchel, Vaina.
Satisfy, Boka hakunua.
Saturday, Satadei. (*Introduced.*)
Saunter, Laka metailamctaila.
Savage, Dagedage.
Save, Hamauria.
Saviour, Ihamaurina tauna
Savour, Mamina.
Saw, Iri.
Sawdust, Au dimura.
Say, Koau.
Scab, Taoha.
Scald, Goua.
Scale, *s.* Una.
Scale, *v.* Unahia.
Scalp, Qara kopina.
Scamper, Heau.
Scar, Kipara.

Scarce, Hoho lasi.
Scarcity (*of food*), Dōe.
Scare, Hagaria.
Scarify, Hekisi.
Scarlet, Kakakaka.
Scatter, Gigiarohoroho. (*As fowls scratching*), Petapeta.
Scent, *s.* Bona.
Scent, *v.* Bonana kamonai.
Scholar, Hadibaia mero.
School, Ahediba karaia.
Schoolmaster, Ahediba tauna
Scissors, Pakosi. (*Introduced.*)
Scoff, Gonagona.
Scold, Koaukoau.
Scoop, *v.* Kadoa.
Scorch, Halaka.
Scorn, Lalo dika henia.
Scour, Hagoevaia.
Scourge, *s.* Dadabaia gauna.
Scout, *s.* Hasinadoa tauna.
Scowl, Vaira hamue.
Scramble, Hetabubunai.
Scrap, Sisina.
Scrape, Naua.
Scratch, Hekagalo.
Scream, Tai lolo
Screen, *s.* Hametai gauna
Screw, *s.* Mogea ikoko.
Scribble, Revareva torea dika.
Scriptures, Revareva helaga
Scrotum, Apo.
Scrub, Huria.
Scrutinize, Itaia tarikatarika.
Scuffle, Hetabubunai.
Scull, Qara koukouna.
Sea, Davara.
Seacoast, Kone.
Seasick, Gure.
Seaside, Davara badina.
Seawater, Tadi.
Search, Tahua.
Season, Negana.
Seat, Helai gauna.
Seaward, Atai. Davara kahana.
Secede, Lou.
Second, Ia ruana.
Secret, Hereva ehuni.
Secure, Auka. Kunukakunuka.
Secure, *v.* Koua kunukakunuka.
Sedate. Matau.
Sediment, Nuri.
Seduce, Koia.
Sedulous, Goada.
See, Itaia.
See ! Ba itaia !
Seed, Au nadinadina. Uhe.

SEE (64) SIG

Seek, Tahua.
Seemly, Kara namo.
Seine, Reke.
Seize, Dabaiatao.
Seldom, Nega tamo tamona
Select, v. Abia hidi.
Selfish, Anidika.
Self-restraint, Boka auka.
Sell, Hoihoi.
Semblance, Bamona.
Senator, Tau bada.
Send, Siaia.
Senior, Varaguna.
Sentinel, Ginia tauna.
Separate, Idau.
Sepulchre, Gara.
Serpent, Gaigai.
Servant, Hesiai tauna. Isiai mero.
Serve, Isiaina laoheni.
Set, Atoa.
Set on (as pot), Ahelaiakau.
Set on fire (as grass), Doua.
Seven, Hitu.
Seven times, Hahitu.
Seventeen, Qauta hitu.
Seventh, Ia hituna.
Seventy, Hitu ahui.
Sever, Utua nege. Rahuautu.
Several, Haida.
Severe, Dagedage.
Sew, Turituri.
Shade, Kerukeru.
Shade, v. Hakerukerua.
Shadow, Laulau.
Shake, v. Aheudeheudea.
Shake, v.n. Heudeheude.
Shallow, Guihoho.
Sham, s. Dibaka tauna.
Shame, Hemarai.
Shamefaced, Kopi hemarai.
Shameful (conduct), Hemarai kara.
Shape, Oromana.
Share, s. Ahuna.
Share, v. Hagaua.
Shark, Qalaha. Maleva.
Sharp, Gano.
Sharpen, Segea.
Shatter, Pisi rohoroho.
Shave, Auki huina abia.
She, Ia.
Sheath, Pāu.
Shed, Ruma kalaka.
Shed, v. Hehuhu.
Sheep, Mamoe. (Introduced.)
Sheet, Hetaru dabuana. (Of sail), Idi.
Shelf, Pata.
Shell, Koukouna.

Shell-fish, different kinds of; see Appendix.
Shelter, s. Metai gabuna.
Shelter, v. Hametaia.
Sherd, Ataka.
Shield, Kesi.
Shield, v. Nari. Gima.
Shin, Toratora.
Shine, Hururuhururu.
Ship, Lakatoi.
Shipwreck, Lakatoi tataiakohi.
Shirt, Hedoki gauna.
Shiver, v.n. Heudeheude.
Shoal (of fish, &c.), Serina. (Water), Guihoho.
Shoe, Ae palapala gauna.
Shoot, v. Ipidi karaia.
Shoot, Au tuhutuhu.
Shop, Hoihoi rumana.
Shore, Kone.
Short, Qadogiqadogi.
Shortly, Nega dia daudau. Sevanaha.
Shortwinded, Laga tuna.
Shot, Ipidi nadina.
Shoulder, Paga.
Shoulder-blade, Larolaro.
Shout, Lolo; Lagigi. Gaba. (as when carrying anything heavy) Isidae.
Shove, Hesede.
Shovel, Ikadona gauna. Gaga.
Shovel, v. Kadoa.
Show, v. Hadibaia. Ahedinaraia.
Shower, Batugu.
Shred, v. Toia.
Shriek, Tāi lolo.
Shrimp, Pāi.
Shrink (from cold), Hegogo. (Clothes or food), Hedikoi.
Shrivel, v. Magugu.
Shudder, Heguguba. Hihinana.
Shun, Heirilaia.
Shut, Koua.
Shutter, Ikouahu gauna.
Shy, Kopi hemarai.
Sick, Gorere.
Side, Kahana. Ohena.
Side (by the), Badina.
Side to with, Kahaia.
Siege, Koua hegege.
Sigh, Ganagana.
Sight (eye), Mata hapapai.
Sight, v. Itaia.
Sightly, Namo.
Sign, Toana.
Signal, s. Toana.
Signal, v. (with eyes), Hekunumai.
Signify, Anina.

Silence, Asi regeregena. Hereva lasi.
Silence! Eremui!
Silly, Kavakava.
Silver, Ario. (*Introduced.*)
Similar, Bamona. (*Preceded by the thing compared with*), Na heto.
Simile, Hereva hegeregere.
Simple, Aonega lasi.
Sin, Kara dika.
Since, Ema bona.
Sincere, Momokani.
Sinew, Varovaro.
Sing, Ane abia.
Singe, Duduria. (*Hair*), Dedea.
Singer, Ane abia tauna.
Single, Tamona. Sibona.
Single file, Ilua.
Singly, Ta ta.
Singular, Sibona.
Sink, Mutu.
Sinner, Kara dika tauna.
Sip, Kuri ta ta inua.
Sir! Lohiabada e!
Sister (*woman's younger*), Tadina. (*elder*), Kakana. (*man's*), Taihuna.
Sit, Helai.
Site, Gabuna.
Six, Tauratoi.
Sixteen, Qauta tauratoi.
Sixth, Ia tauratoina.
Sixty, Tauratoi ahui.
Size, Badana.
Skilful, Aonega.
Skin, Kopi.
Skin, *v.* Kopaia.
Skinny, Varotavarota.
Skip, Roho.
Skipper, Lakatoi tauna.
Skirt (*a woman's*), Rami.
Skull, Qara koukouna.
Sky, Guba.
Slack, Hetū.
Slacken, Tūa.
Slander, *v.* Hadikaia.
Slant, Sehe.
Slap, Pataia.
Slap thigh or buttocks (*in defiance*), Valea.
Slaughter, Bua. Buatari. (*of animals*), Mahu.
Slate, Nadi.
Slay, Alaia.
Sleep, Mahuta.
Sleepy, Mata garaia.
Slender, Maragimaragi.
Slide, Dedi.

Slight (*not bulky*), Maragimaragi, Varotavarota.
Slim, Maragimaragi, Varotavarota.
Slime, Qari.
Sling, *s.* Vilipopo.
Sling, *v.* Vilipopo davea.
Slink, Laka magogomagogo. Laka helada.
Slip, Dedi. (*out of*), Puki.
Slippery, Dedikadedika.
Slit, Hapararaia.
Slope, *s.* Dala hekeihekei.
Sloth, Lahedo. Boka mate.
Slough, Kopukopu.
Slow (*in work*), Lega metau. (*in walking*), Laka metau.
Sluggard, Mahuta tauna.
Slumber, Mahuta maragi.
Slut, Sisia hahine.
Small, Maragi. (*of thread, &c.*), Maimu.
Smart, *v.* Hegara.
Smear, Hedahu.
Smell, Bonana.
Smell, *v.* Bonaia.
Smile, Kiri.
Smite, Huaria.
Smoke, Qalahu.
Smoke, *v.* Kuku ania.
Smooth, Manada.
Smut (*from burnt grass*), Banidu.
Snake, Gaigai.
Snare, Idoa.
Snarl, Gigi.
Snatch, Dadia.
Sneeze, Asimana.
Sniff, Iluhai.
Snip, Sisina utua.
Snore, Udu gogona.
Snout, Kurukuruna.
So, Ini heto. Bamona.
Soak, Hadaia.
Soap, Sopu. (*Introduced.*)
Soar, Roho.
Sob, Lagadae.
Sociable, Manada.
Soft, Manokamanoka.
Soil, *v.* Hamiroa.
Soil, *s.* Tano.
Sojourn, Noho.
Solace, Tauhalō.
Sole (*of foot*), Ae lalona.
Solicit, Noinoi.
Solicitude, Kudou hetaha.
Solitary, Sibona noho.
Some (*people*), Haida. (*things*), Taina.
Somebody, Tau ta.

E

Something, Gau ta.
Sometimes, Hata.
Son, Mero.
Son-in-law, Ravana.
Song, Ane.
Sonorous, Regena bada.
Soon, Nega dia daudau.
Sooth, Hamarumaru.
Sooty, Guma karaia.
Sordid, Harihari lasi.
Sore, *adj.*, Hisihisi.
Sore, *s.*, Toto.
Sorrow, Boka hisihisi.
Soul, Lauma.
Sound, Regena.
Sound, *adj.*, Namo. Goevagóeva.
Sour (*acid*), Iseuri ; (*paste*, *&c.*), Bakobako.
Source, Badina.
South, Diho kahana.
South-east, Laulabada kahana.
South-east wind, Laulabada.
South-south-east about, Atu diho.
South wind, Diho.
Sovereign, Gaubada. Hanua pavapavana.
Sow, *v.*, Gigiarohoroho.
Sow, *s.*, Boroma hahine.
Space (*between*), Ihuana. Padana.
Spacious, Lababana bada.
Spade, Gaga.
Spare, *v.*, Mia.
Spatter, Petapetalaia.
Spawn, Bila.
Speak, Koau. Hereva.
Spear, Io.
Specify, Koaulaia maoromaoro.
Speckle, Toutoudia.
Spectator, Itaia tauna. Herarai tauna.
Spectre, Vāda. Vadavada.
Speech, Hereva.
Speed, Heau.
Spell (*a word*), Hagaua.
Spew, Lori.
Spider, Magela.
Spill, *v.*, Hebubu.
Spine, Turiamava.
Spirit, Lauma.
Spit, Kanudi.
Spite, Badu.
Spittle, Kanudi.
Splash, Pisipisina.
Splendid, Namo Herea.
Splinter, *s.*, Au tahana.
Split, Hapararaia.
Spoil, *v.*, Hadikaia.

Spoil, *s.*, Dadidadi kohu. Dinana.
Sponge, Puta.
Sport, Kadara. (*In the sea*), Bulubulu.
Spot, Toutou.
Spotless, Toutouna lasi.
Spotted (*as yam, &c.*), Budubudu.
Sprain, *s.*, Dorua.
Sprain, *v.*, Hadorua.
Spray, Pisili.
Spread (*as a cloth*), Lahaia.
Spring, *v.*, Roho.
Syrinkle, Nevaria.
Sprout, Tubu.
Spurn, Dadaraia. Hihihiraia.
Spy, Kito tauna. Hasinadoa tauna.
Spy, *v.*, Kito.
Spyglass, Varivari. (*Introduced.*)
Squabble, Heai, Heatu.
Squalid, Dika.
Squall, Guba. Ore.
Squander, Davedavelaia. Piupiu laia.
Square, Derekadereka.
Squat (*on heels*), Idori.
Squeak, Tāi.
Squeeze (*in the arms*), Gugubaia ; (*between boards, &c.*), Kapuatao.
Squint, Mata gegeva.
Squirt, Larilari.
Stab, Qadaia.
Stable, Hosi ruma.
Staff, Itotohi.
Stagger, Raraga.
Stagnant, Ranu duhu.
Stair, Vatavata.
Stale, Idaunegai gauna.
Stalk (*of banana, &c.*), Qasi ; (*of mango, &c.*), Adana.
Stallion, Hosi maruane.
Stammer, Lanalana.
Stamp, *v.*, Panadagu.
Stanch, Momokani.
Stanched, Vada doko.
Stand, Gini.
Star, Hisiu.
Starch, Rabia.
Starch, *v.*, Rabia karaia.
Stare, Raraia.
Start, Hoa. Laumadaure.
Startle, Dagu.
Starve, *v., n.*, Hitolo mate.
Stay (*to a mast*), Hadeolo ; (*at home when others go*), Auasi.
Steadfast, Badinaia tarikatarika.
Steady, Tutukatutuka.
Steal, Henao.

STE   (67)   SUP

Stealthily, Helada.
Steam, Varahu.
Steep, v. (in water), Hadaia.
Steep, Hagahaga.
Steer, Tari karaia.
Steersman, Tari tauna.
Stem, Badina.
Stench, Bodaga.
Step, v., Laka.
Sterile (of ground), Gesegese.
Stern (of a ship), Gabena.
Stick, s., Au. (Fencing, small), Adira ; (large), Pulu.
Stick (a walking), Itotohi.
Stick, v., Hekahi. Hekamo ; (as door or window), Kaki.
Sticky, Hekamo.
Stiff, Auka. Lokaloka ; (as starched clothes), Kenkakeaka.
Stiff neck, Aio gageva.
Stile, Ikoukou.
Still, v., Hatuia.
Stillborn, Mara dika.
Stimulate, Hagoadaia.
Sting, v., Koria ; (hornet), Talaia.
Stingy, Harihari lasi.
Stink, Bodaga.
Stir, Giua.
Stomach, Boka.
Stone, Nadi.
Stone, v., Nadi hodoa.
Stony, Nadigabuna.
Stool s. (to sit on), Helai gauna.
Stool (go to), Kuku.
Stoop, Haigo.
Stop, v., Hadokoa ; v.n., Noho.
Stop ! Vadaeni ! Noho !
Storm, Ore. Guba.
Story (narrative), Sivarai.
Stout, Tau gaubadabada.
Straight, Maoro.
Straight v. (to make), Ahemaoro.
Straighten (as a stick), Bena.
Strait, adj., Hekahihekahi.
Strait, s., Kadaha.
Strand, Ere.
Strange, Idau.
Stranger, Idau tauna.
Strangle, Hemata.
Stratagem (to deceive), Koia kara.
Stray, Laka kerere.
Stream, Sinavai. Dogo.
Stream forth (as blood), Bobobobo.
Strength, Goada.
Stretch, v., Veria.
Strew, Lahaia.
Street, Ariara.

Strife, Heatu.
Strike, v. (with a weapon), Botaia. Lapaia, (with the flat hand), Pataia.
String, Varo.
String, v. (a bow), Rohea.
Stripe, Revareva.
Stripling, Tauhau.
Strive, Goada.
Stroke, s. (with stick), Qadia.
Strong, Goada. Abidadama.
Strumpet, Ariara hahine.
Stubborn, Ura dika.
Stud (of house), Ihuaihu.
Stumble, Heqaqanai.
Stump, Au badibadina.
Stunted, Vara lasi.
Stupefy (as fish with drug), Kekero.
Stupid, Kavakava. Asi aonega.
Sturdy, Goada.
Stutter, Gado lanalana.
Sty (pig), Boroma arana.
Stye (on eye), Usiusi.
Submerge, Burua. Hadaia.
Submission, Tomadiho henia.
Subsequent, Gabea.
Subside, Dodo.
Substance, Anina. Anitarana.
Substitute, Boloa. Ibodohi.
Subtract, Veria. Abiaoho.
Succeed, Abia. Davaria. Qalimu.
Succour, Kahaia.
Such, Unu heto.
Suck, Tohoa.
Suckle, Natuna rata hainua.
Suckling woman, Maraloto hahinena.
Sudden, Hoa. Laumadaure.
Suffer, Hisi ania.
Suffice, Vadaeni. (Of food), Boka kanu.
Sugarcane, Tohu.
Suicide, Sibona heala.
Sulky, Badu. Tudaga.
Sultry, Siahu.
Sum, Haboua.
Summit, Dorinai.
Summon, Boilia.
Sun, Dina.
Sunday, Sabati. (Introduced.)
Sunder, Utua nege.
Sunny, Dina tara.
Sunset, Dina kerekere.
Superior, Namo herea.
Supper, Adorahi aniani.
Supple, Perukaperuka.
Supplicate, Noinoi.
Supply, v. Henia.

| SUP | (68) | THO |

Support, v. (as a tree or house), Imudaia.
Suppose, Lalo koau. (mistakenly) Banava.
Suppress, Koauatao.
Suppurate, Hura karaia.
Supreme, Sibona herea.
Sure, Diba momokani.
Surf (on beach), Rahukau.
Surface, Kopina.
Surfeit, Gado lohilohi.
Surmise, Lalo koau.
Surpass, Herea.
Surplus, Orena.
Surprise, v., Hahoaia. Ahebololu.
Surround, Gegea. Hegege madai.
Survivor, Hoho tauna.
Swallow, Hadonoa.
Swamp, Kopukopu.
Swarm (of ants and the like), Taba. Tabataba.
Sway (by the wind), Haevaia. Helado.
Sweat, Varahu.
Sweep, Daroa.
Sweet, Gaiho.
Swell, Gudu. (of ocean), Sinai. (inside reef), Beubeu.
Swift, Heau bada.
Swim, Nahu.
Swine, Boroma.
Swing, Love ; (low) Taupetaupe.
Swoon, Matelea.
Swop, Hoihoi.
Sword, Ilapa. Dare.
Symptom, Toana.
Synagogue, Sunago (introduced).

T

Table, Pata.
Tail, Iuna ; (of birds), Tupina.
Take, Abia. Abikau. (Away), Abiaoho. Laohaia. (Up), Abiaisi.
Tale, Sivarai.
Talk, Hereva.
Talkative, Udu mauri.
Tall, Gaulatalata. Lata.
Tame, Manada.
Tangle, Heqatu. Hemoge.
Tardy, Halahe.
Taro, Talo.
Tarry, Noho.

Tart, Iseuri.
Taste, Ania toho.
Tattoo, Revareva hatua.
Taunt, Koau henia.
Taut, Rorokaroroka.
Teach, Hadibaia.
Teacher, Ahediba tauna.
Tear, Darea.
Tears, Iruru mata.
Tease, Habadua.
Teat, Rata matana.
Telescope, Varivari. (Introduced meaning.)
Tell, Koau henia. Hamaoroa.
Tempest, Ore. Guba.
Temple, Dubu.
Tempt, Dibagani.
Temptation, Idibaganina.
Ten, Qauta.
Tenacious, Auka.
Tend (as sheep, &c.), Legua.
Tender, Manokamanoka.
Tendon, Varovaro.
Tent, Dabua rumana.
Tenth, Ia qautana.
Termination, Dokona.
Terrify, Hagaria.
Terror, Gari.
Testify, Koaulaia.
Text, Hereva badina.
Thank, v., Hanamoa.
Thank offering, Ihanamona gau.
Thanks (to give), Hanamoa.
That, Enai. Unai.
Thatch, Kurukuru. Biri. (According to material).
Their, Idia edia ; (of food), Idia adia.
Them, Idia.
Then, Unai negana.
There, Unuseni.
Therefore, Inai. Badina binai.
These, Inai.
They, Idia.
Thick, Hutuna.
Thief, Henao tauna.
Thigh, Mamu.
Thin, Severasevera.
Thing, Gau.
Think, Laloa.
Thinking faculty, Aonega. Dara.
Third, Ia toina.
Thirst, Ranu mate.
Thirteen, Qauta toi.
Thirty, Toi ahui.
This, Inai.
Thorn, Gini.

Those, Unai.
Thou, Oi.
Though, Ena be.
Thought, Lalo koau.
Thoughtful, Aonega.
Thoughtless, Kavakava.
Thousand, Daha.
Thrash, Dadabaia. Botaia.
Thread, Varo.
Three, Toi.
Threefold, Eretoi.
Threshold, Ikureahu.
Thrive, Vara rohoroho.
Throat, Gado.
Throat sore, Araturia.
Throb (as the heart), Rohodaerohodae;
(as a gathering), Hodachodae.
Throng, Hutuma bada.
Throng v., Hesedea.
Throttle, Gado gigia.
Through (to go), Hanaia lao.
Throughout, Idoinai.
Throw, Tahoa. (away), Negea. (down, as log from shoulder), Dagaia diho.
Thrush, Mala reho.
Thrust, Doria.
Thumb, Sina bada.
Thump, Tutua.
Thunder, Guba rabua.
Thursday, Tarisidei. (Introduced.)
Thus, Ini heto.
Thwart, Laoahu.
Tickle, Ahemaihemai.
Tide high, Davara bada.
Tide low, Komata gui. Davara maragi.
Tidings, Sivarai. Harina.
Tidy up. Hairavaia.
Tie, Mataia.
Tight, Hekahi.
Till, Ela bona.
Time, Negana.
Time of day or night :—
Sunset, Dina e dogu dobi.
Evening (general), adorahi.
About 7 p.m., Adorahi gama-gama.
,, 8 p.m., Kadara e dihomu.
,, 9 p.m., Kadara e daemu.
,, 10 p.m., Malohevani.
Midnight, Malokihi.
About 1·30 a.m., Malokohia.
,, 3 a.m., Taurahani kaha.
,, 4 a.m., Hisiu bada e daeroha.
Lagani e toia.
Daba e kinia.

Time of day or night (continued) :—
About 4·30 a.m., Daba e rotoa.
Daba e kuroa.
,, 5 a.m., Daba e taria.
Daba vaburana.
,, 5·30 a.m., Daba vada e rere.
Broad daylight, Daba vada e daboraia rohoroho.
About 6·30, Daba gamagama.
,, 7 to 9, Dina atoata.
After 9 to 12, general term, Dina tupua.
Noon, Dina e tupua.
About 2 p.m., Vareai lasilasi negana.
,, 3 p.m., Dina gelona.
,, 4 and on to 6 p.m., general term, Adorahi.
Just before sunset, Dina e kerekere.

Timid, Gari.
Tin, Tini. (Introduced.)
Tingle, Ginigini.
Tinkle, Regena.
Tiny, Maragimaragi.
Tip, Matana.
Tipsy, Muramura heala.
Tiptoe, Aesike.
Tire, Aheqarahi.
To (direction towards), Dekena.
Toe, Ae qagiqagina.
Together, Ida. Hebou.
Toil, Heqarahi.
Token, Toana.
Tongs, Ihakahina gauna.
Tongue, Mala.
Tools, Gau karalaia gaudia.
Tooth, Hise; (double), Gadigadi.
Toothache, Arituma.
Top, Latana. Dorina.
Torch, Kede.
Torment, v., Hahisia.
Torrent, Habata.
Tortoise (land), Gelo.
Torture, Hahisia.
Toss, v., Piuaisi.
Tossed (by waves), Ahekurehekure.
Total, Idoinai.
Totter, Raraga.
Touch, Hedaukau.
Touchwood, Alatutu.
Touchy, Badu kava.
Tough, Auka.
Tow, v., Veria.
Toward (to look), Hagere.
Town, Hanua.
Toy, Kadara gauna.

Track, Taoa.
Tractable, Manada.
Trade, *s.*, Hoihoi gaudia.
Trade, *v.*, Hoihoi.
Trade-wind (s. E.), Laulabad (N.W.) Lahara
Tradition, Tuputama hereva.
Trail, Lamari.
Train, *v.*, Hadibaia.
Traitor, Taotore tauna.
Trample, Aemoiatao.
Tranquil, Vea.
Transact, Karaia.
Transcend, Herea.
Transfer, Laohaia.
Transfix, Laiabou (*preceded by instrument*).
Transgress, Tataiautu.
Translate (*language*), Hahegeregerca.
Transparent, Nega.
Transplant, Ragaia hadoa lou.
Trap, Idoa.
Trash, Gaudika.
Travel *v.*, Laolao karaia.
Traveller, Laolao tauna.
Treacherous, Koikoi.
Tread, Hadaia. (*upon*) Aemoia.
Treasure, Kohu.
Treaty, Taravatu.
Tree, Au.
Trees, different kinds of. (See Appendix).
Tremble, Heudeheude.
Tremendous, Gaubadabada.
Tremulous, Heudeheude.
Trench, Dadaila.
Trepidation, Gari.
Trespass, Doha hadikaia. Laka havara. Abia havara.
Trial (*of canoe, &c.*), Dibaia.
Tribulation, Nega dikadika.
Trickle, Veve.
Trifle, Kadara.
Trim, *v.*, Hagoevaia.
Trip, *v.*, Haheqaqanai.
Triple, Hatoi.
Triumph, *v.*, Qalimu.
Troop (*of soldiers*), Tuari oreadia.
Trouble, *v.*, Haraivaia, Haturiaia.
Troublesome, Haraiva.
Trousers, Piribou. (*Introduced.*)
True, Momokani.
Trumpet, Kibi.
Trundle, Hekeialao.
Trunk, Maua (*of tree*), Badina.
Trust, (*in a person*), Abidadama henia

Try (*to try a thing*), Dibaia; (*to do*), Karaia toho.
Tuesday, Tusidei. (*Introduced.*)
Tug, Veria. Haroroa.
Tumble, Keto.
Tumult, Herouherou.
Tune, Ilatana gado.
Turbid, Duhu.
Turkey (*brush*), Apa.
Turmeric, Raborarabora.
Turmoil, Helogohelogo.
Turn, *v.* (*back*), Lou; (*round*), Ginikerehai; (*over a thing*), Hurea; (*over one's self*), Hehurehanai; (*end for end*), Sivaia; (*away*) Idauhai hagerea; (*over on one side as boat to paint*), Ahekea; *end for side*), Koea.
Turtle, Matabudi; (*green*) Ela.
Tusk, Doa.
Twelve, Qauta rua.
Twenty, Rua ahui.
Twice, Harua.
Twig, Au rakona.
Twilight, Mailumailu. Vaburavabura.
Twins, Hekapa.
Twine, Varo.
Twirl, Davea.
Twist, Mogea.
Twist (*string*), Aloia.
Two, Rua.
Twofold, Ererua.
Tyranny, Dagedage.

U

Ugly, Dika.
Ulcer, Toto.
Umbrella, Tamalu. (*Introduced.*)
Unable (*to do*), Karaia diba lasi.
Unaltered, Dia idau.
Unanswered, Haere lasi.
Unarmed, Ima gauna lasi
Unattended, Bamoa lasi. Sibona.
Unauthorised, Koaulaia utuutu, asi ena siahu.
Unawares, Dagu. Hoalaia.
Unbearable, Aheauka doko.
Unbecoming, Namo lasi.
Unbend (*as bow*), Kokiaoho.
Unbind, Ruhaia.
Unblemished, Se bebekabebekana.
Unbounded, Hetoa lasi.
Uncertain, Diba lasi. Sedila.

Uncivil. Ere dika.
Uncle, Tamana.
Unclean, Miro.
Unclothe, Dabua hadokianho.
Uncommon, Diahoho. Ta ta mo.
Uncover, Hulalaia.
Uncourteous, Gaiho dika.
Uncultivated (*land*), Vahu.
Undecided, Daradara.
Under, Hennai.
Underdone, Maeda lasi.
Understand, Diba.
Understanding, Aonega.
Undertake, Karaia koaulaia.
Undo, Ruhaia.
Undress, Dabua dokioho.
Uneasy, Noho namonamo lasi.
Unemployed, Gau karaia lasi.
Unequal, Dia hegeregere.
Uneven, Dia hegeregere.
Unexpected, Laroa lasi. Hoa.
Unfasten, Ruhaia. Kehoa.
Unfold, Kehoa. Hulalaia.
Unfrequented, Dekedekenarahu.
Unfriendly, Taigana dika. Ere dika tauna.
Ungoverned, Asi edia lohia.
Unhandsome, Dika.
Unhandy, Lega metau.
Unhappy, Se moalemu. Lalona se namomu.
Unhealthy (*place*), Gorere gabuna.
Unhonoured, Se matauraia.
Unhospitable, Heabidae lasi. Se hagerea.
Unhurt, Asi ena bero.
Uniform, Hegeregere.
Unintentional, Koaulaia lasi. (*to kill*) Alaia rea.
Union, Hebou.
Unite (*by tying*), Hiriagau.
Universal, Idoinai.
Unjust, Kara dia maoro.
Unkind, Dagedage.
Unknown, Diba lasi.
Unlawful, Taravatu koauahu kara. Ikoautao kara.
Unlike, Idau.
Unlock, Kehoa.
Unloose, Ruhaia.
Unlucky, Ima lalona asi anina.
Unmarried, Headava lasi.
Unmerciful, Boka hisihisi lasi.
Unmovable, Tutukatutuka.
Unneighbourly, Karakara tauna.
Unobserved, Ta se itaia.
Unpaid, Davana lasi.

Unpardoned, Koauatao lasi.
Unprepared, Dose hagoevaia.
Unripe, Mage lasi. Garugaru.
Unroll, Hulalaia.
Unruly, Koauedeede.
Unsatisfied, Bokana se kunu.
Unselfish in eating, Ani roharoha. Harihari bada.
Unsuccessful, Abia lasi. Davaria lasi. Ima kavakava.
Unthankful, Hanamoa lasi.
Untie, Ruhaia.
Until, Ela bona.
Untried, Dibaia lasi.
Untrue, Koikoi.
Unwilling, Koauedeede. Tau se raiva.
Unwonted, Se manadamu.
Up, Dae.
Up! Toreisi!
Upbraid, Koau henia. Loduhenia.
Uphold, Abiaisi. Durua.
Upon, Latana ai.
Uppish, Dagedage.
Upright, Tupua. Gini maoro.
Uproar, Helogohelogo.
Uproot, Ragaia.
Upsidedown, Kaluhia hebubu.
Upward, Ataiai.
Urge, Ura henia. Noinoi.
Urine, Mei.
Us, Ita (*including those addressed*). Ai (*excluding*).
Use, *s.*, Kara.
Use, *v.*, Abia.
Usual, Taunabinai.
Uterus, Boka.

V

Vacant (*as a house*), Ruma gagaena.
Vain, Hekokorogu.
Vainglorious, Heagi.
Vale, Goura.
Valiant, Goada.
Valley, Goura.
Valuable, Hoihoi bada gauna.
Value, *v.*, Davana koaulaia.
Vanish, Lasihia.
Vanquish, Hadarerea.
Vapour, Ninoa. Valahu (*steam*).
Variance, Hebadubaduheheni.
Variety, Idauidau.
Vast, Bada.
Vaunt, Heagi.

Veil, *s.* Gobaiahu gauna.
Vein, Rara varovaro.
Velocity, Heau.
Vend, Hoihoi.
Venerate, Mataurai henia.
Vengeance, Davana.
Venomous, Mate gauna.
Verandah, Dehe. Ese.
Verify, Hamomokania.
Verse, Siri (*Introduced meaning*).
Versed, Manada.
Vertigo, Mata madaimadai.
Vex, Habadua. Turiariki.
Vexatious, Turiariki.
Vial, Kavapukavapu.
Vice, Kara dika.
Victor, Qualimu tauna.
Victuals, Malamala.
Vigilant, Kito.
Vigorous, Goada.
Vie, Helulu.
Vile, Dika.
Vilify, Hadikaia.
Village, Hanua. (*Small*), Hanua motu.
Vindicate, Hamaoromaoroa.
Violate (*a tabooed thing*), Bokatoto. Abia havara.
Violent, Dagedage.
Violet colour, Dahuludahulu.
Viper, Gaigai.
Virgin, Haniulato rami hebou. ((*Man or woman*), Lalo duhu.
Visit, *v.* (*as a sick person*), Hegoita.
Visitor, Vadivadi.
Vixen, Koaukoau hahinena.
Vocation, Dagi.
Voice, Gado.
Volcano, Qarahu orooro. Lahi orooro.
Voluntarily, Sibona.
Vomit, Mumuta.
Voracious, Aniani bada.
Voyage, Hiri. (*Short*), Daiva.

W

Wade, Tulu.
Wag, Hevaseha tauna.
Wages, Davana.
Wail, Tai.
Waist, Gaba.
Wait, Nari. Helaro.
Wake, Noka.
Walk, Laka.

Walking-staff, Itotohi.
Wall, Magu.
Wallaby, Magani. (*Black*), Kove, and also Vauota.
Wallow, Hekuhihekuhi. Hedilohedilo.
Wander, Loa kava. Loa evaeva.
Want, *v.* Hekisehekise.
Want, *s.* Ogogame.
War, *s.* Alala.
War, *v.* Alala karaia. Tuari lao (*to go to war*).
Warcry, Hone.
Warm, Siahusiahu.
Warm, *v.* Hasiahua.
Warn, Rauaia.
Warp, *v.* Hagegevaia.
Warrior, Alaala tauna.
Wart, Usiusi.
Wash, *v.* Huria.
Wasp, Naniko. (*Carpenter*) Dina matana.
Waste, *v.* Petapetalaia.
Watch, *v.* Gima. Nari.
Watch, *s.* Dina gauna. (*Introduced meaning.*)
Water, Ranu.
Watercourse, Habata.
Waterfall, Dadahekei.
Watery, Ranukaranuka.
Wave, *v.* Aheudeheudea.
Wave, *s.* Sinaia.
Wax, Bata.
Way (*road*), Dara. (*Custom*), Kara
Waylay, Banitao.
Wayside, Dala isena,
We, Ai (*excluding the person addressed*). Ita (*including*).
Weak, Manokamanoka.
Wealth, Kohu.
Weau, Rata dadaraia.
Weapon, Ima gauna.
Weary, Tau e boera.
Weave, Hatua.
Web, Valavala.
Wed, Headuva.
Wedge, Hakahi.
Wednesday, Uenisidei. (*Introduced.*)
Weep, Tai.
Weed, *v.* Avarau.
Weed, Ava.
Week, Hebedoma. (*Introduced.*) (*In counting*), Sabati.
Weep, Tai.
Weigh, Abiatoho baine metau Haragaia.
Weighty, Metau.

Welcome, v. Mata papa.
Well, Ranu guri.
Well, adj. Namo.
Well, adv. Namonamo.
Well nigh, Mokona.
Wellspring, Ranu lohi.
Wench, Kekeni.
West, Tahodiho.
Wet, Paripari.
Whale, Lakara donodono.
What? Dahaka?
Whelp, Sisia natuna.
When? Edananegai?
Whence? Edeamomai?
Where? Edeseni?
Wherefore? Badina dahaka?
Whet, Segea.
Wheat, Sitona. (Introduced.)
Whether, Iava.
Whetstone, Kaia segea nadina.
Which? Edana?
While, Negana.
Whip, Qadilaia gauna.
Whirlpool, Kavabulobulo.
Whirlwind, Koeahilihili.
Whisker, Vaha huina.
Whisper, Hemaunu.
Whistle, Hioka.
White, Kurokuro.
White hair, Hui buruka.
Whitewash, Ahu ranuna.
Whither? Ede lao?
Who? Daika?
Whole, Idoinai.
Wholly, Idoinai.
Whore, Ariara hahine.
Whose? Daika ena?
Why? Dahaka gau?
Wick, Vavae. (Introduced.)
Wicked, Kara dika.
Wide, Lababana bada. Gamoga bada.
Widow, Vado. (In mourning), Vapu.
Wife, Adavana.
Wild, Se manadamu.
Will, Ura.
Willing, Ura henia.
Wind, Lai.
Wind, v. Lokua.
Windbound, Lai e laoahu.
Window, Varivari, (Introduced meaning.) Ikoukou.
Windpipe, Gado baubau.
Wing (of a bird), Hani.
Wink, Hekunumai.
Winkle, Basisi.
Wipe, Hedahu.

Wise, Aonega. Laloparara.
Wish, Hekisehekise. Ura henia.
With, Ida. Hebou.
Wither, Marai.
Withhold, Rūa.
Within, Lalonai.
Without (outside), Murimuri.
Withstand, Laoahu. Koauatubu
Witness, Idibana tanna.
Woe, Nega dikadika.
Woe, int. Inaio.
Woman, Hahine.
Womb, Boka.
Wonder, v. Hoa.
Wont, Kara. Vaia.
Wood, Au.
Wool, Mamoe huina. (Mamoe introduced.)
Word, Hereva.
Work, v. Gau karaia. Heqarahi
World, Tanobada idoinai.
Worm, Biluka.
Worm-eaten, Manumanu ania.
Worse, Dika (following the name of the thing or time with which it is compared).
Worship, Tomadiho henia.
Worsted, v. Darere.
Worth, Davana.
Wound, Bero.
Wrangle, Heai.
Wrap, Kumia.
Wrath, Badu.
Wreath, v. Hiria.
Wrecked, Hurekau.
Wrench, Giua. (up), Giuaisi. (off), Giuaoho.
Wretched, Lalo dika.
Wriggle, Heloge. Hebivahebiva.
Wrinkle, Magugu.
Wrist, Ima palapala loulouna.
Write, Revareva toren.
Writhe, Hegirohegiro.
Writing, Revareva.
Wrong, v.a. Hadikaia. Dagedage henia.
Wrong, v.n. Kererekerere.
Wry, Gageva.

Y

Yam, Maho; (sweet) Taitu.
Yard, Dimona. (A measure of about a yard.)
Yawn, Mava.

Ye, Umui.
Year, Lagani.
Yearly, Lagani lagani.
Yearn, Hekischekise bada.
Yell, Tāi lolo.
Yellow, Raborarabora ; (*deep orange*) Magemage.
Yes, Io. Oi be.
Yesterday, Varani.
Yield, Kamonai. Darere.
Yonder, Unuseni.

You, *sing.* Oi ; *pl.* Umui.
Young (*of animals*), Natuna ; (*of trees, &c.*), Karukaru.
Your, *sing.* Oiemu ; *pl.* Umui emui.
Youth, *s.* Tauhau negana.

Z

Zealous, Goada bada.

NOTE.

IN using the Motu-English Dictionary it should be remembered that *b* and *p* are sometimes undistinguishable to unaccustomed ears. If a word supposed to begin with *b* cannot be found under that letter it may be discovered under *p*. And so with *d* and *t*, and *k*, *l* and *r*; aspirates are uncertain, so it may be worth while to look under both *a* and *h*. The verb in its simple form and with the causative *ha* is not generally inserted in both forms. The one in most common use is put in the dictionary and the other can be formed from it. Nouns which are not used without a suffix have that of the third person singular, as *adavana* on opposite page. Remove the suffix *na* and the root word remains, to which any other suffix can be added, as *adava gu* my wife.

In the same way the transitive verbs have generally the third person singular suffix, as, *adavaia* on opposite page. Remove the termination *ia* and the root word can take any other suffix. The suffixes and infixes are indicated in this edition by a space between them and the root word, as, *Abi a* on opposite page.

MOTU AND ENGLISH.

A

A has the sound of *a* in father. Sometimes it is short, as *a* in mad.
A, *prefix*, causation, generally with verbs beginning with *he*.
A, *conj.* but.
Abae, *s.* the name of a fish.
Abagoro, *s.* breastbone of birds.
Abama, small bag net, as Koe.
Abe, *s.* presence; proximity.
Abi a, *v.* to have, to get, to take hold of.
Abi a dae, to receive hospitably; to believe.
Abi a hanaihanai, continuous line, as houses in street, net stretched out to dry, &c., &c.
Abi a isi, to take up.
Abi a oho, to remove, take out of the way.
Abi a gini, to hold upright.
Abi a hidi, to have by choice, to choose.
Abi a lasi, to take out of.
Abi a toho, to weigh on the hands, to try.
Abidadama, *a.* strong.
Abidadama, *s.* a person or thing to rely on.
Abidadama henia, *v.* to trust in or to, to put dependence on, to rely on.
Abihavara, *v.* to take a thing when told not to; to disregard the taboo of a tree.
Abikau, *v.* to take; *s.* a small lean-to on the verandah.
Abilai a, *v.* to obtain with.
Abi mauri tauna, *s.* a captive.
Abitorehai, *v.* to have on trust.
Abitorehai tauna, a debtor.
Abo, scrotum.
Abo kavari, *s.* clephantiasis in scrotum.
Abo na abia, *v.* to castrate.

Abo na ivaia, to castrate.
Ada na, *s.* stalk of fruit.
Adava ia, *v.* to be married (mentioning the person to whom married).
Adava na, *s.* wife or husband.
Ade, *s.* the chin.
Adehui na, beard on chin.
Ademela, name of a fish.
Adeholo, *s.* the stay of a mast.
Adia, *pron.* for them, theirs (of food); also of enemies, generation, and some other.
Adia, name of a fish.
Adira, a small stick of fence.
Adorahi, *s.* evening.
Adorahi gamagama, *s.* evening, about 7 o'clock.
Ae, *s.* leg (the entire leg and foot).
Ae badau, clephantiasis in the leg.
Ae gabu, a footprint.
Ae gedu, the heel.
Ae komukomu, the ankle.
Ae henuri, to slip with the foot turning out.
Ae kamodae, paralysed or withered legs.
Ae kepo, to slip with the foot turning in.
Ae moi a, Ae moiatao, to tread upon.
Ae moimoi, to rest the feet upon.
Ae palapala, the foot.
Ae qagiqagi na, the toe.
Ae sike, *v.* to stand on tiptoe.
Ae sike tauna, a lame man; walk on tiptoe.
Agavāita, one kind of yam.
Agi, ginger.
Agiagi na, with *itaia*, to use carefully (as food), not wastefully.
Agi na dika, to be selfish, unfriendly.
Agi na namo, unselfish, kind, friendly.
Agu, *pron.* mine, for me (*of food*).
Ahebololu, to be surprised by unexpected arrival of visitors, &c.

Ahaga ia, *v.* to open the mouth; one's own or another.
Ahakara, name of a fish.
Ahava ia, *v.* to drive, to chase, as a dog or kangaroo.
Aheauka, *v.* to forbear; to have patience.
Aheauka, *s.* patience, forbearance.
Aheudeheude, *v.* to shake. See Heudeheude.
Aheboera, *v.* to wear out, to fatigue.
Ahebou a, *v.* to add to.
Ahebubu a, *v.* to turn over, to spill.
Ahediba, *v.* to cause to know, to teach.
Ahediba tauna, one who makes known, instructs, a teacher.
Ahedinarai a, *v.* to manifest, to confess, to expose.
Ahedoki a, *v.* to put on (as clothes).
Ahedu a, to command, to permit.
Ahegani, to command.
Ahegani herevana, *s.* commandments.
Ahegogo, to collect, assemble.
Ahehu a, to rest by lying down, *Doru e ahehu a,* a siesta.
Aheke a, to turn over on one side, as boat to paint.
Ahekora, *v.* to put off on another; to excuse oneself from giving by saying it is another's; to lay blame on another for one's own fault.
Ahekurehekure, *v.* to be tossed about by the waves.
Ahelai a kau, *v.* to set on.
Ahelai a tore, to cause to sit up.
Ahelaga ia, *v.* to make sacred, to consecrate.
Ahelalo a, *v.* to remind, to commemorate.
Ahelaridae, to make signs with eyes from man to woman, or *vice versa.*
Ahemaoro, *v.* to make straight; *s.* judgment.
Ahemauri tauna, *s.* saviour.
Ahemara ia, *v.* to abash, to disgrace.
Ahenamo, salutation; to honour by giving something.
Aheqa, *v.* to tell one to speak.
Aheqina ia, *v.* to pillow.
Aheqaqana ia, *v.* to cause to stumble.
Aherahu, *v.* to smell, from affection, in place of a kiss.
Ahetoni, *v.* to part with friends, to bid farewell.
Abeu a, as ahehua, which see.
Ahonu a, *v.* to fill.

Ahu, *s.* gourd or bottle in which the lime is carried for chewing with betel nut.
Ahu, *s.* lime (quick or slack). Ahu hegara, quicklime.
Ahu, to close (as a fence which completes enclosure).
Ahu, *adv.* in composition, closed.
Ahui, ten (in counting after the first ten, as rua ahui, twenty).
Ahuiahuia, name of a fish.
Ahuota, *s.* a fish so called.
Ahu mianimiani, *v.* to stop a crack in *hodu* with melted gum; to make a vessel water-tight; to be closed (of a door), having no aperture.
Ahu na, *s.* a share, a division, a portion. Ahugu, my share.
Ahunu a, *v.* to make fast a rope.
Ahururu a, *v.* to cause to flame.
Ai, a relative particle of time or place.
Ai, *pron.* we (exclusive of the person addressed).
Ai emai, *pron.* our (exclusive).
Aio, *s.* neck (of person or animal).
Aio gauna, necklace.
Aio gageva, stiff neck.
Aio kekarukekaru, to nod one's head slowly.
Aio mareremarere, to nod.
Aiha, *s.* centipede.
Aina, sign of 1st person singular immediate future.
Aita, sign of 1st person plural (inclusive) immediate future.
Aitaeta, crashing thunder.
Aivara, *s.* pole used for poling in shallow water.
Akarua, one kind of banana.
Akeva, *s.* beads.
Akona, two large canoes lashed together for carrying food.
Ala, *v.* from Lao to go, 1st person plural present.
Alabore, *s.* sinnet (made of cocoanut fibre).
Ala ia, *v.* to kill; to burn (*a house*).
Ala ia ore, to exterminate.
Alala, *s.* war.
Alala heni a, to give battle.
Alala karaia, making war, fighting.
Alala koaulaia, to speak of fighting; the opposite of peace.
Alatore, *v.* to fish with nets on the shore reef.

Alatutu and Halatutu, *s.* a dry tree or touchwood, burning until consumed. *Rei doua alatutuna.*
Aloi a, *v.* to twist (as flax into string).
Amai, *pron.* ours, for us. (Exclusive of persons addressed.) Of food only.
Amo, *prep.* from.
Amo, distributive particle, used in counting or dividing; *rua rua amo,* two each.
Amu, *s.* native oven, covered in with leaves and earth.
Amu, *pron.* yours, for you (sing).
Amui, *pron.* yours, for you (plural).
Anama, a fish.
Ane abia, *v.* to sing.
Ane, *s.* a song.
Ane sisiba ia tauna, a bard.
Aneru, *s.* angel. (*Introduced.*)
Ani, generic name for bananas.
Ani a, *v.* to eat.
Ani gunita, to eat selfishly, secretly.
Ani dika, selfish, eating secretly.
Ani hidi, to be dainty in eating.
Ani ore, to eat up.
Ani bou, to eat together.
Ani rerevarereva, to eat many different things.
Ani rohaisi, unselfish in eating, liberal, generous.
Ani roharoha, as *ani rohaisi.*
Ani une, fancy of pregnant women for different kinds of food.
Aniani, *s.* one kind of mangrove.
Aniani, *n.* food.
Anikaanikana, strong, able, valiant.
Ani na, *s.* flesh of the body.
Ani na, *s.* primarily, something to eat; substance, meaning, contents of a thing. *Hodu mai anina,* the water-pot has water in it; kernel.
Asi anina, empty, hollow.
Anitorehai, to eat borrowed food.
Anitara na, *s.* body; substance; form.
Anivaga, *s.* a fast.
Ao, *s.* a sheltered anchorage.
Aola, *v. imper.* Go!
Aoma, *v.* come.
Aonega, *s.* the thinking faculty.
Aonega, *a.* wise, clever, acute.
Apa, *s.* a brush turkey.
Aqa, mangroves; road along beach by the mangroves.
Ara, *s.* a fence of upright sticks.
Arana latana, height, of house, roof, &c.

Arara, one kind of mangrove, the bark of which is used as dye.
Araturia, sore throat.
Are, *s.* nymphæ.
Areto, *s.* bread. (*Introduced from the Greek.*)
Aria, *s.* a feast made out-of-doors.
Aria, marked, indented, as bottom of canoe with stones.
Ariaoda, a fish.
Ariara, *s.* a street, road through a village (distinguished from *dala,* a road through the bush).
Ariara natuna, a bastard.
Ariara hahine, courtesan.
Aribida, to cook meat alone, without vegetables.
Ariha, *s.* a large lizard, iguana.
Ario, silver. (*Introduced.*)
Arituma, *s.* toothache.
Aroma ia, *v.* to carry a small netted bag round the neck, hanging down the back.
Aru, with *lalona,* nausea. *Lalogu eme aru.*
Aru, *s.* current (of river or sea); multitude; *Liq amnii.*
Aru henia, as *ura henia,* to desire.
Arua mai, *v.* to flock.
Ase or Ate, *s.* liver.
Asease, a trench.
Asease geia, to dig a trench.
Asemo, small wild cucumber.
Asi, *s.* a large canoe. *Asi memero,* crew.
Asi, *adv.* not. Same as *lasi;* but used before the verb, while *lasi* follows it. *Asi tauna,* nobody.
Asi idai na, without an equal, superior, excellent.
Asi karikari na, content, satisfied.
Asimana, *v.* to sneeze.
Asi regerege na, *s.* quiet.
Ata, *pron.* ours, for us (inclusive of person addressed).
Atai, *adv. & prep.* above; the space between earth and sky; seawards (of the course of a canoe or ship).
Ataina, *s.* eminence.
Ataka, *s.* potsherd.
Ataka, caked (as mud), sago cooked in an *ataka;* hence also, biscuit, or anything hard and thin.
Atalata, *a.* ten. (Used in counting long things, as poles, bananas, sugar-canes, &c.)

Ate or Ase, s. liver.
Ato, word auxiliary to verb, 1st pers. plu. exclusive, signifying about to ......but, &c.
Ato a, v. to place, to set.
　Ato a dabe, to put on one side.
　Ato a tao, to give a sigu to another. See Heatotao.
　Ato a hegiro, to turn a thing over.
　Ato a kau, to place, to lade.
Atogu, v. to place me (ato-gu).
Atu a, to press pottery into shape.
Atuahu, s. a painful swelling without matter, a blind boil.
Atuatu, sticks of roof parallel with rafters. See haduhadu.
Atudiho, of wind, about S.S.E

Au, a prefix to numerals in enumerating dishes and things of length.
Au, s. a tree; firewood.
　Au badibadi na, a short stump.
　Au gama na, a small bundle of firewood.
　Au dimura, sawdust, very small particles of wood.
　Au hagaria, to fell a tree.
　Au huahua, blossom, and also fruit.
　Au kopi na, bark of a tree.
　Au kota na, bundle of firewood.
　Au maragi, sapling. Au maragimaragi, brushwood.
　Au momoru. See Au dimura.
　Au huahua nadinadi na, seed.
　Au ragaia aria na, feast for dead, the final feast.
　Au rako na, twig.
　Au rakorako, young trees, saplings.
　Au ramu na, root.
　Au ranu na, sap of heart.
　Au taha, a splinter, a small piece of wood.
　Au tuhutuhu, a shoot.

　Au todena, sap, gum.
　Au tupina, a stump, longer than badibadina.
Aua, to tie, as sticks in a fence.
Auau, s. a stick fork to eat with; handle, as of an axe.
Auasi, s. one who stays when others go on a voyage, or journey. Auasi tau. Auasi hahine.

Auka, a. firm (not loose); hard (as wood); tough (as meat); difficult to open (as a door); secure.
Auka, v. to be strong, firm.
Auka bada, durable, immovable.
Auki, s. the lower jaw.
　Auki bada, swollen lower jaw, mumps.
　Auki huina, beard all round.
Auri, iron, metal. (Introduced from Tahitian.)
Auro, gold. (Introduced.)
Auruaoti, a. two, of long things.
Autuna, s. gall.
Antupua, s. a mast.
Ava, s. weeds. Avana.
　Ava rau a, to weed (when a stick is used).
Ava. Verbal particle, as bava.

B

B is pronounced as in English.
Ba, a particle preceding verbs, indicating the future tense, 2 p. sing. or pl. Ba oma, Come thou.
Babaka, one kind of banana.
Babalau, hahine sorceress; tau, sorcerer.
Bada, a. large, great. Badana, s. size.
Badahobadaho, v. to grow. (Of children).
Badau, s. penis erectio. Usi badau. Elephantiasis. Ae badau.
Badihusi, region between bladder and navel.
Badila, s. red colour of teeth, from chewing betel nut.
Badi na, adv. by the side of. Badibadi na.
Badina dahaka? adv. wherefore.
Badina, s. the trunk or stem of a tree near the root; hence, the root or cause of a thing; foundation.
Badina ia, v. to cleave to; to be faithful to; to keep (as law).
Badiu regena, tail joint of wallaby.
Bado, sandal wood.
Badu, v. to be angry.
　Badu kava, hasty.
　Badu bada, passion.
Badubadulai a, to provoke, tease, make angry.

Badukalo, one kind of yam.
Bae, v. part. indicating fut., 3rd pers. pl. *Idia bae karaia.*
Baela, v. 3rd pers. pl. fut. to go.
Baema, v. 3rd pers. pl. fut. to come.
Bagara, one kind of yam.
Bago a, to mortice.
Bagu, s. forehead.
Bagu, conj. on account of, for the sake of.
Bagu a, v. to carry a netted bag hanging in front.
Bagukoau, v. to forbid to come; to send back by scolding.
Bagu moru, frontal headache.
Bagu tutuna, forehead.
Baha, sometimes used for *ba* or *bae.*
Bahu na, s. food left, and kept to eat cold.
Baia, v., part. indicating fut. 1st pers. pl. *Ai baia karaia.*
Baia, v. to be near death; hopeless, as from sickness or shipwreck, or surrounded by fire and no way of escape. *Vada eme baia.*
Baiama, conditional particle 1st pers. pl. (exclusive) if; past time.
Baimumu, s. owl.
Baina, v. partic. 1st pers. sing. fut. used before verbs. *Lau baina abia.*
Bainala, irreg. v. 1st person. I will go.
Bainama, I will come, 1st per. sing. future of verb *mai*, to come.
Baine, v. partic. 3rd pers. sing. fut. before verbs. *Ia baine abia.* If.
Bainela, irreg. v. 3rd person (see Grammar), he will go.
Bainema, v. partic. 3rd pers. sing. fut. to come.
Baita, v. partic. 1st pers. pl. ft.
Baitala, v. partic. 1st. pers. pl. ft. of the verb to go.
Baitama, v. partic. conditional. 1st pers. pl. (inclusive), past time.
Bakibaki, s. a dumpling. (Generally of sago.)
Bakobako, a. sour (as paste).
Bakubaku, s. roof of verandah.
Bala, s. white wild duck.
Balaheni, adv. steadily, carefully, persistently.
Balaia, to place carefully.
Balala, s. the name of a fish.
Bala ta, a. ten, in counting pigs, dogs, fish, turtle, dugong, &c.

Bama, conditional partic. if; 1st pers. sing. and pl. past.
Bamuhuta, Good-night! *Ba mahuta o!* May you sleep. Also used in the day-time. Good-bye.
Bame, ba, sign of, 2nd pers. sing. fut. with *me* of euphony.
Bamo a, v. to accompany another.
Bamo a lasi, unattended.
Bamo na, adv. like, thus.
Bamo na, s. a companion, friend.
Banaere, one kind of banana.
Banava, to suppose (mistakenly).
Banenebanene, carelessly, heedlessly.
Banene tauna, a careless lazy man, unsuccessful in hunting, fishing, &c.
Bani, s. a patch.
Banilaia, s. to patch with.
Bani, v. to plait; to patch; to kindle fire from a spark, as from tinder.
Bani a, to mend mats.
Bani, v. to lay in wait.
Banitao, to be laid in wait for.
Banidu, s. smut, from burnt grass, any light rubbish, dust, &c.
Baola, v. 2nd pers. pl. fut. to go.
Baoma, v. 2nd pers. pl. fut. to come.
Bara, v. to row.
Bara, s. oar.
Bara hodehode, a very large sea snake.
Baragi, s. lungs.
Baraka, the melt. *Boka barakana.*
Baribara, s. cross. *Au hiri baribara.*
Ba roromamumu. A phrase when quarrelling. "I'll kill you." From roroma to kill.
Baroko, large, as thread or string.
Barua, s. muliebria.
Barubaru, the name of a fish.
Basi, adv. Not (*Ba* and *asi*).
Basi, adv. negative fut. Not.
Basiema, 3rd pers. plural, future of verb *mai.* They will not come.
Basileia, s. (from the Greek) a kingdom.
Basina. 1st pers. fut. sing. negative.
Basinama, 1st pers. sing. fut. of verb *mai.* I will not come.
Basine, sign of 3rd per. sing. fut. negative.
Basita, negative with 1st pers. plural (inclusive), let us not.
Bata, wax, used as finger points on skin of drum-head.

Batata, name of a shell-fish.
Batu, one kind of yam.
Batugu, *s.* a shower.
Baturo, hiccough.
Bau, *s.* bamboo.
Baubau, a bamboo pipe.
Bava, *particle* fut. 2 pers. sing. or pl. Used before verbs beginning with a. *Bava abia. Bava alaia.*
Bava, *s.* a crab.
Be, a connective particle; also used alone with the meaning of Why? What's up?
Be a, sometimes used with verb instead of *baia.*
Bebe, a fish.
Bebekabebeka, blemish. Generally used with negative, of canoes, &c.
Bedaina, where?
Bedebede, name of a shell-fish.
Bedi, *s.* a spoon.
Bedu, one kind of spear, similar to *karagoda.*
Bekere, one kind of sword-fish.
Bema, conditional particle, if, 3rd pers. sing. and pl. past time.
Bena, as *ena,* there.
Benai, as *enai,* there.
Benaini, *adv.* just so; all right; now now.
Bero, *s.* a wound. *Iena beroghida?* How many wounds has he.
Bese, descendants, used of tribe as nation; *Motu besedia, Maiva besedia.*
Besele, cedar.
Bea a, to straighten, as a stick by bending.
Beubeu, swell of ocean, less than *sinai.* Generally of swell inside reef.
Biaguna, *s.* master, owner.
Bio, *s.* cocoanut-shell cup. (Deeper than *kehere.*)
Biobio, *s.* small cocoanut charm.
Bibi a, to move a little way. *Bibia lao.*
Bibi na, *s.* lips. Udu bibina.
Bigu, *s.* the fruit of the banana.
Bila, *s.* spawn.
Bilailo, *s.* one kind of ant.
Biluka, *s.* earth-worm.
Binai, as *inai,* here.
Binubinu, to grub, as pig.
Biri, leaf of bastard palm, used for thatch.

Biriakei, *s.* the name of a month (November.)
Biriabada, *s.* the month of December.
Biribou, trousers. (Introduced.)
Biru, *s.* gardening, work in garden or field.
Biru eno, to work in the garden, and sleep there.
Biru, *v.* to garden, to till; also Biru henia.
Bisini, small sunbird.
Bisisi, name of a shell-fish.
Bisisi, to be small and poor, of banana and other fruit.
Bisiva, ridge cap.
Bita, *s.* native rat.
Bitacla, as Baitala.
Bitu a, *v.* to break, as a stick, spear, &c.; to gather a flower or little branch by breaking the stalk; to gather fruit.
Bivai, *s.* one kind of hawk.
Bo, *euphonic particle,* used much as *bona. Oi ede bo laomu?* Where are you going?
Bobo, *s.* a fool.
Bobo, name of a shell fish.
Bobobobo, *v.* to stream forth, as blood from a wound.
Boboda, name of a fish.
Bohoro, *s.* the hornbill.
Bodaga, *s.* stench.
Bodaga, *v.* to stink.
Bodaga, *a.* fetid.
Bodia, a loop.
Bodo, *v.* to go out, be extinguished, as fire, lamp.
Boe, *s.* sandbank.
Boera, *adj.* fatigued, "done up."
Bogibada, *s.* name of a hawk.
Boga. *See* Boka.
Bogo, *s.* ear of corn when first swelling.
Boha, *a.* bald. *Qara boha,* bald head.
Boi, *s.* night. Generally used with *hanua, Hanuaboi.*
Boiboi, *v.* to call, to summon. Pass. boilia.
Boigagadae, to challenge.
Boioboio, *v.* to be lost.
Boka, *s.* the stomach, the seat of desire and affection; the uterus.
Boka sisia, prolific (of woman).
Bokabada, name of a shell-fish.
Boka ia, *v.* to disembowel.

Boka auka, *v.* to have self-restraint; to be strong to work, and not easily exhausted; to be not nervous and easily frightened.
Bokalau, *s.* entrails, bowels.
Boka hekukuri, diarrhœa.
Boka heudeheude, to desire greatly.
Boka hisi, *v.* to pity, have compassion, &c. *Ia e bokaia hisi.*
Boka hisihisi, colic.
Boka hisihisi, *v.* to grieve.
Boka kunu, to be satisfied with food, bellyful.
Boka mate, lazy.
Bokani, name of a shell-fish.
Bokani bisisi, name of a shell-fish.
Bokaragi. Bokaragina, *prep.* in the midst.
Bokatoto, *a.* lawless, one who violates taboo on food.
Boko a, to cut off trees at top, to lop branches.
Bolo a, *v.* to possess as by an evil spirit, to substitute.
Boloa, *s.* a substitute; a successor.
Boloa tauna, a deputy.
Boloko, *s.* the name of a gum-tree; the bush in which the boloko abounds.
Boma, conditional particle, if, 2nd pers. sing. and pl. past time.
Bomu, *s.* a hole in the top of the mast through which halyards are rove.
Bomaboma, a name of a shell-fish.
Bona, connective particle, used in enumerating persons or things.
Bona, *s.* scent.
Bona ia, *v.* to smell.
Bonana, *v.* euphemism for bodaga, to stink.
Bonana namo, fragrant.
Bone, *v.* to return unsuccessful from fishing or trading.
Bonubonu, name of a tree.
Bora, shrub used with sago for seasoning.
Bore, to be dry as sandbank. *Vada eme bore.*
Bore, *s.* a narrow road on the reef or the sand, dry at low tide.
Borebore, a fish.
Boreta, bows of boat or canoe inside.
Boroboro, *s.* a painful swelling in the face.
Boroma, *s.* a pig; also all large animals, as goats, sheep, cows, &c.

Baroma anina, pork.
Boroma arana, pig-stye.
Boroma huina, a bristle.
Boroma maruane, a boar.
Bosea, *s.* a basket.
Bosi, spear of white wood used in hunting.
Bota, reed like grass growing at edge of river.
Bota ia, *v.* to beat, to thrash.
Boti, boat (Introduced).
Boto, name of sandal-wood at Gaile and some other places.
Bou, *s.* a small round shell neck ornament.
Bou, *adv.* together, as *anibou*, to eat together.
Bou a, *v.* to hammer a rock; to knock off oysters, &c.
Bua, to die in numbers.
Buaki, one kind of mangrove.
Buatari, *v.* to destroy a whole town, to kill wholesale, *Buadiatari.*
Buatau, *s.* areca nut and palm.
Bubu, *s.* hymen.
Bubudare, hym, rupt.
Bubu e! term of address to grandmother.
Bubua, to spill, to pour out.
Bubui, one kind of yam.
Bubuni, *v.* to be covered, as trees with water, overshadowed, with verbs of motion, to disappear, pass away.
Bubunidaiko, very short shower.
Budabuda, name of a tree.
Budia, name of a fish.
Budia lási, *v.* to gush out, as blood, when a spear is withdrawn; to bleed as when finger cut.
Budiabudia, to bleed as when pricked by *hebasi.*
Budibudi, small ulcers round sound centre.
Budibudi, with negative, *asi budibudi*, no sound of coming (when looking out for expected ones).
Budoa, name of a tree.
Budu *v.* to make a hole through the eye of the cocoanut, to bore a hole.
Buduauru, *v.* to bore a hole right through.
Budubudu, *a.* spotted, rough, pitted, as the face.
Budugara, name of a shell-fish.
Buka, book (Introduced).

Bulelamo, *s.* a caterpillar.
Bulo a, *v.* to mix.
Bulu, to immerse.
Bulubulu, *v.* to duck in the sea in sport.
Bulukia, *v.* to gather, as fruit of mango.
Buna, *s.* the name of a fish.
Bunai. See Unai.
Bunu, *s.* husk of cocoanut.
Bunugu, to break charm, cause to be unfortunate.
Bura, *s.* grated cocoanut, after the oil has been expressed.
Bure a, *v.* to blossom.
Bure na, *s.* small blossom bud.
Buru, to immerse.
Buruka, *a.* white. Of hair only. *Hui buruka.*
Buruki a, *v.* to gather by breaking off.
Busisi, *s.* a small winkle.
Busibusi, *s.* clitoris.
Butu a, *v.* to pull up as grass; to pull out, as hair, feathers.
Butu a oho, *v.* to adopt a child when an infant.
Butu a tao, *v.* to catch hold of one.
Butubutu, *a.* coarse, rough.
Butubutu, clam fish.

D

D is sounded as in English. In some words it is scarcely distinguishable from t.
Daba, *s.* (lity. morning). Used in counting, &c., for a day.
Daba matana, early.
Daba hekinia, first appearance of dawn.
Daba e rotoa, next after *daba hekinia.*
Daba e taria, next to *daba e rotoa.*
Daba c taboraia rohoroho, broad daylight.
Daba e rere, morning, after sunrise.
Daba daba idoinai, daily.
Dabaia qaitu, to break off a branch at junction with stem, or fruit.
Dabai a tao *v.* to seize.
Dabara, *s.* banana leaf used as a plate to place food on. Or plaited cocoanut leaf.
Dabarere, morning.
Dabaraia, *v.* to serve up food. *Aniani dabaraia.*

Dabari, *s.* male kangaroo
Dabekau, *v.* to lean against.
Dabi a, *v.* to put a piece of wood or stone under a canoe, &c., so as to raise it from the ground.
Dabu, *v.* to be left out in distribution, to have no share.
Dabua, *s.* clothing (general name), cloth.
Dabua hadokilaia, to clothe.
Dabua mamoe, flannel or any woollen cloth. (Introduced).
Dabua sisina, *s.* rag.
Dabui a, *v.* to pull, as a rope; to drag along, as an unwilling child.
Dabutu, *s.* the name of a fish.
Dadaba, *v.* to flog, to beat, chastise.
Dadadaeroha, to rise, as the sun.
Dadadiho, to descend from tree.
Dadadobi, *v.* to go down, as the sun, as food into the stomach.
Dadaga, a storm of wind and rain.
Dadagila, as Dadaila.
Dadaila, trench, gutter.
Dadami, small stinging ray.
Dadarai a, *v.* to reject, to decline.
Dadaroa, *v.* to drag, as the anchor.
Dadaroha, *v.* as Dadaroa.
Dadaroha, *v.* to uncover an oven of food.
Dadi a, *v.* to snatch.
Dadidadi, *v.* to pillage.
Dadidadi gaudia, *s.* booty.
Dae, *v.* to ascend.
Dae, *s.* the name of a large fish.
Dae a, *v.* to destroy a village, killing its inhabitants.
Daedae, stinging ray.
Daegumi, *s.* a corner.
Daehutu, *s.* a chamber.
Daekau, *v.* to ascend.
Daekobi, *s.* a two or three-pronged comb, a solid stem from which two or more prongs are cut.
Daelai a, *v.* to lift up, to exhalt.
Daena, *s.* the top (as of a box).
Daena, *v.* to be abreast of, or off a place on the coast.
Daenai, *adv.* on the top.
Daetao, to have taken what had been previously bespoke, suffix of person who had bespoken. *Daegutao.*
Daga, material used in preparing *lakatoi* for long voyage.
Dagadaga, *s.* heavy clouds, those not carried by the wind; groin.

Dagadae, to grow, as trees increasing in height.
Daga hanai, v. to get over, as a fence.
Dagahu, a. cloudy, the sun shaded.
Dagahu tauna, s. one sent to watch, lest taboo should be broken. Now used of policemen.
Dagai, s. the name of a fish.
Dagai a diho, to throw down, as log from shoulder.
Dagalo, s. feathery blossom of cane, reeds, &c.
Dagautuna, to carry with cross poles assisting long ones.
Dage, excrement.
Dage tauna, a quarrelsome man, challenging others to fight, &c.
Dagedage, a. cruel and ferocious.
Dagedage tauna, s. a bully.
Dagi, s. occupation, trade, office.
Dagu, v. to startle.
Daha, a. thousand.
Dahaka? pron. what?
Dahaka gau? pron. why?
Dahalaia, v. to carry a small netted bag (vaina) over the shoulder.
Dāhi, v. to crouch or go upon the hands and feet.
Dahu, v. to rub, to wipe.
Dahu a, to rub on, to wipe.
Dahu a kamo, to wipe with the hands.
Dahu a oho, to wipe off.
Dahudahu, s. the name of a large fish.
Dahudahua, redup. of dahua.
Dahulu, a fish.
Dahuludahulu, a bright violet colour, as some fishes' eyes.
Dai, to be becalmed and drifting.
Dai evaeva, to spread, as an epidemic.
Dāi hanai, contagious; also Dai hanaihanai.
Dai lou, to double up tongue when throwing a spear, on making some exertion, to energise.
Daia, v. to rest on, as a foot on the ground, &c.; to build, of houses or a village. *Hanua daia.*
Daia, v. to think.
Daia hegege, to surround, as by troops.
Daiahu, v. to close a bag by sewing up the mouth; used figuratively of the mouth; to enclose by enemies; to wound the eye by throwing a stick.

Dai a kunu, full grown, as *lō.*
Dai a maka, open a little way, of door.
Daiauru, v. to pierce through.
Daiba, s. a yam-pit.
Daidai, v. to boil.
Daidobi, v. to be drifted to sea, as by the current or wind.
Daihanai, v. to be driven out to sea, so as to lose sight of the mountains.
Daika, pron. who?
Dāikau, preceded by *hisi*, to be seized with pain, or an epidemic, as *Hisi eme dāikau, Hisi taina lau taugu ai eme dāikau.*
Daili a, v. to water (plants); to pour water on a sick person, &c.
Dai na ai, on account of, for the sake of. *Daigu ai, Daidia ai.*
Dainamo, a. convalescent, as *Taugu eme dainamo,* I am better.
Daipa, a wide space weeded round garden fence.
Dairia. See Dailia.
Dairiki, lame.
Dāitao, s. a canoe or ship making but little progress from current, head wind, &c.
Daiva, s. a short voyage, as to Maiva or Hula.
Dakaia, to throw spear harmlessly.
Daki a lasi, to draw off, as finger ring.
Dākidāki, s. a very large arm-shell.
Dala, s. a road.
Dala korikori, highway.
Dala katakata, cross-roads.
Dala, name of a shell-fish.
Daladala, a fish.
Daladedi, slippery road.
Dalaia, s. the name of a fish.
Dalagi, s. the name of a fish.
Damena, s. salt.
Damu (takes suffix, *damugu,* &c.) trading goods taken on a voyage also goods brought back in return.
Danu, conj. also.
Dapai a, to strike downwards, as with a sword.
Dapia a oho, to cut off by down cut.
Daqa dobi, to fall from height, head first.
Daqai, s. a bag-net.
Daqaihu, to enclose, as by a fence.
Daqala, s. a sea-eel.
Dara, mind. See daradoko below.
Daradae, v. to ascend, as mountains.

Daradara, v. to doubt, to hesitate.
Daradara, s. indecision.
Daradara mo, a. querulous.
Daradoko, v. to be sad, on account of absent or dead friends; to be speechless from fear; to mourn silently; to miss. *Lau daragu eme doko.*
Darahu, v. to feel, to grope.
Daralai a, v. to take up, carry up hill or mountain.
Dare, a sword.
Dare a, v. to tear.
Darere, v. to be vanquished, conquered, weak.
Daria, v. to husk a cocoanut with the teeth. *Ise daria.*
Daria, s. lanyards.
Dari a oho, to burn up suddenly, as powder on the ground.
Darima, s. outrigger.
Daro a, v. to sweep; to trim off knots, &c., to adze a plank; to make passes, and perform sorcery over a sick person. *Gorere e daroa.*
Darodae, to return to, to be reconciled, to take to.
Darodaro, s. the name of a month (April, May).
Darodaroa, redup of *daroa.*
Daro lasi, to brush or comb hair down to forehead.
Daro mutu, to put locks of hair through shells for ornament. *Daroamutu daroamutu.*
Daro parara, with *hai*, to part hair.
Dāu, s. one kind of banana (very long).
Daua, v. to net.
Dāuahuahu, v. to bother, as a child or a busybody, in the way, &c. *Dāugu ahuahu.*
Dauatoho, to touch.
Daube, daubedaube, v. to swing on a low swing.
Daudau, a. distant (place or time).
Daudobi, v. to dip into.
Daukau, v. to touch.
Dāulao, moon just past full.
Daure, intensive, with negea.
Dautu, s. the name of a fish. (The porcupine fish.)
Dava, water in chasm, or ditch; also lagoon in atoll.
Davadava, s. the name of a fish.
Davaha, s. coarse cloth worn in mourning

Davalai a, cost.
Davana, a. full, as a house; sufficient, as sticks for a fence; each having a portion in division of food, &c.
Davana, s. a payment, a ransom.
Davana henia, to compensate, to punish.
Davana korikori, punishment.
Davara, s. the sea.
Davara hadaga e dihomu, very high tide.
Davara bada, s. high tide.
Davara maragi, low water.
Davari a, v. to find, to obtain.
Dave a, v. to drag, to haul up.
Dave a dae. to launch.
Dave a isi, to lift up and swing round, as stick to strike.
Davedavelai a, to waste.
Davelai a, v. to throw a thing or person on to the ground, away from one; to swing laden *kiapa* round on to the forehead; to raise a heavy box on to the shoulder.
Dea Dea ia, v. to bark a tree by inserting a wedge into a slit.
Deadea, name of a tree.
Dedi, v. to slip.
Dedi dobi, to backslide.
Dede a, to singe.
Dedeari, sago-palm leaf.
Dedidedi. Dedikadedika, a. slippery, of the ground, or hands, or object held.
Degiro, sleeping place of wild pig or wallaby. "*Magani dègiro inai.*"
Dehe, s. the verandah at the end of a house facing the street.
Dehoro, s. oil of the cocoanut, fresh, mixed with a little water.
Dekea, v. to dodge (as a spear, &c.)
Dekedekenarahu, s. a quiet, deserted place; a. noiseless.
Deke na, *prep.* near to, by the side of. *Lau ia dekena nala.* I went to him.
Dekena tauna, neighbour.
Demademа, the work of caulking.
Demaia, v. to calk.
Demai a toho, v. to taste.
Demari, v. to lick.
Demokademoka, smooth, perfect, of hair or skin.
Demoni, demon. (*Introduced.*)
Dene, s. sandfly.
Depuru, small crayfish.
Dera, s. hair on the body, the arms, chest, &c.

Dera tauna, a hairy man.
Dere, back and belly fins of fish.
Deredere, s. the square edge of a board, &c.
Derekadereka, s. square edged.
Derekaka, s. the name of a fish.
Deruha, the well in a canoe.
Deure, one kind of banana.
Dia, s. a kind of pudding made of sago and bananas.
Dia, negative used before noun or verb.
Dia bada, s. anything very small or light.
Dia maragi, s. anything very big or heavy.
Dia daudau, s. proximity, nearness.
Diagau, a. many.
Dia hoho, a. not many.
Diaranu, s. clear oil.
Diari, s. light (as opposed to dark); diaridiari, brightness.
Dia tau dikana, s. a good man.
Diba, s. an arrow.
Diba, v. to know, to comprehend.
Dibagadi, a long grass.
Dibagani, v. to tempt.
Dibaka tauna, s. a dissembler, one clever to snare and catch fish, birds, &c.
Dibu, a small light spear used in war.
Dibu a, v. to carry a bag, &c., suspended from the forehead (as the women do their kiapas).
Dibura, a. dark.
Dibura taudia, heathen.
Dida, prep. with; syn. Ida.
Didi, to enter, or go out in numbers.
Didi dae, to ascend, or go out to sea.
Didi dobi, to descend in numbers.
Didi lasi, to go outside, a number together.
Didi vareai, to go into a house, or inland, a number together.
Didika, an occasional plural of dika, bad.
Didiki, s. near the edge of a thing, as a table, chair, &c.
Didikididiki, v. to be far out to sea.
Digara, a. fat; good (of food or drink); lard.
Digu, v. to bathe.
Dihi na, s. a man's sons who will perpetuate his name and character; hence sometimes used of inherited skill or character.

Diho, v. to descend; to land from a boat.
Diho, a. south.
Diho havara, dae havara, going to and fro from house to house instead of working.
Diholoa, v. to beat boards and shout, as a sign of rejoicing, as when a lakatoi comes.
Dihotani a, v. to be deserted by a wife.
Dihu, s. a bowl or bath of wood.
Dihudihu, name of a shellfish.
Dika, a. bad, foul.
Dika, s. a calamity; guilt.
Dikadika, adv. intens. very much. Goada dikadika, very strong.
Dikoana, units, in counting, ten mai dikoana toi.
Dikoi, followed by vareai or dae, all gone inland, to sea, to church, &c., as didi.
Dilaha, s. an old garden (not this year's).
Diledile, s. a small flying squirrel.
Dilidilia, to jet, squirt. Used in indecent joking.
Dima, s. grass seed; bait for small crabs.
Dimadima, of pig, to eat snuffling along on surface of ground.
Dimaili, s. a small ant.
Dimakau, to catch fire by train of dry grass, &c., or by contact, as a grass petticoat.
Dimona, s. a measure of length, less than a fathom, one yard or less.
Dimuradimura, a. anything very small, as grains of sand.
Dimura na, measure of length less than dimona, about a span.
Dina, s. the sun; a day.
Dina atoata, about 8 a.m.
Dina gelona, afternoon.
Dina kerekere, little before sunset
Dina namo, fine weather.
Dina tara, glare of the sun.
Dina tupua, mid-day.
Dina v. to be visible, apparent, as the bone in a wounded leg. Turia vada dina.
Dina, prey; also contribution to feast, &c., as Lau dinagu inai.
Dina, spear of white wood used principally in hunting.
Dinaha, a fish.
Dina idoinai, a. habitual.

Dinamatana, carpenter wasp.
Dinika, *s.* a fork.
Diraha, *s.* all children after the first-born. Old garden, see *Dilaha.*
Dirava, *s.* spirit ; god.
Dirava kara, religion.
Diu, *v.* to hit, as with an arrow or gun.
Diu, *s.* elbow.
Diua, *v.* to put up the sail of a canoe.
Diuaisi, to lift up, as hands.
Diudiu, successful in fishing, &c.
Divaro, *s.* the name of a month (May).
Divoi, one kind of yam.
Do, a particle marking future time.
Do and doho, contractions of dohore.
Dōa, *s.* collar-bone.
Doa, *v.* to pole a canoe.
Doa, *s.* a boar's tusk ; a horn.
Doadoa, *s.* a scorpion.
Doadoa, *s.* a cage in *lakatoi* for the pottery of the captain.
Dobe, a sago dumpling with ripe banana inside.
Dobi, *v.* to be lost in the bush. (Of pigs or dogs.)
Dobi, *adv.* downwards.
Dobi, *v.* to fruit. (When hanging down, as bananas.)
Dobi, to go inland, or to sea. *E dobi be vada ela.* To sail as fleet to west.
Dobili, wind rushing through between two mountains.
Dobitani a, to sail away from a place.
Dobosere, a white wallaby.
Dobu, *a.* deep.
Dobukadobuka, deep, as a soup plate, generally shortened to *Dobuna.*
Dodi, *s.* a debt, *v.* to owe.
Dodō, *s.* very high tide, coming over the street. (Higher than *utubada.*)
Dodo, *v.* to soak up, to absorb, to subside.
Dodoma, dog's teeth necklace.
Doe, *s.* famine, dearth.
Doga, to alternate, take every other one, *abi doga, abi doga.*
Dogagi, new moon, cresent shaped.
Dogo, *s.* anchor.
Doga atoa, Dogo negea, *v.* to anchor.
Dogo gabuna, anchorage.
Dogoro, *s.* dry banana-leaf packing.
Dogoro, liberal, generous friend, *Egu dogoro.* Also postfixed to relationships, *Tamagu dogorona,* my father, but not real father ; uncle
Dogu, *s.* a deep bay.

Dogudogu, *s.* a hollow, depression.
Dogu dobi, to set (as sun).
Doha, *v.* to prohibit.
Doha *s.* to taboo, a law which forbids.
Doholodoholo, *a.* dry (of cooked food), blood no longer dropping from joint.
Dohore, *adv.* by-and-bye.
Dohore, *v.* to postpone.
Doini, still, *doini mia,* still left, *doini helai,* still sitting.
Doka, a tributary stream.
Dokaimo, ceremony of poling large canoes (*lakatoi*) about when ready for sea.
Dokia, to take off clothes.
Dokiaoho, *v.,* to pull down a skin without cutting it, as the skin of lizard, or a kangaroo tail ; hence to take off one's clothes.
Doko, *s.* anchor.
Doko, *a.* maimed. *Ima doko.*
Doko, to end.
Doko a tao, *v.* to hold, restrain.
Dokokadokoka, *adj.* following *dara,* lonely, distressed.
Dokona, *s.* conclusion, end. *Asi dokona,* endless.
Doku, *s.* the calf of the leg. *Lau dokugu.*
Dola, *s.* penis erectio.
Dolu, *s.* back.
Domaga, *a.* one hundred thousand.
Domena, *s.* resin.
Domu a dae, to put in mouth.
Dona, name of a fish.
Dori a, *v.* to push, to nudge, to jog.
Doria dobi, to depose.
Dori duduna tau, captain of one end of native ship (*lakatoi*) ; mate.
Dori na, *s.* the top.
Dorinai, *prep.* on. Also *adv.*
Dorivadoriva, *a.* very high in the air. *Guba dorivadorivana ai.*
Doro, *v.* to stop crying, to be pacified.
Doru, *s.* the back.
Doru laoho, crooked back.
Doru qagugu, *a.* humpback.
Dorua, sprained.
Dosema, for *dosi ema,* not yet come.
Dōsi, *v.* to take care of, to cherish, especially of a wife or child when the husband is away.
Dosi, negative, do *asi.*
Doua, *v.* to set fire to, as dry grass.
Doua, to ring (as a bell).

Dounu, particle future time, not yet.
Duadua, s. the name of a fish.
Duahi a, v. to count, to read.
Duahi hanai or hanaihanai, to count wrong.
Duahi lasi, countless.
Duba, brown colour, dark cloud.
Dubaduba, black; the colour of the skin of Elema natives.
Dubara, small land crab.
Dubu, s. chief's platform; sacred house; church; a pointed mound.
Dubu, to hit (of a missile); to reach to.
Dubi na, s. the tail of a bird.
Dudi, v. to leak (of a canoe).
Dudu, v. to gather up, as a squall; to form as fruit after the blossom falls; to form as an abscess; to grow, as the teeth of an infant.
Dudu, the name of a shell-fish.
Duduia, v. to point.
Dudukau, adv. with verb to give, constantly, again and again, and no payment.
Duduri a, v. to singe, to sweat.
Duha, name of a plant, the root and leaves of which are used to stupefy fish.
Duhi a, v. to prepare yams, &c., for cooking, to pare.
Duhu, a. thick, muddy, as water; gross, boka duhu.
Duhukaduhuka, thick, muddy.
Dui, s. banana (tree).
Dulua duiduina, to light fires all along the beach to attract or guide vessel at sea.
Dumu, the name of a fish.
Dumu sisia, the name of a fish.
Duna, s. the name of a bird of prey.
Dura, s. the back end of a house.
Duri, sting, as of stinging ray, &c.
Duribaroko, the name of a fish.
Duru a, v. to help in lifting a weight, to help generally.
Durua, waves caused by wind, as on a river; waves breaking on shore when sea is smooth.

E

E is pronounced as a in cake.
E, sign of past tense, 3rd pers. sing. and plu. See Grammar.
E, sign of present participle, followed by verb and suffix mu. See Grammar.
E, adv. Yes.
E, the sign of the vocative following the noun.
E, conj. or.
Eda, pos. pro, ita eda, ours.
Edana, pron. interr., which?
Edana negai, adv. when?
Edaseni, adv. where? in what place?
Ede, adv. where? oi ede lao? how? ede heto?
Ede amo mai, adv. whence.
Edeede. See Koau edeede.
Ede karatoma? how was it done?
Ede koautoma? what was said?
Ede lao? whither?
Edeseni? where? in what place?
Ia edeseni? where is he?
Edia, pron. theirs, for them.
Egediho, v. to recline on the side.
Egu, pron. mine, for me.
Ehea, v. to carry on the shoulder, as a water-pot.
Ehinana, to stretch one's self on waking.
Ehona, to chant or sing.
Ehona kurea lao, dirge for dead.
Ehona kurea lao, kurea laomu.
Ehurjehuni, } a. hidden; adv.
Ehuni, } privately.
Ehuni, v. to conceal.
Ehuni mamata, choice, reserved, given to visitors by a liberal man.
Ekidadiho, to throw down carelessly, to drop or leave on the road.
Ekidaela, v. to lie on the back.
Ela, e. green turtle.
Ela, v. went.
Ela bona, adv. till.
Elakaelaka (geme), broad chest.
Elaseni, adv. where? See Edeseni.
Eleguna, adv. long ago.
Eleseni, adv. where? See Edeseni?
Ema, v. came.
Ema bona, until, of past time only.
Emai, pron. ours, for us (exclusive of person addressed).
Emaimu, coming.
Eme, sign of past tense, 3rd pers. sing. or plu.
Emu, pron. for you, yours (sing.)
Emui, pron. for you, yours (plural).
Ena, pron. his.
Ena, there, that.

Ena. *See* Dekena.
Ena be, *conj.* although, notwithstanding.
Enai, *pron.* that.
Eni, *s.* chunam stick.
Eno, to lie down, generally of confinement from sickness. *Nega daudau ia enolaia.*
Enoeno, *s.* leeside.
Enoeno, *v.* to stay out all night.
Eno a tao, *v.* to overlay, as an infant, &c.
Enobou, *s.* cohabitation. (A respectful term.)
Enodele, *v.* to lie on the side.
Enokererekerere, *a.* not sacred, as a man newly married.
Enoraiva, to move, as infant in womb.
Erava, a raft of logs.
Ere, *s.* a row; a line drawn. *Ere rua*, two rows. Thicknesses, strands. *Ere hani*, fourfold.
Ere dagedage, *a.* impudent.
Eredika, *a.* discourteous.
Ere gabe, *a.* early manhood, middle-aged.
Eregabe eregabe, or, Eregabe maragi, younger than *eregabe*.
Eremui! Silence!
Ere na, *s.* speech, voice.
Erere, *v.* to spread, as light at dawn.
Ererua, *v* to be double, as boards, mat, &c.
Eretoi, *a.* threefold.
Erupi, a wild mint.
Ese, *s.* verandah at side of the house; gangway outside of the bulwarks of *lakatoi*.
Ese, particle between a pronoun and verb. *Ta ese e ka raia.*
Etai, *s.* a fish so called.
Eto, suffixed to verb in 3rd person to signify about to, but prevented. *Ia e karaia eto.*
Etomamu, *adv.* indeed. (Emphatic word.)
Eu, name of a small fish caught in great quantities on the reef after heavy rain.
Eu nege, or hanege, to fish with branches of trees for *eu*.
Evaeva, following *lao*, to go about, to roam.

G

G is always hard, as g in good. In some words the g approaches so nearly to k that it is very difficult to distinguish between them.
Gāba, *s.* loins above the hips; a belt.
Gaba, native drum, a feast.
Gaba, to shout, yell (without words).
Gabai a, to put on plaster, poultice, &c.
Gaba doua, *v.* to ring a bell.
Gaba na, circumference, waist, mountain side.
Gabani, *v.* to be barren (of a woman).
Gabe, gabea, *a.* last; *adv.* after, hereafter.
Gabele, *s.* a children's game of spearing cocoanut husks.
Gabena, *a.* last. Gabenai, next.
Gabena, *s.* the stern of a ship, or canoe.
Gabeta, *s.* a charm.
Gabili, to fill ill and shivery, as at beginning of illness.
Gabi na e lahaiakunu, to be courageous and strong in spite of difficulties.
Gabiruma, bush near a village or garden.
Gabu, *s.* place.
Gabu a, *v.* to roast over the fire.
Gabu na, a site.
Gabugabu, *s.* to talk imperfectly.
Gabugabu ("g" harder than above), to roast, &c.
Gabugabu, *s.* a breaking-out on the lips (as when recovering from illness).
Gaburu, the name of a fish.
Gāda, *s.* between the fingers or toes; fork of tree.
Gada, *adv.* quickly, nimbly.
Gada, *v.* to be quick, nimble. *Ba gadaia mai.*
Gadara, to play.
Gade, *s.* penis. Syn. Usi.
Gadea, *s.* a cable, a chain.
Gadegade, *s.* eye of a rope, link of a chain, &c.
Gādegāde, *v.* to annoy by constantly asking questions, or talking when busy.
Gadibaragara, to bite the under lip as sign of anger or strength.
Gadigadi, *s.* double teeth.

Gadigadi, *v.* to speak with deep, gruff voice, as in anger.

Gadigadi, *adv.*, with *tai*, to cry out as on death of friend, recounting his virtues, &c.

Gadigadi hahedai, *v.* to grind one's teeth.

Gadili, *a.* thin, ill-looking, either from sickness, fatigue, or any other cause.

Gadiva, *s.* knife of bamboo.

Gãdo, *v.* to be hungry for meat or fish.

Gãdo, *s.* the throat; voice; language; speech.

Gãdo baubau, windpipe.

Gado lohilohi, *v.* to nauscate, to belch, eructate.

Gadoi, *a.* few.

Gadobada. Gãdo, *s.* the ocean, the deep sea.

Gadogau gadogau, to gad about as a busybody.

Gado gigia, *v.* to choke.

Gado hahegeregerea, to translate, interpret.

Gado hanai, *a. v.* to learn a foreign language or dialect.

Gadogagadoga, *a.* light green, as young leaves, &c. ; blue.

Gado lānalāna, *v.* to stutter.

Gado dika, hoarse.

Gado namo tauna, *s.* a good-tempered man, a courteous man.

Gado roho, tattoo on chest of young girl.

Gadu dae, *v.* to comply, to consent.

Gaegae, *s.* the name of a green parrot.

Gaga, to turn face towards. *Lau hagaga henigu.*

Gaga, *s.* a wooden spatula used for sago; hence, a spade.

Gagaena, *a.* unoccupied, waste (of land).

Gagaia, *s.* coition.

Gagaisi, *s.* to look up with the head back, as when looking at the sky.

Gagado, *s.* very young cocoanut, before any kernel has formed.

Gagado, *s.* short tie-beams on the roof.

Gagalo, *v.* to scratch. Also Hegagalo.

Gagama, *s.* large cocoanut leaf basket.

Gagare, a light brown colour.

Gagatao, *v.* to be looked up at, as dogs waiting for a piece of food.

Gageva, *v.* to be crooked (inwards); as the bough of a tree towards the tree.

Gageva (of conduct), crooked, erratic.

Gagevagageva, to curve.

Gahi, *s.* flat stone club.

Gahu, *s.*, ashes, dust, mist, fog at sea, haze.

Gahukagahuka, albino.

Gahuko, *s.* the name of a bird.

Gaiagaia, the name of a shell-fish.

Gaigai, *s.* a snake.

Gaigai bamona, reptile.

Gaigo, isthmus.

Gaiho, *a.* sweet, pleasant to the taste.

Gaiho namo tauna, *s.* a hospitable kind-hearted man.

Gaiho dika, inhospitable.

Gaihona dika tauna, *s.* an abusive churlish man.

Gaili, *s.* a plain or level place on a mountain side.

Gaima, *a.* calm (at night).

Gaima, *v.* to be becalmed (at night).

Gaiva, *s.* a projection in the roof over the end of the house.

Gãlo, *s.* the name of a bird.

Galugalu, to joke together, unseemly mirth.

Galuna, *s.* early morning.

Gama, *au gamana*, a small bundle of firewood carried with other things.

Gama, to cut end of post so as to rest wall-plate on it.

Gamagama, following *adorahi*, evening, about 7 o'clock.

Gamiga, the large sinew of the thigh.

Gamoga, *a.* wide, as a doorway, river's mouth, &c.

Gamoga bada, broad.

Gãna, *s.* plaited armlet.

Gana luluna, midway between elbow and shoulder, measure of that length to tip of middle finger.

Ganai a, *v.* to warm oneself at the fire.

Ganagana, *v.* to groan, to sigh, to beg, to ask for in prayer.

Ganaganana (*ima*), just above wrist.

Gani, *v.* used with *mata*, to learn from reproof, to take warning.

Ganiahuota, name of a fish.

Ganikau, to burst out in flame; also of sudden energy of lazy man.

Ganiva, *s.* cane plaited round the waist or arm when mourning.
Gāno, *a.* sharp, keen edged.
Gānokagānoka, the sharp edge of a board when cut square; sharpish.
Ganotao, unsociable, disagreeable.
Ganunu, a shower.
Gao, *s.* voice. Syn. Gado.
Gaova, phosphorescent.
Gara, *s.* sepulchre, descendants, seed.
Gara ia, burnt, as mouth, from acrid food, or quick-lime, &c. *Udu garaia.*
Gara ia, *v.* (proceeded by mata) to be sleepy.
Gerabi, *s.* thorn of the sago palm.
Garagara, *v.* to be very hot (of the sun or fire; also, of anger). *Dina garagara.*
Garekagareka, crooked, running down as paint or tattooing ink.
Garia utu, to cut through, as with shell.
Gari, *v.* to be afraid.
Gari, *s.* fear.
Gari tauna, a coward.
Gari, *v.* to fall, as a tree, house, &c.
Garia tao, *v.* to be fallen on, as by a tree.
Garina, *conj.* lest.
Garokoni, one kind of banana
Gāru, *s.* See Karu.
Garugaru, *s.* a joint. A hinge.
Garugaru, *a.* immature; babyish, childish.
Garugaru bamona, *s.* dotage.
Gāsibobo, to spear two fish, or wallaby, with one spear; to kill two birds with one shot.
Gata, one kind of yam.
Gau, *s.* a thing.
Gāu, roots of grass or weeds, when ground is dug up.
Gauai a, *v.* to chew, masticate.
Gaubada, *s.* a great chief, a king.
Gau badabada, *a.* copious, hugh, weighty.
Gau kara ia, *s.* employment.
Gau kara memero, workmen.
Gau kara tauna, workman.
Gau ta, something.
Gau lata, *s.* height.
Gauka, old (of men or women).
Gaulatalata, *a.* high, tall.
Gatoi, *s.* egg.
Gava, name of a tree.

Gava ia, *v.* to run after one, in order to overtake.
Gave, *s.* feelers of octopus.
Gavena, a lull in wind; moderate, as of sun not yet high.
Gavera, *s.* edible mangrove.
Gea, *s.* the name of a tree: waste land where such trees stand. *Gea mo.*
Geahu, uncultivated.
Geakone, name of a tree.
Gebi na dika, selfish, unfriendly.
Gebi na namo, unselfish, friendly, equal to *T'aigana namo.*
Geda, *s.* a mat, a sail.
Geda, plant in river edge, of which mats are made.
Gedu, *s.* back of the head, also heel.
Gedua, preceded by *bagu,* to do up hair, as young girls at feast time. *Bagu e gedumu.*
Gedu vakovakona, as *gedu.*
Gege a, *v.* to surround, enclose, to gird.
Gegeva, *v.* to be crooked (outwards). See Gagova.
Gei a, *v.* to dig, as a hole; to dig up, as yams.
Gei a, *v.* to carry a person on the back (g. harder than in *geia,* to dig).
Geia asease, to dig, or trench.
Gēlo, *v.* to swing with a long rope from a cocoanut tree.
Gelo, *s.* fresh water tortoise.
Gelo, turned (as sun), to cant over (as a house).
Gelo, streamer from hair at back of head.
Gelona, *s.* the time of day, about 3 o'clock. *Dina gelona.*
Geme, *s.* bosom, chest.
Geme elakaelaka, broad chest.
Geme lasikalasika, projecting inflated chest.
Gemegeme, *s.* breast-bone of animals.
Gerebu, *a.* ten thousand.
Geregere. Gerekere, *s.* pandanus tree.
Geregere, *a.* equal, even.
Gesegese, *a.* sterile (of ground.)
Gete, one kind of yam.
Gibo a, *v.* to gouge out, as the eye.
Giboa, *s.* muliebria.
Gida, *s.* charcoal, embers.
Gidu u, to distribute.
Gigi, *v.* to snarl.
Gigi, to shed down, to scatter.

Gigi a, *v.* to squeeze, to shampoo.
Aio gigia, to throttle.
Gigi a, *v,* to scatter, to spread out, as gravel.
Gigia lasi, to fall out and down.
Gigiarohoroho, to scatter abroad.
Gigiakau, to throw something on to or into.
Gilaki, the name of a tree.
Gili, name of a shell-fish.
Gima, *v.* to look, to watch, to protect.
Gima tauna, sentinel ; a protector.
Gimata, *s.* a single white feather comb ornament.
Gini, *v.* to stand, to be erect.
Gini gunana, first.
Gini gabena, last.
Ginitore, to stand up (from a sitting posture).
Gini, *s.* a thorn, tatooing instrument.
Gini aheveri, to stand abreast in line.
Ginibou, to stand together.
Ginibo kanabo, good looking, handsome (of young men).
Ginidae, to arrive, to appear in sight, of words, to fulfil.
Ginidiho, to stand down.
Ginigini, *a.* stinging, prickly.
Ginigini, *a.* (the g a little harder than the proceeding word) prickly, thorny.
Gini hetabila, *v.* to adjoin (of houses).
Gini hekapa, to join (of houses with no passage between).
Ginikaginika (of cloth, &c.) prickly, rough to skin.
Ginikerehai, *v.* to turn round.
Ginilaiadae (of words), to cause to appear, *i.e.*, to fulfil.
Gini maoromaoro, to be perpendicular.
Gini sehe, to stand aslant, at an angle.
Giro a, *v.* to turn round, as the handle of a machine, &c.
Girogiro, *v.* to spin (as a top).
Giu, *s.* large long paddles, let down at the side of *lakatoi,* acting as centreboard.
Giu a, to stir.
Giua, *v.* to take up young bananas. *Dui giua.*
Giu a isi, *v.* to prize up (as the lid of a box).
Goada *a.* strong, clever, bold, valiant.

Goadagoada, very strong.
Goada bada, zealous, energetic.
Goada, *s.* courage.
Goai, term of respect to a widower, *Kevau goai.*
Goegoe, *v* to be dinned by the noise of talking, &c.
Goegoe, an outsider who helps in feast, &c.
Goeahu, lowering, as sky.
Goeva. *a* clean, prepared.
Goevagoeva, *adv.* thoroughly ; *a.* clean.
Gobaiahu, *v.* to veil, to obscure.
Gobagoba, *s.* to break thin shell of young cocoanut between the hands.
Gobe a, *v.* to catch.
Gōdi, small stone hatchet.
Gōgō, *s.* a creeping plant. The leaves are used in incantations, and to make yams fruitful.
Gogoa, *v.* to pick up.
Gogo a oho, to gather out of.
Gogo a bou, to gather together.
Gogori, *s.* young cocoanut with very soft kernel.
Gogosi a, *v.* to keep intact.
Goha, *s.* the name of a month (February).
Gohu, *s.* a lake, a lagoon.
Gohu, small cocoanut shell in which lamp black solution is put for tattooing ; an inkstand.
Gohumānu, *s.* water-birds.
Gole a oho, to burn up, consume by fire.
Gonagonalaia, *v.* to deride, to mock.
Gore, *v.* to deny.
Goregore, *s.* shelf or rack, formed by the wall-plate at each end of the house.
Gorere, *v.* to be ill.
Gorere, *s.* disease.
Gorere siahu, fever.
Gori, *s.* legend.
Goroahu, to pray on account of misfortune, &c., when all ancestors are invoked.
Goroahu, small bag net.
Goroto, *s.* gray clay.
Goru, *v.* to lie on the belly, to be prone.
Goru, large flat piece of sago frond at base.
Goru a, *v.* to entice or deceive with food, and then kill while eating.

Goruahu, *v.* to overshadow.
Goru a tao, *v.* to be laid on; to be overlaid, as an infant; to be sat on, as eggs by a hen; to fall prone on.
Gorudiho, to fall prone; a suppliant for mercy would *gorudiho* at feet of conqueror.
Gorugoru, large package of sago, enclosed in two palm fronds, and containing from 6 to 14 *kokoara*.
Gorukau, to lean on a table or box on the elbows, with the face downwards.
Goruparapara, *v.* to fall prone; with arms and legs out, "spread eagle."
Gou, to roar, to low.
Goua, *s.* to scald, to blister.
Goua, *s.* a blister.
Goula, *s.* a smooth place for anchoring, as between two reefs, &c.
Goura, *s.* a valley.
Gova ia, to cover over from head to feet, also used of veil for face.
Guara, the name of a tree.
Guba, *s.* sky, heavens; heaven; a squall.
Guba dokona, the horizon.
Guba rahua, *s.* thunder.
Gubagohu, a lake or pool caused by heavy rain, and soon dried up.
Gubaguba, short cocoanut tree.
Gudu, *v.* to swell, as the hand or leg.
Gudu, one kind of banana.
Gududu, *s.* the name of a fish.
Gugu, *s.* the river bottom, where there are deep holes.
Gugu, to clasp.
Gugu, to struggle, to get away.
Guguba, *v.* to hold tightly, to grasp with tight fingers.
Guguba ia, *v.* to squeeze by embracing; to break, as a cocoanut shell between the two hands; figuratively, of one broken by distress.
Gugugugu, *adv.* slow, loitering (*Laka gugugugumu*).
Guguru, *adv.* completely, entirely.
Guhi, *s.* the roof of a house.
Guhi nese, to be elated, puffed up, boastful.
Gui, *v.* to go on board a canoe or ship; to ebb; to ride.
Gui a, *v.* to tie, as the hands or feet; to prepare a torch.
Guia gauna, a band.

Guiahu, aground with shallow water all round.
Guikau, to embark on someone else's ship.
Guioho, shallow.
Guiohoa, aground.
Guitau, *s.* the season of S.E. monsoon.
Gula, native oven of hot stones.
Gula, *v.* to cook in oven of hot stones, differing from *Hamudo* in being covered in with leaves only.
Guma, *s.* lamp-black, bait for fish.
Gumaulu, the name of a shell-fish.
Guma karaia, *v.* to blacken oneself, to be sooty.
Guma karaia ariana, feast for dead made when mourners blacken themselves.
Guna, *a.* first; *adv.* before.
Gunaguna, intens. of guna, first of all (in time).
Gunalaia, *v.* to go before, to lead.
Gunana, *a.* old; former.
Guni, *s.* inland.
Gunita, *v.* to eat alone, not sharing, to be selfish.
Ani gunita (an abusive term).
Gunita tau, a stingy, greedy man.
Gure, *v.* to be sea-sick.
Guri, *s.* a pit; a grave.
Guri *v.* to bury; Guria (G har almost *kuria*).
Guri, *s.* a drink, a draught. *Gu tamona*, one draught.
Guri, a deep inlet of the sea.
Guri a, *v.* to pray. *Dirava guria* (softer than *g* in *guria*, to bury.)
Guriguri, *s.* a prayer.
Gurita, *s.* a draught (of drink).

H

H is not sounded by natives of Pari, and some others; Hohodae, for instance, a part of Hanuabada (Port Moresby).
Ha, also He, *interj.* warning, forbidding, look out!
Ha, causative particle.
Ha, prefixed to *hani* in counting persons.
Habada ia, to enlarge.
Habade, *v.* to accuse.
Habadelai a, *v.* to be accused.

Habadu a, *v.* to displease, to enrage, to provoke.
Habapatiso, *v.* (*introduced*) to baptize.
Habata, *s.* a rain stream.
Habero a, *v*, to be wounded.
Habidi a, *v.* to rub the eye.
Habodo a, *v.* to extinguish, as a fire.
Habogo, to stretch out one's neck so as to see better.
Habou a, *v.* to collect, to gather together, to assemble.
Habou a kahinaikahinai, to gather things together and have close at hand.
Habua, to kill many. *Magani habuaia lao.*
Habubuni a, to cover, as with water.
Hadabu a, to lack, to be left out.
Hadadai a, *v.* to make to enter, or go through (as a nose-stick).
Hadaea, *s.* ceremony of a sorceror to find and bring back the spirit of a sick person. *Laulau hadaea.*
Hadagedage a, *v.* to make savage, to exasperate.
Hadaia, *v.* to place on, as the foot on a mat; to soak, to steep.
Hadaia heni, to consider, to think.
Hadaia kunu, to ram down, as earth on newly-made road.
Hadai bara, to give smaller portion than to others.
Hadaihadai, *adv.* slowly, to grow slowly, as tree.
Hadamena, to salt.
Hadamlai a, *v.* to put *vaina* over the arm on the shoulder.
Hadaro a dae, to cause to return to one after estrangement.
Hadava ia, *v.* to marry. *Inai kekeni lau na hadavaia.*
Hadebedi, to salute by chucking under chin, a sign of friendship.
Hadedea, *v.* to frizzle, to burn fat; to fumigate.
Hadehuina, *s.* beard, a goatee.
Hadelea, *adv.* sideways.
Hadeo, a stone hatchet, used for inside of canoes, &c.
Hadeolo, *s.* stay (to mast).
Hadetari, *v.* to brood over, to be pensive.
Hadetarihadetari, *adv.* humbly.
Hadiari a, *v.* to make light, to enlighten.
Hadiba ia, *v.* to teach.
Hadibadibaia, as *Hadibaia.*

Hadidi, phosphorescent.
Hadigu a, *v.* to bathe.
Hadiho a, *v.* to divorce a wife.
Hadika ia, *v.* to culumniate, to contemn.
Hado, Hadohado, to plant.
Hadobi, to cause to fruit.
Hadokilai a, *v.* to put on clothes.
Hadoko a, *v.* to conclude, to stop.
Hadoko dae, a number to ascend to house or church together.
Hadoko vareai, a number to enter a house together, or go inland.
Hadono a, *v.* to swallow.
Hadoru a, to sprain.
Hadu a, *v.* to tell someone to do a thing; to give permission.
Hadua ia, to command.
Hadudua, *v.* to give food out of respect, as to a chief, or out of compassion to a lazy man.
Hadudu, relations, adherents.
Haduhadu, small wood on roof parallel to rafters to which thatch is fastened.
Haduhu a, to make thick, or gross.
Haege a diho, *v.* to cause to recline.
Haererua ia, *v.* to make of two thicknesses, as boards, mats, &c.
Haeno, moon, two or three nights after full.
Haere, *v.* to answer.
Haese a, to hold, or carry, carefully on hands.
Haeva ia, *v.* to sway (by the wind).
Haevai a tari, to cause to pass away; disappear.
Haga, *s.* craig, high rock.
Haga, open (as wound).
Hagaia, *v.* to open the mouth.
Hagabi a, to fill partly.
Hagadoi a, *v.* to dwindle.
Hagageva ia, *v.* to bend, to crook; (morally) to lead astray.
Hagahaga, *s.* steep rocks, cliffs, precipice.
Hagani a, *v.* to command. Preceded by *matana,* to reprove or punish so as to reform.
Hagara, to meet in combat; to hold on to.
Hagari a, *v.* to daunt.
Hagaru, *s.* rising tide.
Hagau a, *v.* to count (mentally), to distribute to all of a party.
Hagauhagau, *a.* each one of a company.

Hagava, v. to bother, to hinder, to be called away before work is finished, or turned back by wind before fishing.
Hagavara, one kind of banana.
Hagegeva, a. (with the face vaira hagegeva), sorrowful, on the point of crying.
Hagelo, to fasten a streamer to lock of hair at back of head. Gedu ai hageloa.
Hagere, v. to look towards, to receive a person. Hagerea.
Hagini a, v. to cause to stand, to raise up.
Hagoada ia, v. to stimulate.
Hagoeva ia, v. to cleanse.
Hagoi a, to imitate.
Hagoi na, a pattern, example.
Hagori a, v. to steer seawards, to luff.
Haguguru a, to complete, finish.
Haguhi, v. (with lalo) to reflect, to consider.
Haguma ia, to blacken.
Hahala adv. lightly, gingerly. (With the verb to hold.)
Hahane, v. to invoke, to call upon absent friends. O vagi o!
Hahatai a isi, v. to lift and train up, as yam vines.
Haheadava ia, v. to give in marriage, to cause to be married.
Haheduaisi, v. to lift up from the ground, as the tomato vine.
Hahealo, v. to constrain, to encourage, to exhort.
Hahebou a, v. to add to, to combine, to congregate.
Hahedai, v. to grind (as the teeth), to gnash.
Hahedaibara, not to have a share, or smaller than others.
Hahediho, feast on occasion of birth of first child.
Hahedinarai, v. to cause to be manifest, to cause to show.
Hahedua, v. to exhort, to urge to be be quick, to command.
Hahegaraheheni, to meet in combat, quarrelsome. See Hagara.
Hahegeregere, v. to compare with, to make equal to. Syn. Hahetoho.
Hahelahu a, s. coïtio.
Hahenamoheheni, v. recipr. of namo.
Haheqaqanai, v. to trip.

Haherahu, v. to smell, to rub noses (instead of kissing).
Hahetoho, v. to compare.
Hahetoho gauna, measure.
Hahidaoti, some men chosen from others.
Hahisi a, v. to cause pain, to afflict, to hurt.
Hahitu, seven times.
Hahoa ia, a. to disturb, to surprise.
Hahoho, v. to respire.
Hahoho a, to make plentiful.
Hahururu a, v. to make a fire blaze.
Hai, preceded by idau, adv. away from.
Haida, a. some, any, more (of persons).
Haidaulai a, v. to alter.
Haidita ia, v. to make bitter.
Haigo, x. to peep, to stoop.
Hahine, s. woman; female.
Haino, s. small white snake.
Hainu a, v. to give drink.
Hainu a, to hang pearl shell or other ornaments round neck.
Hāiraina, s. adornment. Hāiraina karaia.
Hairava, to put in order, tidy up.
Haitalai, to be made a spectacle Haitalaimai.
Hakahi, v. to jam; to cut wedge shape. Tarai hakahi.
Hakala, v. to lean forward so as to catch every word, to listen attentively.
Hakapu a, v. to shut, to close.
Hakara, v. to have killed some one (of returning warriors); also of fishing, hunting, &c.
Hakaroho, v. to cause, to scatter.
Hākau, to reach, to be in contact.
Hakau a, v. to lead.
Hakaua taudia, s. escort.
Hakede, v. to bend forward the ear so as to catch every word.
Hakede a, v. to light with a torch.
Hakerukeru a, v. to shade.
Hakeruma ia, v. to chill.
Hako regena, leg joint of wallaby.
Haketo a, to cause to fall.
Hakoe a, v. to turn round side for end.
Hakudima ia, to make deaf.
Hakunu a, v. to cause to be satisfied.
Hakurokuro a, v. to make white.

Hālā, s. the platform of sticks on which meat is grilled ; a gridiron. A *Koitapu* word.
Halababana ia, v. to make broad.
Halagāu a, to be disrespectful, rude.
Halahe, v. to delay, to linger, to be tardy.
Halahu a. See Hahelahua.
Hala ia, v. to broil (*Koitapu*).
Halaka, v. to burn in cooking.
Halaka, one kind of seaweed.
Halaka ia, v. to scald, to burn.
Halala, v. to hold lightly or carelessly. *Abia halala. Kahua halala.*
Halao a, v. to become, to be transformed into.
Halata, projection, or shelf in native house. On this the offering to the gods was placed.
Halata ia, v. to elongate, to lengthen.
Hālatutu, s. fire continuing to burn, after that in the surrounding bush has gone out. *Rei doua hālatutuna.*
Halasi, s. banana-leaf caulking the third row of caulking in *lakatoi.*
Halasi a, v. to expel, to take outside.
Haliga na, an example, pattern.
Halō, v. to comfort.
Haloakunu, v. to grate on a rock (as a boat).
Halohia ia, v. to praise, to laud; to help a chief with presents ; to honour.
Halou a, v. to cause to return ; to bring or send back ; to convert.
Hamage a, v. to ripen on the tree.
Hamaka ia, to break edge (of knife or axe).
Hamakohi a, v. to be dilapidated.
Hamanada ia, v. to habituate.
Hamanau a, v. to abase.
Hamane, s. a tree from which oars are made ; the gum of the tree ; glue, gum, paste.
Hamanoka ia, v. debilitate, to dispirit, to enfeeble.
Hamanu, v. to send for (persons or things when absent from house).
Hamaoro a, v. to show, to make known.
Hamaoromaoro, v. to make straight, to justify.
Hamara, hammer. (*Introduced.*)
Hamaragi a, to decrease, to abate, to lessen.
Hamarumaru a, v. to conciliate, to pacify.
Hamatamata a, v. to mend, to renew.

Hamate a, v. to efface, to kill.
Hamau, v. give no answer ; not to speak to.
Hamauri a, v. to save, to heal.
Hametai, to shelter from wind.
Hametau a, v. to encumber.
Hamiro a, v. to defile, to soil.
Hamoale a, v. to cause to rejoice; to amuse.
Hamomokani a, v. to confirm.
Hamomokanilai a, v. to fulfil ; to prove.
Hamu, s. the heated stones for cooking ; a foreign oven.
Hamūdo, v. to cook with hot stones, and covered in with leaves and then earth.
Hamūe, v. (used with the face, *vaira hamūe*) to look away from any one, as a sign of displeasure ; to receive a visitor with disrespect.
Hamumutaia, s. emetic.
Hanai, v. to cross, to go over, to pass through.
Hanai a, with *gado*, to learn a foreign language.
Hanai a lao, v. to pass. See *daga hanai. Tulu hanai, &c.*
Hanaihanai, a. eternal.
Hanamo a, v. to commend, to give thanks.
Hanaipa koikoi, to cajole.
Hanamoa henia, to salute.
Hane,' s. a woman. Used only (instead of hahine) with the place or tribe to which she belongs, as *hane motu;* or first in a sentence, as *hane namo,* a good-looking woman.
Hane, see *Hahane,* to invoke, call upon.
Hane qana, term of address to a widow.
Hani, s. the wing of a bird, &c.
Hani, the sign of a question. *Oi gorere hani ?*
Hani, a. four.
Hanihi, to see a dead person in a dream.
Hanihi a, v. to appear as a dead person in dream.
Haniulato, s. a maiden, a young woman.
Hauogo, to stretch out neck, so as to see better.
Hanua, v. village, town.
Hanua motu, a small village.
Hanua taudia, populace.

Hanuaboi, s. night.
Hao a, v. to arouse.
Haoda, v. to fish. Haoda tauna, fisherman.
Haoda eno, v. to go fishing, and stay out all night.
Haodi and Hahodi, v. to take breath, as when going up hill.
Haodi, s. a deep breath; a sigh.
Haore a, v. to demolish, exterminate, to finish.
Hapa, s. the side of a house.
Hapaeatao, to make fast a canoe to pole on shore.
Hapapai, v. to be bright (of the eyes).
Hapapaia, to give sight to.
Haparara ia, v. to split, to separate, to cleave, (of mind) to understand.
Haparipari a, v. to moisten.
Hapoporaia, to cause scarcity, or bring misfortune upon others.
Hapou a, v. to explode.
Haqadogi a, v. to make short, to clip, to abbreviate.
Haqalimu a, to help an ally and so cause him to conquer.
Hara, s. brains. *Qaru harana.*
Haraga, adv. quickly, easily. Haragaharaga, promptly.
Haraga. Haragaharaga, v. to be light in weight, to be quick.
Haraga ia, to hurry.
Harahu a, v. to be kissed. (Lit. to be smelt.)
Hara ia, v. to light a fire or lamp.
Haraiva, v. to trouble, to disturb, to bother.
Hare, v. to brandish a spear, to defy.
Hari. Harina, s. a report, fame. Harina dika, a. infamous.
Hari, adv. now, at this moment. Used also as a definite article. *Hari ira*, the hatchet, just used, or spoken of.
Hari ahui, forty.
Hari gau, cat's cradle.
Hari kava, to give away foolishly, uselessly.
Hari a, v. to divide.
Harihari. As *hari*, but oftener used of to-day; not so immediate or present as *hari*.
Harihari ela, henceforth.
Harihari, favour.
Harihari gauna, a present.
Harihari bada, liberal.
Hario a, to gird.

Hariolai a, to gird with.
Haroho a mauri, to cause to escape, to save from death.
Haropo a kau, to run into as a ship or boat, to collide.
Haroro, v. to proclaim, to preach, to make a speech.
Haroro tanna, missionary, a preacher.
Haroro a, v. to haul on, to pull taut.
Harotono ia, to make narrow.
Harna, v. to be carried away by a current or flood.
Haruа, a. twice.
Haruaia heidaheida, to divide into two equal parts, preceded by *dala*, half way.
Haruaoho, v. to be washed out and carried away.
Hasatauro, v. to crucify (from the Greek).
Hasiahu a, v. to warm, to heat.
Hasinadoa, v. to look intently at so as to know again.
Hasinadoa tauna, one who knows a road, place, &c., from previous observation; a spy.
Hata, adv. sometime, another time, presently.
Hatai a, v. to clang, to rattle, to play on any instrument.
Hataisi, v. to grow up as a yam vine by clinging to a stick or tree.
Hataka, to cake (as mud), see also *Ataka.*
Hataora ia, v. to level.
Hatatadaeroha, v. to cause to rise, as the sun.
Hatata ia kerebai, to cause to turn about, as horse with bridle.
Hato a, v. to pronounce a name.
Hotobo a, to give suck.
Hatolai a, to crown, to put on (as hat).
Hatolo, Cycas palm tree and fruit.
Hatoni a, v. to take leave of friends, leaving on a journey.
Hatono, v. to gulp, to swallow.
Hatore a isi, v. to raise up.
Hatorotororo a, v. to stiffen.
Hatu a, v. to plait, as mats; to weave, to beat a bamboo drum, to tattoo, to twist small rope.
Hatubu a gauna, s. leaven, v. to cause to ferment.
Hatui a, v. to quell, to still.
Haturi, v. to tire, vex, trouble.

Haturia ia, *v.* to trouble, to tire. See Haturi.
Haulumoa, general rejoicing.
Haunu, to finish. Syn. *Hadokoa.*
Haura ia, to cause to desire, to teaze a child by showing him a thing and then refusing to give it.
Hava ia, *v.* to chase.
Havara, havarahavara, against command or law, to do or take without authority.
Havara ia, *v.* to cause to grow.
Havareai a, *v.* to take inside, to insert.
Havaseha, *v.* to banter.
Havave, to send to call some one. *Vagi ba haravea.*
Haveri, to pull, equal to *veria.*
Haveve, *v.* to liquify.
Haveve a, to be deliberate in taking aim, to straighten carefully, slowly.
Hē. See Ha.
Heabiabilai a, to receive visitors gladly, to take into houses of the village.
Heabidae, *v.* to receive into one's house, to show hospitality (with suffix of person so received). *Lau heabigu dae.*
Heabidae tauna, one who is hospitable.
Heabiahu, *v.* to go off to meet a ship coming in.
Headava, *s.* the state of marriage. *Oi headava?* Are you married?
Heagi, *v.* to boast.
Heagi herevana, to brag.
Heagi tauna, *a.* conceited.
Heagilai a, *v.* to ascribe strength, wisdom, &c.; to praise.
Heahu, *v.* to bring about one's death by obstinacy in not listening to others. *Ia sibona heahu.*
Heai, *v.* to quarrel. (Without coming to blows.)
Heai karaia, a disturbance.
Heaiva, *s.* payment to a sorcerer for causing rain, restraining wind, &c.
Heaiva ia, *v.* to fee a rainmaker, &c.; to pay tribute.
Heala, *v.* to be intoxicated.
Healaheheni, *v.* recipr. of alala, to fight.
Hearuru, to rush together.
Heatolai a, *v.* to praise, to extol.
Heatotao gauna, *s.* the payment given to betray or kill another.

Heatotao tauna, the one that pays another to betray or kill a third person.
Heatu, *s.* a combat.
Heau, *v.* to run; to go fast as a canoe or ship; to escape.
Heau dae heau diho, to beat against head wind.
Heau dara, *v.* to run up, as a mountain.
Heau hekei, to run down.
Heau hekapu, to run two together competitively.
Heau helulu, to run together, to see which can get in first.
Heau kau, to arrive, as canoe, ship, &c.
Heaulai a, to run off with.
Heautatatata, to run with short steps, like a child just beginning to walk.
Heautani a, to be outrun.
Hebadubaduheheni, *v.* recipr. of badu, to be angry one with another, to be at variance.
Hebagu, to do up hair as young girls at feast time, to do it often a sign of prosperity. *Hebagu ai e gedua.*
Hebedoma, a week. (*Introduced.*)
Hebasi, *v.* to puncture the forehead with a small flint-pointed arrow, so as to draw blood, to relieve headache.
Hebibi lao, to move a thing or person along a little way.
Hebibi vasi, as *Hebibi lao.*
Hebirihebiri, *v.* to sit or stand close together, as trees standing close together.
Hebiri matemate, *a.* to be squeezed, crowded.
Hebivahebiva, to wriggle.
Hebodohi, *v.* to substitute.
Hebokahisi, *v.* to compassionate.
Hebokahisi tauna, a compassionate merciful man.
Hebokahisi, *a.* humane.
Hebolo, *v.* to take the place of another, to be a substitute.
Hebore, envy.
Hebore karaia, to be envious of success or prosperity of others.
Hebou, *v.* to add to, together with.
Hebouauru, tide turned from low.
Hebubu, *v.* to spill.

Hebulohcbulo, *v.* to be mixed up; also of the mind, and several stories mixed up in it.
Hedaedae, to dispute.
Hedahu, *v.* to besmear, to wipe.
Hedahu muramura, liniment.
Hedai, well, strong, of a sprained joint.
Hedai, *v.* to dive head first.
Hedai dobi, to dive feet first; to fall from a height feet first.
Hedāiahu, to enclose (as trees growing all round, troops, &c.); to close, as mouth.
Hedāiriki, lame.
Hedaqadobi, *v.* fall from height, to throw oneself down from a tree or cliff.
Hedalo boubou, to live together in peace and harmony.
Hedalo kuboukubou, as *Hedalo boubou.*
Hedalo daudau, to be separated, not friends, the opposite of *Hedalo boubou.*
Hedalokepokepoa, *v.* (preceded by *taia*) to disbelieve; to reject a story as false.
Hedamena, to coagulate, to set, as cocoanut oil from cold.
Hedaraune, *v.* to remember to call to mind (especially when reminded by the sight of something).
Hedare, *v.* to rend.
Hedarehedare, *a.* ragged.
Hedau a toho, *v.* to touch, to lay hand on.
Hedaukau, *v.* to place the hand on, to touch.
Hedava, to do by turn.
Hedavari, *v.* to meet.
Hedave a, *v.* (following hoihoi) to exchange different things in barter.
Hedea, *a.* only, *vara hedea*, only begotten.
Hedibagani, *v.* to dissemble.
Hedibagani, *s.* a temptation, hypocrisy.
Hediho, *s.* a divorcement.
Hediho hahine, a divorced woman.
Hedikoidae, *v.* to shrink (as clothes, or food in cooking).
Hedilohedilo, to wallow.
Hedinarai, *adv.* openly.
Hedinarai, *v.* to make manifest, to show openly.

Hedoahedoa, to live in a place as a foreigner.
Hedogodiho hedogodiho, to anchor at many places along the coast.
Hedogo gabuna, *s.* anchorage.
Hedoisi, *v.* to kneel on one knee.
Hedoki gauna, *s.* a shirt.
Hedoko, *v.* to part combatants.
Hedoriahu, *v.* to push away or down.
Hedorihedori, *v.* to crowd, to jostle.
Hedudutari, to sting, as a wasp.
Hegabi, partly full.
Hegagaheheni, opposite.
Hegagalo, *v.* to scratch.
Hegagiudac, *v.* to throw the arms round neck, to embrace. Cramp.
Hegame, *v.* (following noi) to beg.
Hegame tauna, beggar, to look on in hope of getting a share.
Hegamehegame, *adv.*, with *hereva*, to speak to one quietly not in anger, to reprove quietly.
Heganai a, to warm oneself.
Hegani, *v.* to desire (only used with lalona). Used with *henia* of object.
Heganotao heganotao, one who is unsociable, who rarely comes, and doesn't talk.
Hegara, *v.* to smart, as the tongue, or a wound.
Hegara, *a.* caustic, pungent.
Hegege, *v.* to encompass.
Hegege madai, *v.* to enclose.
Hegera, *v.* to coquette.
Hegeregere, *a.* even, equal.
Hegerehegere lasi, *a.* contradictor
Hegigi, *v.* to nip, to pinch.
Hegigi lasi, to fall out and down.
Hegigi a rohoroho, *v.* to scatter, to throw about.
Hegigibou, *v.* to be full, as a village with people, or a box with goods.
Hegigirai a, to strike with claws (as cat, &c.)
Hegida, to hoist sail, of *lakatoi.*
Hegilo, *v.* to turn.
Hegilohegilo, to revolve.
Hegiurāi, too long, jammed at ends.
Hegoita. Hegodiaita, &c., *v.* to visit in order to inquire after the welfare, to go to see a sick person.
Hegogo, *s.* a congregation, an assembly.
Hegogo bada, a concourse.
Hegogo, *v.* to shrink (as from cold).
Hegogo gabuna, good anchorage, harbour.

Hegomogomo, v. to gargle.
Hegore, v. to deny.
Hegore, s. denial.
Heguguba, v. to shudder.
Hehe a, v. to squeeze hard in the hand, to knead in the hand; to milk.
Hehe a, v. to carry the waterpot on the shoulder.
Heheni, suffixed to verb to make it reciprocal.
Hehihiraia, v. to reject.
Hehona, a recitative song.
Hebuhu, v. to shed, to cast leaves.
Hehurehauai, v. to turn over oneself.
Heidaida, s. resemblance, likeness.
Heidaida, a. alike.
Heidioro, to stretch one's self boastfully. (*I am here!*)
Heiga, one kind of yam.
Heigaiga, to fight.
Heilu, v. to float; to slip or slide into; to be swift.
Heinana, to stretch one's self on waking.
Heinugaiho, sexual desire when mutual.
Heinaru, v. to cook food for workers.
Heiri, to refuse to allow to accompany, &c. *Idia lau heirigumu.*
Ieiriheiri, to dissent, to disagree.
Heirilai a, to avoid, shun.
Heita, v. two to look at each other. *Oiemu heita tauna.* To see one's self in a mirror. *Lau sibogu heita.*
Heita tao tauna, one who watches or looks after anything; an overseer.
Heitalai na, a spectacle.
Heiva, with *sibona*, to cut one's self. *Ia sibona e heivamu.*
Hekaba, v. to help with food or goods when visitors come, or at a feast.
Hekabi, a. half-full.
Hekagalo, v. to scratch.
Hekaguri, obstinate, persists in taking a thing and will not give it up.
Hekalia, to help.
Hekaha na tauna, s. a helper. As Ikaha na tauna.
Hekahi, v. to stick, to be tight.
Hekahihekahi, a. narrow, straight.
Hekaki, thick, as arrowroot, made with too little water.
Hekakari, as Herarai, onlooker at feast, &c.

Hekakati, v. to scratch the face in grief, so as to fetch blood.
Hekalo, v. to beckon.
Hekamo, v. to stick; a. sticky.
Hekamokau, v. to take hold of a thing, to touch, to cling to.
Hekamonai, v. to have labour pains.
Hekamotao, v. to clutch.
Hekapa, v. twins.
Hekapu, adv., with *heau*, to run competitively.
Hekarakaraheheni, a. reciprocal of kara, generally of bad conduct.
Hekei, v. to descend a mountain.
Hekei a lao, v. to trundle, to go round and round, as a wheel.
Hekeihekei, slanting ground.
Hekeikau, v. to be crushed, fallen upon.
Hekenilaia, v. to be raised up by the tide or a flood.
Hekida, v. to hoist sail on a native ship (*lakatoi*).
Hekidadiho, v. to throw down carelessly; to fall down as one dead, or in a fit.
Hekidaela, or Hekidaera, v. to lie on the back.
Hekini a (*daba*), peep of day.
Hekinitari, v. to pinch.
Hekiqo, to boast, to praise.
Hekisehekise, v. to desire.
Hekisebekise henia, to covet.
Hekisi, to scarify, to cut.
Hekisi a, v. to cut oneself with a shell or flint in grief.
Hekonuheheni, v. to converse, to talk and answer.
Hekoho, v. to break off an engagement to marry.
Hekohutani a, v. to leave, to desert a village.
Hekoka, v. to be prevented, to be hindered by what one is doing from going at request. *Lau revareva na tore name hekoka.*
Hekokorogu tauna, a. conceited, proud.
Hekopa, a. excoriated.
Hekori, savage, untamed.
Hekuhihekuhi, to wallow.
Hekukuri, s. diarrhœa.
Hekunilaia, same as *Vagoaia,* which see.
Hekunumai, v. to wink, to make signs with the eyes.
Hekure, v. to lie down.

Hekuredobi, to throw oneself down, to lie down carelessly.
Helada, *adv.* stealthily.
Heladadae, *v.* to creep up stealthily, as a thief.
Heladadua, to draw back, as hands from anything hot.
Heladahanai, *v.* to slip out unseen, to escape.
Heladaoho, *v.* to dislocate.
Heladalou, *v.* to start back from fear.
Heladatao, to stay while others go.
Helado, *v.* to sway, by the wind.
Heladohelado, *a.* loose.
Helaga, *a.* sacred, taboo.
Helagāu, *v.* to pass before a chief, to be disrespectful. *Misi Lao helagaua gurina.*
Helaha, *v.* to kick out behind, as a horse.
Helai, *v.* to sit.
Helai gauna, a seat.
Helai diho, to sit down on the ground or floor.
Helaikau, to sit on, to place, as a pot on the fire.
Helai magogo, to sit in a shy, ashamed manner.
Helai tore, to sit up, from lying down.
Helai dagadaga, to sit astride.
Helaiabou, to transfix.
Helaorealai a, a being mindful of, a thinking of, and so prevented from going with others, on account of sick child, &c.
Helalo, *v.* to reflect, to consider.
Helalo dae, *s.* to think only of lover, fishing, &c.
Helalo karaia, *v.* to repent.
Helaloune. See Hedaraune.
Helaoahu, *v.* to avert, to stop.
Helaqahanai, *v.* to turn a somersault, to fall down on the head.
Helaqahi a, to graze, as leg, &c.
Helarihelari, to make signs with eyes between man and woman.
Helaro, *v.* to wait for, to expect some one.
Helarutao, *v.* to sit together with one piece of cloth round both.
Helata, *v.* to moult, to cast skin, as snake.
Helavahu, *v.* to be hidden by an intervening object.

Helegu hahine, a nurse, one who takes care of a child.
Helide, *v.* to put out of joint.
Heloduhenia, *s.* an accusation.
Heloge, *v.* to enter with difficulty, to wriggle through.
Heloge, *adv.* with difficulty.
Heloge a, Heroge a, *v.* to store, to garner.
Helogeheloge, to work as a ship in seaway.
Helogohelogo, *s.* clamour, discord, turmoil.
Helogologoahu, contention, disputation, clamour.
Helogosidae, to shrink, as clothes from wet, or of food cooked.
Hemadoi, *v.* to be entangled, or detained in a crowd. *Hemadoia matemate.*
Hemaduala, unwilling, indifferent.
Hemai a, *a.* tasteless, insipid, of no relish, as food to the sick. *Lau ania hemaia.*
Hemaihemai, *v.* to itch, to tingle.
Hemani. See Hetari.
Hemarai, *v.* to be ashamed, to be coy.
Hemarai kara, *a.* disgraceful.
Hemata, *v.* to commit suicide by hanging, to strangle.
Hemataurai, *v.* to reverence.
Hemaunu, *v.* to whisper.
Hememeru, *v.* to warm oneself by the fire. Used by those exposed to wind and rain. Let us go ashore and *hememeru.*
Hemoitao, *v.* to tread upon.
Hemomokāni, *v.* to fulfil, to prove true.
Hemumuse, to exaggerate.
Hemumuselai a tau, one who goes about telling exaggerated stories.
Henamo, a term of address from man to man, or from a woman to a woman. *Henamo e!*
Henanadai, *s.* inquiry.
Henao, *v.* to steal.
Henaohenao, *v.* to have intercourse with the opposite sex, to ravish.
Henaohenao, *s.* illicit intercourse, adultery.
Hene, spear of white wood used for hunting.

Henega, a council, a compact or agreement between two or more persons.
Henega, *v.* to make a compact or agreement.
Heni, *v.* to give, to hand to.
Heni a, *v.* to contribute.
Heni dava, to give in payment.
Henidoa, to give without payment.
Heni dudukau, to give constantly and no return.
Heni haganhagau, to distribute.
Henigagae, *v.* to give without expecting payment.
Henimai, to pass along, to hand to speaker.
Henitao, to give for use and then return.
Henitao henitao, to give constantly and no return.
Henitorehai, to give a thing on credit.
Henivasi, to pass along, away from speaker.
Heno, *adv.* aslant, as *abia heno*, to hold a pen slantingly.
Henu, *prep.* beneath, under. Also Henunai.
Henu, *adv.* seawards (in steering), westwards.
Henuai, *adv.* downwards, under.
Henugu, *hereva henugu*, muttering, grumbling to oneself.
Henukahana, in a westerly direction.
Hepalare, *a.* lazy. *Hepalarea tauna* (term of abuse.)
Hepapahuahu, *s.* contention, *v.* to contend, to recriminate. Also of wind, rain, troops, &c., to oppose, *hepapaiahuahua.*
Hepede, to chip, as edge of shell or plate.
Hepetehepete, noise of work, &c., preventing conversation.
Hepididae, *v.* to come to mind, to be reminded of.
Hepuhihepuhi, *a.* foolish, erring, crooked (of speech or conduct.)
Hepuni, *v.* to sink in, as the feet in mud or sand.
Hepurai, *v.* to run over.
Hepuraidobi, *v.* to boil over, to overflow.
Heqada, to brandish spear, &c., as a demonstration.
Heqaqanai, *v.* to stumble.
Heqarahi, *s.* labour, work.

Heqarahi, *v.* to work, to be busy, to be tired.
Heqarai, as Heqarahi.
Heqaroto hahine, midwife.
Heqatu, *v.* to tangle.
Hera, *a.* personal adornment. *Hera karaia.*
Hera gauna, *s.* ornament for personal adornment.
Herage, to take food to women whose husbands are gone on a voyage.
Herabe, *v.* to commit fornication.
Herahia, *s.* a present, an offering.
Herai, *v.* to put on the girdle. *Sihi herai.*
Herarai, to look on, to be a spectator.
Heraraho, to take food to women whose husbands are away on voyage, in payment for taking armshells, pottery, &c., for trade.
Herariherari, *v.* to talk about a thing without understanding or knowing the truth. Used with sivarai and koau.
Herariherari, *s.* a "cock and bull" story.
Herea, *v.* to overlap, project, to excel.
Herea, *adv. or adj.*, excellent, surpassing, very.
Herea dae, to exceed in height, overtop.
Heregeherege, *v.* to be unwilling.
Hereqahereqa, to forget, to be of forgetful careless mind.
Hereva, *s.* speech.
Hereva, *v.* to talk.
Hereva, euphemism for *gayaia*, sexual intercourse.
Hereva haevaiatari, to put aside, drop on account of someone more important.
Herevaherava, to confer.
Herevaheheni, to talk together.
Hereva hegeregere, fable.
Hereva hemoge, to pervert, misrepresent.
Hereva lanalana, to stutter.
Herogea, *v.* to store.
Herohemaino, *v.* to pacify, intercede, to conciliate.
Heroho, *v.* to wash off, to come out (as dirt), to rub of.
Heroiheroi, *v.* to rub oneself against a post.
Herouherou, *v.* to be excited, to be in tumult (of a village.)

Heruruki v. to let slip through the fingers; to strip by drawing through the fingers, as an ear of corn.
Hesede a, hesedesede, to be crowded, to push with the shoulder, to jostle, as in a crowd.
Hesede matemate, to stand crowded, jammed.
Hesese, v. to be cracked, as the skull, or pottery.
Hesiai, s. a message, an errand. As isiai. Hesiai taudia, embassy.
Hesiai mero, a servant.
Hesiai tau, a servant.
Hetabubunai, v. to scramble.
Hetaha. See Kudon.
Hetahahai, v. to marry a woman who has left her husband.
Hetahu, v. to daub, to anoint the body.
Hetāiuduri, v. to cry after, as a child after his father.
Hetapohetapo, to dance as a cock bird, to flutter.
Hetamanu, v. to charge, to admonish.
Hetamanu, s. a charge, an exhortation.
Hetaoahu, v. to put up the hands in forbidding, or in order to save oneself when falling.
Hetaoisi, v. to sit up, from lying down.
Hetari, v. to coagulate.
Hetaribabara, v. to fall backwards.
Hetaru, v. to be covered, clothed.
Hetata matemate, v. to push and jostle in a crowd.
Hetau a dae, v. to hang up.
Hetavauhe, v. to leave, to forget.
Heto, adv. like, as (following the s. Boroma na heto).
Hetoa, s. boundary.
Hetoa, to land.
Hetoi hedavari, v. to meet on the road.
Hetoisi, to kneel on one knee.
Hetohotoho, to mock, to try, to test.
Hetotao, v. to lean one's weight, as on a stick.
Hetouhetou, to hang back from fear or laziness, unwilling to go first.
Hetu, a. slack.
Hetū, v. to lie off, as a ship from the beach, to be anchored.
Hetubuahu, confined (of bowels), as Boka hetubuahu.

Hetudiho hetudiho, to call at many places on coast in canoe voyage.
Hetutu, v. to smite oneself in grief.
Hetutuqada habinena, the wife with whom a man has lived from her maidenhood, hence principal wife or wives of a polygamist.
Hetutuqada tau, husband with whom wife has lived from his youth.
Hetuturu, v. to drop (of liquids).
Heubu, v. to make a pet of; to feed.
Heubu mero, s. a boy kept and fed, as servants in a family. Nao heubu memero.
Heubu sisia, a pet dog.
Heudaabi, to commit adultery or fornication.
Heudahanai, to commit adultery or fornication.
Heudeheude, v. to tremble, to shake. With boka, to desire.
Aheudeheude, to cause to shake.
Henduri, v. to follow about, as a man after a woman, or to beg something; to go after to overtake.
Heukeheuke, s. a throbbing headache.
Heunahi, to rub against post.
Heuraheni, v. to desire someone to come to or go with the speaker.
Hevago, v. to be skinny from illness and refusing food.
Hevago tauna, one who feeds children or destitute.
Hevalavala, v. to be mildewed.
Hevarure, landslip, wall falling down.
Hevaseha, s. fun, jest.
Heveri, a. powerless,- paralyzed (of an arm or leg).
Hi, interj. See Hina.
Hia na, s. sister or brother-in-law.
Hida, adv. how many ?
Hidai, an equal.
Hidaoti, some (of fish, &c., chosen from others).
Hidi, v. to choose. (Preceded by ita, abia, &c.)
Hidio, s. See Idiho.
Hido, s. a wild cane growing by the river side; also, a comet.
Higo, name of a tree.
Hihiri a, v. to blow with the mouth, as Ihili a.
Hila, s. a large species of edible arum.
Hilai, two large canoes (asi) lashed together.

Hili, *v.* to go a long voyage.
Hili lou, to go a long voyage and return quickly.
Hili a, *v.* to twist round and round; to tie up a parcel or bundle by twisting string all round it. Also Hiri a.
Hilia dabuana, a bandage.
Hili a kau, *v.* to fasten by tying or lashing.
Hilua, *hilua e ani tauna*, a cannibal.
Hina, *interj.*, aha!
Hinere, *v.* to deceive.
Hineri, a hinge. (*Introduced.*)
Hioka, *v.* to whistle.
Hiri, *s.* a voyage.
Hiri boroma, to lash box, &c., so as to carry suspended between two.
Hiri a, *v.* See Hili a.
Hisi, *s.* pain; an epidemic.
Hisi eme daikau.
Hisiai. See Isiai.
Hisi ania, *v.* to suffer.
Hisihisi,*v.* to ache, to be in pain.
Hisi mo ania, to be in constant pain.
Hisiu, *s.* a star.
Hisiu bada, *s.* morning star.
Hitolo, *a.* hungry.
Hitolo, *v.* to hunger.
Hitolo mate, famished.
Hitu, *a.* seven.
Hituahui, seventy.
Hoa, *v.* to be surprised, amazed.
Hoihoi, *v.* to barter. *Hoihoi davana maragi*, cheap.
Hoihoi tauna, merchant.
Hobe, *s.* houses at each end of *lakatoi* for packing pottery.
Hodachodae, *v.* to throb, as an abscess.
Hodahoda ia, to sprinkle, using a bough or bunch of leaves.
Hoda ia, *v.* to be shaken, as by wind; to shake out, as cloth.
Hodaia gari. Hodaia keto, *v.* to be blown down by the wind.
Hodaia kohu, *v.* to be blown down and broken to pieces by the wind.
Hodara, *v.* to have two or more wives. Also Hodala.
Hodava, name of a tree.
Hode, *s.* a paddle.
Hodo a, *v.* to throw, as stones.
Hodu, *s.* native waterpot; pl. Hodudia.
Hogohogo, *s.* rust.

Hoho, *a.* complete, sufficient, plenty.
Hoho lasi, scarce.
Hoho a, *v.* to be blown by the wind, to be carried away, or to be swaying about in the wind, *Lāi hohoa.*
Hohoa, to inhale, as tobacco smoke.
Hohoga, *s.* a large hole, as in the end of a canoe, where the heart of the wood is.
Hohotauna, *s.* the survivor, after all the others are killed.
Holo, to be forceful (of spear), to enter.
Holo a, *v.* to make a hole in the ground with a pointed stick or crowbar.
Hona, only.
Hone, war shout.
Honehone, a short grass.
Honu, *v.* to be full, as *hodu*, with water, &c.
Honuhonudae, quite full.
Honu, *a.* full. Honuhonu.
Hore, to be above water, as the reef at low tide, or a rock standing up, &c.
Horea ia, to overtop others.
Horetao, *s.* a man higher than his fellows, *Sibona horetao.*
Hori, *v.* to grow. Syn. Vara.
Horo to anoint the head. *Ia qarana e horoa.*
Hosi, horse. (*Introduced.*)
Hotamu, name of tree similar to cedar.
Hou a, *v.* to paint the face red, when going to fight.
Houkahouka, *a.* rotton, as wood.
Houkahouka, *v.* to be rotten.
Houkahouka, *s.* pith.
Hu, *s.* the noise made by the wind. *Lai huna.*
Hu, to hum.
Hua, to increase, as an ulcer.
Hua, *s.* the moon; a month.
Hua dāulao, moon soon after full.
Hua dogagi, new moon.
Hua haeno, moon next to *dāulao.*
Hua karukaru, young moon.
Hua lokaloka, moon about half full.
Hua matoa torea, moon after *hæno.*
Hua. Huaia, *v.* (used with the face, *vaira hua*), to look angry, not to smile with others. *Ia dahaka vaira hua.*
Hūa, *v.* to cough.

Hūadaehuadae, v. to throb, as an abscess.
Hualahuala, of fire burning at a distance, or of a lamp burning in house.
Huahua, s. fruit.
Hua ia, v. to carry on the shoulder.
Huaia boroma, to be carried by two or four.
Huaia tauna, a bearer.
Huaiakau, to carry on shoulder.
Huarara, v. to shine (of the moon and stars).
Huararua, v. to carry on a pole between two.
Huaria, v. to smash, as pottery; to strike on the head or limbs in falling; to clash.
Huda, full, as sail with wind.
Hudo, s. navel.
Hudo. See Udo.
Hudu na, a. thick, as a board or mat.
Hūbū, s. single bananas, broken from different bunches, and taken or given to some one.
Huhula, a fish.
Hui, s. hair.
Hui daroa, to search in hair for lice.
Hui demo, slightly curly hair.
Hui gavekagaveka, hair curly at ends.
Hui kaki, hair matted, difficult to comb.
Hui lau, straight hair.
Hui tubikatubika, hair twisted into strings.
Hui tuma, s. hair curly.
Hui a, v. to put a child or anything large in a netted bag.
Huikahuika, hairy, as blanket.
Huinaimi, a fish.
Huiraura, s. the name of a month (January).
Huitabu, one kind of banana.
Huke a, v. to break off, as single bananas; to gather.
Hula. See Hura.
Hulalai a v. to open up, as a parcel, to uncover, to unroll.
Hulekau, v. or Hurekau, to be thrown up by the waves on to the beach.
Hulo tauna, a. industrious.
Huni, v. to cover, to hide.
Huni, ringworm.

Huni boroko, a malignant skin disease.
Honu, s. dew.
Hunu a, v. to make fast, as a rope.
Hunu a, to beat out fire.
Huo, s. a kangaroo net.
Hura, s. matter, of an abscess.
Hura bamona, purulent.
Hura karaia, to suppurate.
Hure, v. to drift, to float.
Hure, of day or feast close at hand. On Saturday evening, *Sabati ita vairada ai eme hure.*
Hure a isi, to be lifted up by tide or flood.
Hure a dae, as Hure a isi.
Hurehure, v. to be rough, of the sea.
Hurekau, to be wrecked, as *Hulekau* above.
Huri a, v. to wash, to scrub.
Huro, s. grindstone.
Hurokahuroka tauna, an albino
Hururu, v. to lighten with a torch.
Hururu, s. a flame.
Hururuhururu, a. bright, shining.
Hururuhururua, v. to burnish.
Husihusi, s. wart or pimple.
Hutuma, a. many (of people).
Hutuma, s. company.
Hutuna, a. thick.

I

I is sounded as ea in east.
Ia, *pron.* he, she, it.
Ia, both letters with hard breathing, an exclamation of dissent or disapproval.
Iabi na, s. one who takes; a servant.
Iahu, s. a woman who is sacred, and who performs certain rites during the absence of voyagers to ensure their safe return.
Ialata, s. the name of a fish.
Iana, *pron.* his, hers (*of food only*).
Ianimaina, one kind of food to eat with another as a relish, to kitchen.
Iareva, s. brush.
Iatuatu, the small piece of flat wood used for beating pottery into shape.
Iava, *conj.* or, whether.
Iena, *pron.* his, hers.

Ibadibadi hahine, a man's female friend, a woman who fetches water, &c., for a neighbour.
Ibamo na, one who accompanies another, a companion for the time.
Ibasi, *s.* small bow and arrow, an instrument used for doing the *hebasi*.
Ibodohi,) *s.* a substitute, an ex-
Ibodohina,) change.
Ibondiai, all.
Ibounai, *a.* all, every one.
Ibudu gauna, *s.* gimlet.
Ibuni mata, *s.* eyebrows.
Ida, *conj.* together with.
Ida, *prep.* with. (It follows the noun or pronoun of the person accompanied.) *Lau ia ida lao. Oi daika ida?*
Idabubu na, a bunch, a cluster.
Idai na, to be equal to, to be like.
Idau, *a.* different, other, foreign, strange.
Idauhai lao, *v.* to depart.
Idaunega, usually Idaunegai (past time); just now; a long time ago.
Idaunegai gauna, stale.
Idavarina tauna, finder.
Idi, *s.* the sheet of a sail.
Idia, *pron.* thy, they.
Idia edia, *pron.* theirs.
Idiba, *a.* right (as opposed to left).
Idibaganina, *s.* temptation.
Idibana tauna, one who knows, a witness.
Idiho, flesh, lean of meat, grain of wood.
Idita, *a.* bitter (as gall); salt (as sea water.
Ido, a comet.
Idoa, *s.* a snare.
Idoa, *v.* to ensnare.
Idoa, *v.* to throw a spear or stick by putting the finger on the end.
Idoidiai, *a.* every.
Idoinai, *a.* the whole, all.
Idoinai, *adv.* quite.
Idori, *v.* to sit on the heels, to squat. Idori evaeva, to *idori* from place to place in the house. *Oi dahaka idori evaeva helai diho lasi.*
Iduara, *s.* doorway; end of the house facing the street.
Iduara dehe, verandah at the end of the house facing the street.
Iduari, *s.* a comb.
Iduhu, *s.* tribe or family.

Iduka, *s.* headland.
Iduka matana, a point of a headland.
Idume, *s.* payment to a doctor.
Igara, *s.* a barb.
Igāu, *a.* hooked.
Igedu, *s.* large lashing of the foot of the mast in a native *lakatoi*.
Igigirohorohona tauna, *s.* one who scatters seed.
Igimana tauna, a watcher, a protector.
Igiri, *s.* ornamental marking on the edge of pottery bowl. (Trade mark of the maker.)
Igo, *v.* to stoop down. *See* Haigo.
Igodae, *v.* to throw the head back a little so as to look up at something, as on a verandah.
Igodiho, *v.* to bow one's head; to look down abashed; to bow down; to render homage.
Igodiho haniulato, *s.* a bashful young woman, *a.* chaste.
Igogoita, to visit or send food to sick person.
Igoisi, *v.* to look up.
Igunalaina, *s.* one who leads.
Ihaboulai na, offerings taken to *varo tauna's* house to make gods propitious and cause dugong net to be successful; used now for offering and sacrifice to God.
Ihaboulai na boroma, a sacrifice.
Ihaboulai na pata, an altar.
Ihabou na, same as *ihaboulaina.*
Iha dogoro, brother's son's wife. As *Iha rahai.*
Ihakauna tauna, a leader.
Ihana, *s.* a brother-in-law.
Ihaporoina, Ihopoporana tauna, one who causes scarcity or brings misfortune upon others.
Iharahai, *s.* a cousin by marriage; a man's wife's cousin in his *iharahai* (of opposite sexes).
Ihareha, *s.* an orphan.
Ihareha, *a.* forlorn.
Ihiihi, a nettle.
Ihihira ia, *v.* to spurn, reject.
Ihiria, *v.* to blow with the mouth, as a fire or dust.
Ihoga, *v.* to whistle.
Iholulu, *s.* a boil.
Ihuaihu, *s.* side posts of a house.
Ihuana, *s.* the space between two things, as trees and posts.

Ihuanai, *prep.* between.
Ihui, a netted bag used as a cradle.
Ikau, *s.* the joining of two nets.
Ikahana tauna, *s.* a helper.
Ikahi, pole which keeps down the thatch of roof.
Ikarana tauna, one who makes.
Ikede tauna, one skilled in canoe making.
Ikeroikero, *s.* the fourth, or top row of caulking on large canoes of *lakatoi.*
Ikoautao na, forbidden; also forgiveness.
Ikoda, *s.* a pole along each side of the canoe in *lakatoi,* caulked between it and the canoe.
Ikoko, *s.* uprights driven into the outrigger of a canoe, to which the cross pieces connecting it with the canoe are tied; hence a nail, a screw.
Ikokosi na, covetous, grasping.
Ikokou, *s.* a gateway, a stile.
Ikokou, entrance to lakatoi when palm leaf bulwarks, or small door used as window.
Ikoro tauna, *s.* a skilful canoemaker.
Ikou, *s.* an enclosure, as of mats round a newly made grave, in which the widow stays.
Ikou karaia, *v.* to ripen, as bananas.
Ikoulaina, an enclosure.
Ikumi, *s.* bale, bundle, parcel.
Ikureahu, sill of door.
Ila, *s.* a hatchet.
Ilau (*generally Ilauta*), small quantity of rice, sago, clay, &c.
Ilaha, *s.* deck.
Ilaila na, with *itaia,* to use wisely (of food), not wastefully or carelessly.
Ilapa, *s.* sword.
Ilaqaibo, harlot (indecent word).
Ilata na gado, a tune.
Ilava, *s.* pieces of wood laid across to connect the canoe with the outrigger. In *lakatoi,* cross poles on the top of *ikoda.*
Ileguna, *v.* to watch, to tend.
Iliili, *s.* file.
Ilimo, name of tree and wood of which canoes are generally made.
Ilimoirana, *s.* one kind of hatchet or adze, used after the tree is cut down, and before using the *matapala* or smoothing axe.

Ilua, *adv.* single file (with verb to go) *Ilua lao.*
Iluhai, *v.* to blow down, as the nose, *Udu iluhai.*
Iluhai vareai, to sniff up.
Ilukailuka, crooked, twisted.
Ilulu, track in long grass or shrubs.
Ima, *a.* five. Ima ahui, fifty.
Ima, *s.* the arm (including the hand).
Ima gauna, a weapon.
Ima ganaganana, just above wrist, and measure of that length to tip of middle finger.
Ima helapuroro, to throw out arms vigorously.
Ima honu, handful.
Ima kavakava, empty handed.
Ima laloani tau, contracted from, *ima lalona anina tau,* one who is successful in hunting, &c., fortunate, prosperous.
Ima lalona anina tau, see ima laloani tau.
Ima lauri tauna, left-handed.
Ima loulouna, inside of elbow, and measure of length to top of middle finger.
Ima mauri, mischievous.
Ima mamano, clumsy.
Ima nuana, the lower part of palm of hand.
Ima palapala, the hand; also measure of length.
Ima patapata, to clap the hands.
Ima qagiqagi, finger.
Ima palapala loulouna, inside of wrist joint.
Ima tabuana, thick part of arm between wrist and elbow, measure of length to tip of middle finger.
Ima qagiqagi vagivagina, finger ring.
Ima dava, *s.* a return present, as when a friend gives a spear, and the friend to whom he gives it returns him a knife.
Imaguna, *v.* to begin a quarrel or fight.
Imahalataia, *v.* to help with food or goods when visitors come, or when a marriage, &c., is to be paid for.
Imea, a grove of cultivated trees.
Imodai, *s.* a very large native canoe or ship (*Lakatoi*); renowned, as house, ship, or men.
Imodai, to exalt, magnify, praise.

Imoga, *s.* pain or sickness supposed to be caused by sleeping in the place where visitors have slept the night or two previous. *Idia imogana ai ese e alamai*
Imuda, *s.* a prop used to support bananas in a strong wind; also a prop to a fence.
Imuda, *v.* to prop. *Dui vada imudaia.*
Inā, *interj.* Oh!
Ina, same as *inai*, this.
Ina, address of child to its mother. *Ina e.*
Inai, *pron.*; this, as opposed to *unai*, there; also here; an introduction to a speech.
Inai, *adv.* therefore.
Inai, *s.* enemy.
Ināi, *interj.* (with a rough breathing before I). Behold! What!
Inaio, *interj.* woe be to.
Inamama, address of child to its father and mother; a stranger speaking to a child would say, where are your *inamama*?
Ini *adv.* here, as opposed to *unu*, there; as *Ini mai*, Come here. *Inimai unu lao.* hither and thither.
Inia, as *ini*.
Iniheto, *adv.* like this, so, thus.
Inika, ink. (*Introduced.*)
Inikaratoma, *v.* to act thus.
Inikoautoma, *v.* to speak thus.
Iniseni. *adv.* here.
Initoma, *adv.* thus. Showing at the same time how.
Inu, *v.* to drink.
Inua toho, to taste by drinking.
Io, *adv.* yes.
Io, *s.* a spear.
Iohara, one kind of spear.
Ioheni, *v.* to give a spear to one to kill another with.
Iohururu, *s.* a boil.
Iorimuni, star-shaped stone club.
Ipidi, *s.* a gun, a rifle.
Ipidi anina, a gun charge.
Ipidi nadina, a bullet.
Iqadu, a knot.
Iqadu tauna, a man who has power of sorcery.
Iqahina kara, respectful conduct.
Iqodobe, *s.* a cork, a stopper.
Iqina, *s.* a pillow.
Ira, *s.* hatchet, adze.
Irava, to tidy up, put in order, &c.

Iri, *s.* handsaw.
Irigi, *s.* one kind of coral.
Irohona, one who scatters, destroys, or rubs out.
Iroiro, impatient, *noho iroiro*, impatient to be off.
Irurumata, *s.* tears.
Irutahu na, centre of floor in house, the sacred place where children must not play.
Ise, *s.* tooth. Ise hahedai, to gnash the teeth.
Iseda, as *ita eda.*
Iseise, *s.* gunwale.
Iseisena, *s.* edge, brink.
Isena, *s.* border, brink, edge, hem.
Iseuna tau, one skilful in housebuilding or in directing any work.
Iseuri, *a.* sour, acid, as unripe fruit.
Isi, in composition, up, as *abiaisi*, to take up.
Isi, *s.* wall-plate.
Isia, *v.* to husk a cocoa-nut; to bite off rind of sugar-cane; to break a row of bananas from a bunch.
Isiai, *s.* one who is sent either on a message or to do something.
Isiai manoka, willing, as one sent and not needing to be told twice.
Isiai mero, a servant, see *Hesiai mero.*
Isiai tau, a servant, see *Hesiai tau.*
Isiaina tauna, one who is sent.
Isiaina, *v.* (used with *laoheni*) to serve.
Isidae, *v.* to shout.
Isiriu, *s.* a scarf or join in wood.
Isiva, *s.* a planting stick; a crow bar.
Ita, *pron.* we (including person addressed), us.
Itadara, *s.* mallet for beating out native cloth.
Ita eda, our (inclusive).
Itaita, to look one to another, when told to do a thing, who should get up to do it.
Itahidi, *v.* to choose by inspection.
Itahuna tauna, a searcher.
Ita ia, *v.* to see, to look. The root ita is rarely used except with suff.
Itagu, to look at me.
Itaiatao, to look at steadfastly, to watch.
Itama, *s.* bows of a canoe.
Itauu, *s.* the small lashing at the foot of the mast in the native *lakatoi.*
Itapo, *s.* fan.

Itari, ground plate; *Itari auna*.
Itatauta tauna, one who transgresses.
Itohona (with nahuana), *s.* one who looks after, &c.
Itohona gau, something to test or measure with.
Itohona revareva, a writing copy.
Itoreahu, *s.* lid, of a pot, &c.
Itorena, *s.* writing.
Itorena tauna, a scribe.
Itotohi, *s.* walking-stick; a prop to a house.
Itotohi karaia, *v.* to prop a house.
Ituari, a fish.
Itudobina, *s.* a thing to let down with (followed by varona), a string to draw water with from a well.
Itulu, *s.* small basin with a little knob or leg used to hold the lamp-black for tatooing.
Itutuhina au, a pestle for mashing ripe bananas.
Iubuna, *adj.* (followed by *tauna*), a cherisher, a feeder.
Iuna, *s.* a tail.
Iutuna tauna, *s.* one who cuts down.
Ivadivadi, visitors.
Ivago memerodia, those who are fed by others.
Iva ia, *v.* to cut, as one's finger; to cut up, as a pig; to mutilate; to flay.
Ivirikou, *s.* a reed musical instrument, a flute, a trumpet.
Ivitoto, a hammock.

K

K is pronounced as k in kettle.
Kabaede, to marry another than betrothed.
Kabaia. *See* Gabaia.
Kabana. *See* Gabana.
Kabukabu, one kind of yam.
Kadaha, a strait, channel.
Kadara, *s. See* Gadara.
Kadava, *s.* platform between a double small canoe.
Kadidia, *s.* armpit.
 Kadidia ramuna, hair of the armpit.
Kado a, *v.* to dip up water. *Ranu kadoa*, to shovel.
Kaekae, *s.* a green parrot.
Kaemadahu, *s.* sweet potato.

Kagiu a, *v.* to put an arm round a post, &c.
Kaha, *v.* to help.
Kahai, *v.* to spit for roasting, as Hūla fish.
Kaha na, *s.* side, part of; a district.
Kahau, *s.* claw; nail (finger or toe).
Kāhi, *v.* to be jammed, to be too big to enter.
Kahi, *s.* a fence made with sticks, or split bamboos placed lengthwise, hurdle fence.
Kahi a tao, to press down tight, as thatch with poles lashed.
Kahikahi, *adv.* near, not far.
Kahilakahila, as Kahikahi.
Kahinai kahinai, close at hand, as baggage ready for a start, to call to come close to one.
Kahoda, *a.* soft, well done (of cooked yams).
Kahu a, *v.* to hold in the clenched hand, to hold tight.
Kahu a kubolukubolu, clenched fist.
Kahu a tao, to hold in the clenched hand.
Kahu a nege, *v.* to let go, to part.
Kahugo, one kind of yam.
Kāi, little pieces of wood or grass used as tokens in counting.
Kaia, *s.* a knife. (*Introduced*).
Kaiakiri, one kind of banana.
Kaipu, name of a tree (good redwood).
Kaiva, *s.* a cooking-pot, with a rim for the lid; a shell-fish.
Kaivakuku, a dancing mask; an idol.
Kakabeda, name of a tree.
Kakainege, to stop sucking from surfeit. *Rata kakaianeye*.
Kakakaka, *a.* red; any bright colour, purple.
Kakala, afraid of falling, dizzy.
Kaka na, *s.* elder cousin, elder brother of brother, or sister of sister.
Kakare, white wild pig.
Kake, *s.* sharp ends of a canoe, &c.
Kaki, to stick, as window long closed.
Kakoro, *a.* dry, as withered leaves.
Kalai, *s.* white cockatoo.
Kalaka, *s.* hut; a lean-to; a shelter made for sleeping under.
Kalava, name of small fish little larger than *eu* and caught with them.

Kaleva, *s.* club (wooden).
Kalo, *v.* to paddle.
Kaloa helulu, to compete in paddling.
Kaluhi a. Kaluhiahu, *v.* to put the lid on, to cover up.
Kaluhia gauna, lid.
Kaluhia hebubu, upside down.
Kaluhioho, *v.* to take off the lid or cover.
Kama, term of respect added to name when calling, *Vagi kama e.* (A Kabadi word).
Kamalau na, sound of, as footstep or voice.
Kamea, one kind of banana.
Kamea moa, one kind of banana.
Kamela, *s.* the camel. (*Introduced.*)
Kamika, *s.* *See* Gamiga.
Kamo, *a.* sticky.
Kamo, to gather, as clouds, tree about to fruit, &c.
Kamo tarikatarika, to mark well, as pencil, ink, &c.
Kamo a, *v.* to adhere; to mark well as pencil, paint, &c.
Kamokamo, *s.* that which sticks to the inside of the pot, as when arrowroot has been cooked. *Aniani kamokamo.*
Kamokamo, *s.* a kind of grass resembling wheat.
Kamonai, *interj.* hark!
Kamonai, *v.* to hear; to obey; to believe.
Kamonai, *s.* faith.
Kanigi, very strong stormy trade wind. *Laulabada kanigina.*
Kanudi, *v.* to spit; *s.* spittle.
Kanudi a, *v.* to be spit on.
Kāpa, *s.* frontlet.
Kapa, scaffold on which some feasts are hung.
Kapakapa, *s.* small canoes joined together without space between.
Kapu a tao, *v.*, to press down on.
Kaputi, teacup. (*Introduced.*)
Kara, *v.* (with a suffix, karagu) to catch by contagion.
Kara, *s.* conduct, custom, habit.
Kara dika, sin.
Kara haraga, make haste!
Kara kererekerere tauna, one who errs.
Kára lebulebu tauna, a profligate, dissolute man.

Karagoda, palm from which spears are made; also name of spear made from it.
Karai, *s.* white cockatoo.
Kara ia, *v.* to make, to do.
Karaia diba, can.
Karakara tauna, a worker.
Karaia toho, to endeavour.
Karakara, redress, of *karu*, acts, continued work.
Karakara, *a.* fierce, as a wild pig; quarrelsome (of village or individual).
Karatoma, *v.* to do thus. (Preceded by ini or unu).
Karaudi, *s.* a fish spear with many points; harpoon.
Karikari, *s.* barb of arrow.
Karina, generally with negative. *Asi karina,* contented, quiet.
Karite, *s.* barley. (*Introduced.*)
Karo a, *v.* to divide, when there are many divisions.
Karoa, *s.* a division. *Karoa rua,* to divide in two.
Karoho, *v.* to be scattered, as troops defeated and retreating; to disband. *Karohorohoro.*
Karohu, ridge cap.
Karu, *s.* a young cocoanut (fruit).
Karukaru, *s.* babe.
Karurakaruma, of skin, soft, smooth.
Kasikasi, *s.* hard-cooked sago in cakes; (brought by Elema people from the Gulf).
Kasili, raw, uncooked.
Kasilikasili, dark red-brown colour.
Kasiri, *adv., abia kasiri,* to catch unexpectedly, as fish without a net; to take without wounding.
Kasiri vahoro, untatooed.
Katakata, *s.* (preceded by dala), cross-roads.
Kau, *v.* to reach a place. *Eme kau.* To be in contact. (In composition it is added to verbs of placing, sitting, &c.)
Kau a, *v.* to plait a cocoanut leaf round a tree in order to taboo it.
Kaubebe, *s.* a butterfly.
Kaukau, *a.* dry.
Kaukau, a prickly creeper.
Kāva, *v.* to be out of mind, crazed.
Kāva, *a.* crazed. *Kāva bamona* frantic.
Kavaitoro, a fish.
Kavakava, *s.* folly.

Kavakava, a. foolish, empty, *Hodu karakava*; without purpose; only. *Ranu karakava*, water only.
Kavabu, s. a bottle; a smooth white stone used as a charm; a pearl.
Kavabulubulu, s. eddy.
Kavabukavabu, dim. of kavabu.
Kavarikavari, to scrape smooth and . clean, as bananas, yams, &c. *Naua kavarikavari*.
Kavera, edible mangrove.
Keadi, name of a shell-fish.
Keakakeaka, stiff, as of cloth starched.
Keavaro, name of a tree.
Keboka, s. megapodius. *See* Kepoka.
Kede, s. a torch.
Kede a v. to adze a canoe.
Kehere, s. *See* Kepere.
Keho a, v. to open. (The opposite of *koua*.) To unfasten.
Keho maka, a little way open (as door).
Kei a, v. to roll over and over, as a heavy box.
Kei a tao, to be struck by a stone rolling down a mountain side.
Keikei, s. a small cooking-pot.
Keke a, v. to coil (as a rope on the deck).
Kekeni, s. girl. (Kenikeni at . Kapakapa, &c.)
Kekenikekeni, s. diminutive of kekeni.
Kekerema, name of a shell fish.
Kekero, to be stupefied, as fish with *duha*; to be drunk.
Kelero, to cast lots. *(Introduced.)*
Kema, s. the name of a bird, a coot.
Kemaiore, one kind of yam.
Keme, s. the chest.
Kemerosi, v. to fold the arms on chest.
Keni, to float (of wood, &c.)
Kenidae, to rise to surface and float.
Kepere, a cocoanut shell; hence, any small vessel for holding liquid; also with *adj*. of kind, for plates and other crockery.
Kepilakepila, crooked; similar to *gagevagageva*.
Kepoka. *See* Keboka.
Kepokepomu, with *taia hedalo*, v. to disbelieve.
Keporāi, v. to turn away the head from one speaking. (A sign of disapproval.)

Kepulu, a. blind.
Kerehai, to turn round.
Kerekere, s. sun nearly down. *Dina kerekere*.
Kerenoi e vara, born small and prematurely.
Kerenakerena, small.
Kerepa, s. small native ship, consisting of four or five *asi*.
Kerere, a. something in the eye. *Mata kerere*.
Kererekerere, v. to do a thing carelessly, heedlessly, without authority; to blunder; to err.
Keri, accumulation of drift, brought down by current or flood.
Keroro, name of a tree.
Keru, a. cold; fever and ague. *(Introduced meaning.)*
Kerukeru, adv. to-morrow.
Kerukeru, s. shade.
Kerukeru, a shady (of place).
Keruma, Kerumakeruma, a. as Keru, cold. (Generally used of food.)
Kesi, s. a shield.
Ketara, s. fresh cocoa-nut oil, without water added; the same cooked as sauce.
Keto, v. to slip; to fall.
Keto dele, to slip or fall sideways.
Kevau, s. rainbow.
Kevakeva, name of a shell-fish.
Kevakulu, name of a shell-fish.
Kevaru, s. lightning.
Kevaru a isi, v. to lighten. From Kevaru.
Ki, a key. *(Introduced.)*
Ki karaia, to lock.
Kiamakiama, s. aglow (as embers); bright.
Kiapa, s. native netted bag.
Kibi, s. a quail; a shell trumpet.
Kibo, s. a large round basin.
Kibobo, small hole in end of canoe where heart of wood was.
Kibokibo, s. a small basin.
Kibulu, s., a carved cocoanut shell pot with cover, for holding oil or fat.
Kida ia diho, to throw down on ground.
Kidului, s. porpoise.
Kikina badana, old and young, big and little. *Kikina badana baoma*.
Kikitaka, knobbed stone club.
Kila, a fish.
Kilara. *See* Kirara.

Kili. *See* Kiri.
Kili, *s.* sinkers to fishing-net.
Kilima, name of a tree.
Kiloki, *s.* the name of a bird, a parrakeet.
Kimai, *s.* a hook.
Kimagoi, *v.* to rob; to steal continually (a term of abuse).
Kimore, Kimorekimore, *a.* bright; polished.
Kinigohina, *s.* early morning light, before the sun appears. (Preceded by *daba.*)
Kinigohina, used in praising a man and comparing him to morning light. *In vairana daba kini gohina na heto.*
Kinoa, to shoot an arrow.
Kinokino, *s.* a vane; streamer.
Kio, *s.* muliebria.
Kipa, midrib of sago frond.
Kipara, *s.* a scar.
Kirara, *v.* to open.
Kirara, *s.* an attentive ear.
Kiri, *v.* to laugh; used also of fruit ripening, as *buatau*; also of surf breaking on a reef. *I'ada e kirinu.*
Kirikirilaia, to laugh at.
Kiriagaibogaibo, name of a shellfish.
Kirima, one kind of mangrove.
Kiririkiriri, *s.* a chrysalis.
Kiroki, *s.* the name of a small parrot. *Kiloki.*
Kiroro, to inflate.
Kisikisi, name of a bird (he spurwinged plover).
Kisiri, with *taia*, discharging ear.
Kito, *v.* to watch, as for an enemy or a thief; to spy; to guard.
Kito a, *v.* to swoop down and pick up, as a hawk.
Kitokara, *s.* black cockatoo.
Kiulai, to turn back suddenly in anger. *Laka kiulai.*
Koau, *s.* the cause. *Oiemu koau, you are the cause. Lau koauyu, &c.*, always of wrong-doing.
Ko, to shout from a distance, ending in a cooey.
Koau, *v.* to speak.
Koau a tao, to forbid; to forgive;
Pl. koaudiatao.
Koauahu, to forbid.
Koautubu, to counteract; to frustrate; to withstand.

Koauedeede, to be disobedient; to refuse to do as told; to be unwilling.
Koaubou, to concur; to agree.
Koauhamata, to promise.
Koau hemurihemuri, to refuse.
Koaukau, *s.* a message; an errand.
Koaukava koaukava, to guess.
Koaukoau, to growl; to scold.
Koaulaia, to be spoken of; to confess; to bear witness.
Koau laloalaloa, to praise with the view of getting something; to cajole.
Koau maoro, to say good-bye to friends before starting on voyage or journey.
Koaulai a anina anina, to speak from knowledge; with authority.
Koaulai a utuutu, to speak without knowing perfectly; without authority.
Koautao. *See* Koauatao.
Koautoma, to speak thus. (Preceded by *ini* or *unu.*)
Koautora tauna, churlish.
Koautorehai, to borrow; to have on credit.
Koauna, *s.* the cause. *See* Koau.
Kobi, *s.* a needle; the name of a fish.
Kobiokobio, to shave head close.
Kobo, Kobokobo, *s.* the firefly.
Kobo, *v.* to sprout.
Koda, *s.* a man-catcher (a weapon used by Hula natives); a pig-net.
Koda, net in which fish are sometimes boiled.
Koda, tack, of sail, native rope.
Koda, a burden of firewood. *Au kodana.*
Kodaia, to boil in a net.
Kodu, to cease, of wind.
Koe, *s.* a small bag net, shorter than *daqai.*
Koea, *v.* to be turned end for side, to be turned half round.
Koeahilihili, whirlwind.
Koekoe, *s.* loins, hip, waist.
Koekoe torana, belt over hips.
Koekoe. *See* Goegoe
Koge, *s.* a projecting point on a roof; pinnacle.
Kogurogu, *s.* domestic fowl.
Kogurogu, *v.* to be proud, boastful.
Kohe, name of a tree.

Kohena, *s.* a priest. (From the Hebrew).
Kohi, one kind of yam.
Kohia, *v.* to break (of hard things).
Kohoro, *s.* tower.
Kohu, *v.*, to be wrecked; broken to pieces (of a house).
Kohu, *s.* property; wealth; riches.
Kohudia, booty.
Kohu dobi, to pour down as rain.
Kohua, *s.* a cave; also large hole in end of canoe where heart was.
Kohutania, *v.* to leave, desert, as a village, on account of sickness.
Koi a, *v.* to betray, to cheat, to mislead.
Koikoi, *v.* to lie.
Koikoi, *s.* a lie.
Koikoi, *a.* untrue.
Koke, *v.* to creak.
Kokia, *v.* to draw out; to extract; to gather by breaking stalk.
Koki a oho, *v.* to uncork, &c.; to unstring a bow.
Koko, *s.* a baler of wood.
Kokoa, *v.* to nail; to drive in, as a nail; to grip ground, as anchor.
Kokoauru, *v.* to break open a cocoanut for drinking.
Kokoara, a native package of sago, weighing 30 or 40 lb.
Kokokoko, *s.* the cassowary.
Kokome, one kind of banana.
Kokopa, *s.* a crab.
Kokorogu, one kind of yam.
Kokosi, *v.* to gather together, collect.
Kokosi a, *v.* to keep intact. *See* Gogosia.
Komata gui, *s.* low water.
Komoge, *s.* the peak of a mountain top; the top of a tower, spire, &c.
Komu, *v.* to hide.
Komukau, a bud.
Komukomu (preceded by *ae*), an ankle.
Komuta, *s.* a hill rising from plain. *Orooro komuta.*
Komutu, *s.* the core of a boil.
Konaka, *s.* the name of a bird.
Kone, *s.* the beach, the sea-coast.
Kopa, region between navel and chest.
Kopai a, *v.* to skin.
Kopi, *s.* the skin; surface of the earth, sea, &c.
Kopi auka, *s.* a fearless climber, &c.; indifferent to cold, &c.

Kopi hemarai, *v.* to be ashamed.
Kōpi, a dagger.
Kopukopu, *s.* mud, swamp.
Korema, *a.* any dark colour, brown, black.
Korema, *s. bêche de mer.*
Koremakorema, *a.* black.
Kori a, *v.* to bite, to gnaw, to sting.
Korikori, *a.* true, real, original, native, genuine.
Koroa, *v.* to break off twigs or blaze trees, so as to mark the road; to carve, to notch.
Koroha, a short spear.
Kororo, *v.* to subside, as water.
Kororokororo, *a.* all (generally used with mate).
Korua, one kind of yam.
Kou a, *v.* to enclose; to block, as a road; to close, as a door; to fasten, to shut.
Kouahu, *v.* as Koua.
Kouaka, *s.* the name of a bird.
Koukou, *s.* outside shell or hard covering. *Niu koukouna.*
Koukou, name of a tree.
Koukou rereva, sea snake.
Koupa, *s.* a chasm; a ditch.
Koura, *s. See* Goura.
Kove, black wallaby.
Kuadi, name of a shell-fish.
Kuarakuara, *v.* to froth, as a fast boiling pot.
Kuomenau, the name of a shell-fish.
Kubabakubaba, fat, round.
Kubolukubolu, *a.* globular, round.
Kuboukubou (with verb, to dwell), peaceably, amicably.
Kudekude, a long grass.
Kudima, *a.* deaf.
Kudou, *s.* the heart (physical).
Kudou hetaha, consternation.
Kuhi, *s.* a skin disease (frambœsia).
Kuhikuhi, *s.* a painful skin disease, with intense itching.
Kui a, to knead.
Kuku, *s.* tobacco.
Kuku ania, to smoke.
Kuku, *v.* to go to stool.
Kuluha, name of a tree.
Kumi a, *s.* to wrap; enfold.
Kunamaka, *s.* the name of a bird.
Kunu, *v.* to be satisfied (always used with *boka*).
Kunu, *s.* anus; keel of a ship, &c.
Kunu haraga, willing, obedient.

Kunu metau, unwilling, slow to obey.
Kunu rahubou, to slap buttocks in defiance.
Kunukunu, name of a shell-fish.
Kunuiabiahuna, s. the last born.
Kunukakunuka, adv. of intensity, added to verbs signifying to tie, to close, &c.; a. secure.
Kurea, v. to turn over.
Kureaoho, to roll away.
Kureadobi, to drop down from one's hand.
Kureahu, to turn over.
Kurea lao, See Ehona
Kureatao, v. to be struck by a large mass, as a landslip; to be overwhelmed by it.
Kurebou, s. a heap of stones, yams, &c.
Kuri. See Guri.
Kurita, a little water, oil, &c. See Gurita.
Kurokakuroka, a. pale.
Kurokuro, a. white.
Kuroro, v. to inflate, to swell, to distend.
Kuru, v. to run at the nose.
Kururu, the name of a shell-fish.
Kurukuru, s. long grass used for thatching.
Kurukuruna, s. snout.
Kusita, one kind of banana.

L

L is sounded as in English.
La, a prefix to five when counting persons. Laima.
Laba, s. an ornament of a house or ship, to fly in the wind. The distinguishing mark of the Mavara family.
Lababana, a. wide, as cloth, road, &c.
Lababana, s. breadth.
Labana, v. to hunt.
Labana cno, to go hunting, and sleep out.
Labolabo, s. wild bee.
Labolabo bata ranuna, wild honey
Ladaia, to strike camp.
Ladaiaisi, to lead singing.
Lādā, s. gills.
Lada na, s. name.

Lade, s. one kind of coral.
Ladi, a fish.
Lado, to bear down as in labour, to bow the head in dance.
Lado henia, } v. to assent by a sign,
Lado tari, } a nod.
Ladorāi, to nod from sleepiness.
Lāga, s. an earthquake; the name of a month (September).
Lāga, v. to breathe.
Lagaani, lit. to eat one's breath, to rest. Laga takes suffixes.
Lagadae, to pant.
Lagadobu, to be long-winded.
Lagaga, to be frightened, nervous, not speak from fear.
Laganege, to breathe stertoriously, as a dying person.
Lagatuna, a. breathless.
Lagadaelagadae, v. to pant, to sob.
Lagāi, s. the name of a fish.
Lagalaga, name of a shell-fish.
Lagalaga, region just below armpit.
Lagani, s. year.
Lagatuna, s. dyspnœa, short-winded.
Lagāu a, s. disrespect.
Lagere, a fish.
Lagigi, to shout (of one person).
Lagugu, ears stunned, ringing, as from blow, or gun report.
Laguta, s. salt-pans.
Laha, s. large native ship, consisting of ten or twelve asi.
Lahai, s. subordinate, opposed to korikori, real; hence, with Tama it means uncle, and so with all relationships; with chief, friend, &c.
Lahai a, v. to spread a cloth, mat, &c.; to strew.
Lahalaha, the name of a fish.
Lahara, s. north-west wind, and season.
Laharai a, to prepare large sail of lakatoi, by renewing strings, patching, &c.
Lahedo, v. to be lazy.
Lahedo, a. lazy.
Laheta, a fish.
Lahi, s. fire. Lahi alaia, a burn. Lahi hururuhururu, a flame.
Lahi āuna, fuel.
Lahi dairi ariana, feast for mourners, grave-diggers, &c.
Lahui, ignorant, unenlightened.
Lahui tauna, a heathen, an ignorant benighted man.

Lahulahu, *adv.* imperfectly (with verb, to hear).
Lāi, *s.* breeze, wind.
Laia, name of a shell-fish.
Laia, *v.* to get ready a large canoe for a voyage.
Lailai a, to prepare, to clear the road.
Laia, postfixed to verbs to mark the instrument.
Laiabou, to transfix.
Laiaisi, to keep boat or canoe off shore with pole, head to sea.
Laikolaiko, to shake, stagger under heavy weight.
Lailai, *s.* the name of a month (March).
Laima, *a.* five (men).
Laina, name of a shell-fish.
Laka *v.* to step, to walk, to go.
Laka aheveri, to walk in line, to march.
Laka diho, to go down to the bottom of the water feet first. (Opp. to *edui*, to dive.) *Davara lalona lakadiho.*
Lakadua lakadua, to walk with fear, as of ghosts, troops, &c.
Laka haheguna, to walk in single file.
Laka heidiroro, to walk several abreast.
Laka hekako, to walk side by side, with linked fingers or joined hands.
Laka hekapu, to walk side by side.
Laka henia, to go to or after someone.
Laka ia hanai, to walk past.
Laka helada, to walk stealthily.
Laka hetaoahu hetaoahu, to come or go unwillingly, hesitatingly.
Laka kahila, to draw near.
Laka kava, friendless.
Laka kerere, to lose oneself, to mistake the road.
Laka lasi, to go outside, to walk out.
Laka magigi, to walk gingerly, as on a tree over a stream.
Laka magogomagogo, to slink.
Laka metailametaila, to saunter.
Laka muri, backwards; to walk backwards.
Laka roho, to take long steps, to stride along.
Laka siri, to step aside.
Lakatania, to be left, left behind.

Lakatao lakatao, to show disrespect to a gentleman by walking in front of.
Lakatua, to walk backwards.
Lakatoi, *s.* a ship, a native vessel, made by lashing three or more large canoes together.
Lakatoi anina, freight.
Lakatoi tauna, captain.
Lakatoi gabana, side of ship.
Lakatoi vairana, bows of ship.
Lakara, *s.* a whale, or some sea monster larger than a dugong.
Lakara donodono, as Lakara.
Laketo, the name of a shell-fish.
Laki a, to draw a pipe. *See also* Rakia.
Lakolako. *See* Rakorako.
Laku a, to mend fire.
Laku a dae, to push in firewood when end is burnt off.
Lala, woman's brother's children, woman's mother's brother, a father's sister.
Lalo, *s.* the inside; the mind.
Lalo a *v.* to think, to remember.
Lalo na, the inside of a thing; the mind, the seat of the affections.
Laloani, to desire.
Lalo auka, to be self restrained, fearless.
Lalo e ani, to be persuaded or to persuade another, *Lalogu eme ania*. *Lalona name ania.*
Lalo hadaga, to consider, to devise, to encourage one's self.
Lalo duhu, a virgin, male or female, literally, a desireless mind.
Lalo hadaia, to consider, to think
Lalo haguhi, to cogitate.
Lalo haraga, to desire a thing from seeing, or to do a thing because others are doing it.
Lalo hereqa, to forget.
Lalo hesigu, perturbed, worried disheartened.
Lalona keru, comforted, pacified.
Lalo hakerua, to comfort, console, pacify.
Laloalu, to cloy.
Lalo a tao, to bear in mind, to treasure up in the mind and wait for an opportunity of revenge; to keep a thing to oneself, to keep a secret.
Laloatao, *adj.* secret.
Laloboio, to forget.

Lalo bubu, hymen irrupt. With kekeni, a virgin.
Laloharaga, v. to do cheerfully, willingly. See above.
Lalohegani, to desire from seeing. Lalogu hegani. Laloyu hahegania.
Lalokau, to be beloved, endeared ; (of things or food) to be satisfied, or have pleasure in.
Lalokau henia, v. to love, to delight in.
Lalokoau, to think, to conjecture.
Lalometau, to do unwillingly.
Lalouamo tauna, cheerful.
Laloparara, to be intelligent, to understand.
Lalo qani, int. of surprise, disdain.
Lalo siahu, angry.
Lalo tamona, to agree.
Lalumi a, to wet hard ground.
Lamaboha, s. bald head.
Lama hehuhu, bald head.
Lama kepere, bald on top of head.
Lamadaia, v. to wipe off mud from the feet, &c.
Lamanu, s. resin washed ashore, used when burnt as lamp-black for tattooing.
Lamari, to leave a trail, as turtle on beach.
Lamepa, s. a lamp. (Introduced.)
Lanalana, v. to stammer.
Lao, s. a fly.
Lao, v. to go.
Laoahu, to stop, to turn back, to prevent.
Laoevaeva, to go about from place to place.
Laohai a, to take away, to clear away.
Laoheni, to render, to give to.
Laoho, s. preceded by doru, humpback.
Laolao, s. a journey.
Laorea, to be mindful of. See Helaorealaia.
Laoreana, something for person or thing of which subject is mindful. Sabati laoreana aniani benai.
Laorealai a, to think of some one so as to stop from fishing or go hunting on his account. God was mindful (laorealaida) of us, and gave His Son, &c.

Lapai a v. to strike as with a sword or flat weapon.
Lapaiaoho, to smite off.
Lāqa, s. flax, from which small fishing-nets (reke) are made.
Laqa, food for voyage or journey.
Laqa, to graze (as leg).
Laqai, to heap, to place firewood previous to lighting.
Laqahia, v. to strike in falling, as the head, arm, &c.
Lara, s. a large mat sail of lakatoi ; a ship's sail.
Lara, v. to move about while sitting, by propelling with the hands.
Laralara, s. the bottom row of chalking in the native ship (lakatoi).
Larelarelarea, v. to jet out, as blood ,from a cut artery. (Indecent word.)
Larea, to adjust arrow on string.
Lareba, v. to build up stones. Nadi larebaia.
Lari, s. rash, as in measles.
Laria, Raria, s. fine sand.
Laro, s. one kind of shell-fish ; the shell is used for cutting and paring, &c.
Laro a, v. to wait for, to expect.
Laro a, to be lifted and carried away, as canoe by flood, &c.
Larolaro, s. shoulder-blade.
Larolaro, battens on roof lengthways
Lasi, v. to arrive.
Lasi, adv. no ; not.
Lasi, adv. (the a is slightly shorter than in the negative) outside, as to walk outside, pull outside, &c. Lasilaia.
Lasihi a, v. to be gone, disappear ; Pl. Lasihidia.
Lasi henia, v. to receive visitors with respect.
Lasihi, v. to be finished and gone, as a year. Eme lasihi.
Lasikalasika (geme), inflated chest.
Lasilāi, s. wind from between north and east.
Lasiatao, to come upon, overtake.
Lāta, s. length.
Lāta, a. tall.
Lataba, name of a tree.
Lataia, v. to condemn to death some one who is absent. Also, Rataia.
Latalata, a. long, tall.
Latana, s. the top side, on the top of.
Latanai, prep. on. Also, adv.
Lau, pron. I.

Lauagu, *pron.* my (of food.)
Laubada, one kind of mangrove.
Lauegu, *pron.* my.
Laugogo, *s.* leaf of banana cut with the fruit,—a superstitious ceremony.
Laugogogogo, to gather a lot of things together, to grab selfishly.
Laulau, *s.* a shadow, a spirit; a photograph; a picture, image.
Laulabada, *s.* south-east monsoon.
Laulabada kahana, *a.* south-east.
Lauma, *s.* a spirit; formerly used only of ghosts of those killed, who appeared in terrible form.
Laumaere, a fish.
Laumadaure, *v.* to be startled, surprised, to be confounded.
Laumea, *v.* to mend nets.
Laura, cone-shaped piece of wood, used to plug hole in end of canoe.
Lauri, *a.* left (hand).
Lāva, *s.* a message sent to warn a village of an arranged attack. *Lāva Koiari e mailaia.*
Lava, *s.* joists.
Lavara, *s.* a large serpent.
Lave, *s.* halyard (of ship).
Lavu, *s.* a mallet.
Lebulebu, *s.* boisterous, unseemly mirth.
Lebulebu, *v.* to make mirth of any one, to make fun of.
Lebulebu tauna, a profligate, dissolute man.
Lega haraga, *v.* to be quick in doing things, or in coming and going.
Lega haraga, *adv.*, quickly.
Lega metau, *v.* to be slow in doing things.
Legu, Legulegu, *v.* to tend, take care of, as a sick person, animal, goods, &c.
Legua, to nurse sick person, to tend.
Leilei, *s.* a board.
Leilei abiaoho ariana, feast for dead, when boards are taken away from grave.
Lele, *v.* to swim, as fish.
Lelealelea, *adv.*, with verb to dwell, to go from place to place, not stay long in any place.
Lepeta, *s.* farthing. (*Intro. from the Greek.*)
Leta, *s.* cocoa-nut leaf.
Lili a, *v.* to grate, as yams.

Lo, *a.* ripe, mature, also of human beings, full grown.
Lo, to be comforted.
Loa, *v.* to walk about.
Loa evaeva, to walk about.
Loa magogomagogo, to walk about in shrinking, sneaking fashion.
Loa rere, to roam, not stay at home.
Loalai a, to walk about with, as with a sick child.
Lobu, *s.* the name of a fish, grey mullet. *See* Robu.
Lodu or Lotu, a fishing term, to take net round so as to enclose fish.
Loduhenia, *v.* to accuse, to reproach.
Loge. *See* Roge.
Logea tauna, or rogea tauna, *s.* an industrious man, one who stores.
Logologo, *v.* to talk imperfectly, as a young child.
Logora, *a.* the whole of, many. (Used of numbers.) Great, all.
Lohala, *s.* the edge of a net. *Uto lohala,* the top edge. *Kili lohala,* the bottom edge. The small line which fastens the two edges together.
Lohia, *s.* a chief.
Lohiabada, chief, a gentleman, a courteous term of address.
Lohia lahai, a chief who has been appointed, or who acts in place of real chief.
Lohilohi. *See* Gado lohilohi.
Lohilohia, *v.* to bubble up.
Lokaloka, *a.* ripe, mature; stiff.
Lōki, *s.* pain in the limbs, rheumatism.
Lokohu, *s.* the name of a bird, *Paradisea raggiana.*
Lokoru, *s.* the spine at the back of the neck.
Loku, papaw tree and fruit. (*Introduced.*)
Loku a, *v.* to double up, to fold, to roll up.
Lolo, *v.* to shut out, to call out in a loud voice, to brawl.
Lolodagu, to startle by shouting.
Lorekaloreka, pliant, flexible.
Loria, *v.* to vomit, to throw up.
Lou, *adv.* again.
Lou, *v.* to return.
Loulaia, to take back.
Loulou, *adv.* constantly.
Loulou, *s.* spathe enclosing the cocoa-nut blossom.

Loulai a, *v.* to restore.
Lovai, one kind of yam.
Love, *s.* a swing.
Love, *v.* to swing.
Lulu a, *v.* to drive away, to banish.
Lulu a oho.
Luludoa, to arrive too late.
Lulululu, to drive away continuously.
Lulu a, *v.* to put on the shell armlet.

M

M pronounced as in English.
Ma, before verbs, marking continued action.
Ma, and, another, used with *ta* (one) as, *ma ta.* another.
Mabau, *s.* the pouch of a marsupial.
Mabui, a fish.
Madaimadai, *a,* giddy.
Madava and Madavamadava, smooth sheltered place for anchorage.
Madi be, *conj.* because.
Madimadi, *adv.* with *hereva,* to speak to one quietly by himself, not angrily.
Madinamo, plenty (of food), good harvest.
Madina, one kind of yam.
Mādu, *s.* opening.
Maduna, *s.* a burthen, with the carrying pole ; *plu. madunadia.*
Maela, *s.* the name of a fish.
Maeta, *v.* to be done, of things cooked.
Māga, *a.* brackish.
Magadimagadi, *adv.* tremblingly, fearfully.
Magani, *s.* the wallaby.
Maganibada, *s.* ridge-pole.
Magasi, *s.* very low night tide.
Māge, *a.* ripe, as bananas.
Magela, *s.* a spider.
Magemage, *s.* the name of a bird ; also a colour, deep orange.
Magi, name of a tree.
Magigi, to be in awe, to submit to, to render homage and obedience. *Ia magigina e magigi.*
Magigi, *adv.* gingerly, carefully.
Magogo and Magogomagogo, crouching along in an ashamed shy manner.
Magu, *s.* fortress.
Magugu, *a.* creased, wrinkled.

Magugu, *v.* to crease, to wrinkle.
Maho, *s.* yam.
Maho kavabu, *s.* a smooth stone used as a charm, to make yams grow.
Mahu, to slaughter, as wallaby, pigs, or men, *e mahudia.*
Mahuta, *v.* to sleep. Mahuta tauna, sluggard.
Mahuta gauna, a bed.
Mahuta maragi, to slumber.
Mai, *conj.* and, with.
Mai, *v.* to come.
Mailai a, to bring.
Maihenia, to fetch.
Mai, prefixed to nouns or pronouns signifies possession, as *Ia mai ira,* he has a hatchet.
Mai bokana, cowardly, afraid.
Mai bokana tauna, a coward.
Maiali or Maiari, *s.* white feather head-dress.
Maikumaiku, *a.* very small.
Mailu, *s.* evening twilight.
Mailumailu, *s. See* Mairumairu.
Maimera, a fish.
Mainu, small (of thread, &c.)
Mainumaimu, *a.* very small ; wasted by sickness.
Maino, *s.* peace.
Mairihae, fresh water tortoise.
Mai**a**, *s.* mother-of-pearl.
Mairiveina, *s.* the East.
Mairumairu, *s.* dusk.
Maita, name of a tree. (Rose apple.)
Māka, *s.* a crack, notch, as in the edge of a knife, a crevice.
Māka, *v.* to be broken, as a hole in a fence.
Makoa, a fish.
Makohi, *v.* to break, as crockery.
Makohi, haraga, *a.* brittle.
Makona and Mokona, *adv.* almost, all but.
Mokota, one kind of yam.
Mala, *s.* tongue.
Mala reho, *s.* the thrush.
Mala *s.* edible stem of banana.
Mala harerea, to shout out with loud voice in reading or counting.
Mala iharerena tauna, a loud-voiced man in counting, reading, &c.
Malamala *adj.* with *nadi,* flat, smooth, like paving stone.
Maladoke, to speak imperfectly, to substitute one consonant for another.

Malakamalaka, *adv.* patiently, persistently, carefully.
Malamala, *s.* food generally.
Malamala, *s.* wide platform at the end of *lakatoi*.
Malaua, *s.* the name of a fish.
Maleva, name of very large shark.
Maloa, *v.* to drown, to founder.
Maloa, one kind of yam.
Malohevani, *s.* about 10 o'clock at night.
Malokihi, *s.* midnight.
Malo kohia, a little after midnight.
Mama e! child's term of address to his father.
Mama, jealous (sexual).
Mama, a mouthful chewed such as babies are fed with. *Aniani mamadia.*
Mamana, light from lamp or fire at a distance.
Mamano, name of place where bad spirits are and where all unpierced noses go.
Mamano, *a.* weak, from sickness.
Mami, *s.* spoil; prey, as on returning from fishing, &c. *Idia e mami.*
Māmi, *s.* the name of a fish.
Mami. Mamina, *s.* flavour (of food). *Lau mamia toho ia mamina namo.*
Mami, to fall off, as bananas, blighted and unfit for food.
Mami na, a thrill, sensation, feeling, *Mamina* e abia, also of pain, *Taugu mamina name abia.*
Mamoe, *s.* sheep. (*Introduced*).
Mamu, *s.* the thigh.
Manada, *v.* to be accustomed to, to be tame.
Manada, *a.* even, smooth, gentle.
Manadamanada, to be smooth, tame.
Manada tauna, a good-tempered man.
Managa, *s.* land far away from the village.
Managi, *s.* the name of a fish.
Manahala, *s.* the name of a fish.
Manahuromanahuro, a pale green colour.
Manariha, a fish.
Manau, *a.* humble. Manau tauna, lowly.
Manaumanau tauna, shy, slow of speech.
Mane, a shoal of fish. *Robu maneana.*
Manea, to knead in hands, so as to break lumps.

Mani, prefix to many verbs in the present tense, *Lau mani baina itaia.* Sometimes it has the meaning of, to try, *Oi mani a karaia.*
Manoka. Manokamanoka, *a.* weak, cowardly, lazy; of things weak, soft.
Manokamanoka tauna, coward.
Manonoha, one kind of yam.
Manori, *v.* to faint, to be fatigued.
Mānu, *s.* a bird.
Manu rumana, nest.
Manumanu, *s.* beetles, insects; the name of a stinging fish.
Manumaura, *s.* the name of a month (October).
Mao, *s.* gums.
Maoa tauna, *s.* passenger; also, Gui maoa tauna.
Maoaia, *v.* to go as passenger.
Maoheni, *v.* to betroth.
Maora, *s.* bowstring.
Maoro, Maoromaoro, *a.* straight correct.
Mapau. *See* Mabau.
Mara, *v.* to give birth.
Maragi, *a.* small. Maragimaragi slender.
Marai, *v.* to wither; to be exhausted either from work or disease; to be parched by the sun.
Maramara, *s.* umbrella-shaped rock in the sea and on the reef.
Mararoto hahine, suckling woman whose infant is young.
Maraua, *a.* striped.
Maraua, a fish.
Mare a, to pull down as young tree, to bend a bow, &c.
Marere, *a.* bent, slanting.
Marere, of tide, just turned to flow. *Davara e mareremu.*
Mari, *s.* ceremony of cracking fingers to know if a vessel (*lakatoi*) is coming.
Marimari, a sign of some coming calamity.
Mari tauna, one skilled in doing *mari*.
Mariboi, *s.* bat.
Mariva, *s.* after-pains.
Marota, marotamarota, soft feeling, as cloth.
Maroto, marked with pattern, as back from lying on mat.
Maruane, *s.* the male sex, occasional plural, mamaruane.
Mata, *s.* bandicoot.

Mata, *s.* the eye ; point of anything; mesh.
Mata bodaga, to have connection with many women.
Mata bodaga tauna, a lascivious man.
Mata digina, corner of eye.
Mata dika, lascivious.
Mata gani, to take warning.
Mata ganigani, covetous, greedy.
Mata gara, very large mesh.
Mata garaia, sleepy.
Mata gegeva, to squint.
Mata gunina, inner corner of eye.
Mata hanai, second sight.
Mata kani. *See* Mata gani.
Mata kito tauna, quick sighted.
Mata hisihisi, ophthalmia.
Mata kepulu, blind.
Mata lahulu, light coloured eyes.
Mata madaimadai, giddy.
Mata nadinadi, the pupil of the eye.
Mata nuana, middle of eye.
Mata paia, to dazzle.
Mata papa, to look pleased, to welcome.
Mata ranuka, watery eyes.
Mata rauna, eye-lashes.
Mata taia, *v.* to sleep a little when very tired.
Mata valilo, squinting eye.
Mataatu, name of a shell-fish.
Mataboi, *s.* a large rope.
Matabudi, *s.* turtle.
Matadidi, *s.* a whitlow, a painful gathering on the hand.
Mataia, *v.* to tie, to fasten.
Matakaka, a fish.
Matakamataka, sharp, as claws.
Matakamataka, *adv.* with walking or running, to arrive first.
Matalahui, to be heedless, careless.
Matalahui, *adj.* careless, heedless.
Matama, beginning, newly.
Matamaia, *v.* to begin.
Matamata, *a.* new, fresh.
Matana, *s.* tip.
Matana, point, direction, subject, as *Hereva matana.*
Matana tauna, keen sighted.
Matana hagani a, to punish so as to reform.
Matana dika, *v.* to be overcast to windward.
Matanimatani, indifferent, as to food given, to do a thing without interest.

Matapala, a stone hatchet, large and broad.
Matau, grave, sedate.
Matauna, *s.* respect, reverence.
Mataurai, Mataurata, *v.* to respect, reverence.
Mate, *v.* to die.
Mate diba lasi, immortal.
Mate gauna, venomous.
Mate, *adv.* of intensity, as *tahua mate.*
Mate anitu, to die from disease, not a violent death.
Matekamateka, languidly.
Matelea, *v.* to faint.
Matemate, used as an intensive with hebiri, hesede, &c.
Mate mauri, look alive !
Matoatorea, (of moon) about third quarter.
Matohu, of tide, or current, slack.
Matokana, also Matono, " just so," " let be," " we shall see."
Mātu, *s.* a hole, a channel.
Matu na, *s.* orifice.
Maūa, *s.* box.
Maula, or Maura, *s.* a small thing, as a spoon, netted bag, &c., given as a pledge to remind the recipient of his promise to return to same house, a token that the messenger who brings it has been sent by owner.
Maulu, *v.* to make a hole, as in the skull, *hodu,* &c. ; to be spoilt.
Maumau, *v.* to grumble, to complain.
Māumāu, with *habou,* to have things at hand, ready for a start.
Maura. *See* Maula.
Mauri, *s.* life.
Mauri bada, luxuriant.
Mauri bou, cousins on both sides.
Mauri dudu, cousins on both sides.
Mauri maragimaragi, convalescent.
Mauri rohoroho, to grow luxuriantly.
Mava, *s.* white matter on the body of a newborn infant; green on bottom of boat.
Mavamava, *v.* to yawn.
Mavaru, a dance.
Mavaru, *v.* to dance.
Me, particle added to vowel of past time, as *name, eme,* &c. It is also used with other particles, but does not seem to add to their meaning.
Mea, superhuman power, as possessed by sorcerers.

Mea tauna, a sorcerer who has cursing power.
Meamea, *s.* incantation, prayer. Always in a bad sense, to bring misfortune, trouble, or death on the subject of it.
Mede, *s.* the temples.
Medu, *s.* rain.
Medu baroko, rain in big drops, painful to the skin.
Mei, *s.* urine.
Mei, to pass water, pass *Meilia.*
Memeuse, *s.* chip.
Memehute, *s.* a fish.
Meqa, *s.* bread-fruit kernel.
Mereki, plate or dish. Rarotongan word.
Mero, *s.* a boy. Plural, memero. Mero karukaru, a male infant. Meromero, dimin. of mero. Mero bamona, boyish.
Metai, shelter.
Metai, *v.* to shelter.
Metai gabuna, *s.* haven.
Metailametaila, *adv.* carefully, deliberately.
Metsilametaila, *a.* cautious, deliberate.
Metau, *a.* heavy, arduous.
Meuraba, one kind of banana.
Mia, *v.* to leave, to allow. Pl., mimia.
Mia hanaihanai, to continue, to last.
Mia prefixed to nouns or adjectives diminishes the quantity or quality, as *mia bada*, not very big, *mia korema*, black, but not very.
Miara, *s.* female kangaroo.
Mida, a fish.
Midava, *s.* a grave, after boards, &c., have been removed.
Migu, *s.* the echidna.
Mikamika, a intensive word used with *Herea.*
Mimia, *v.* Plural of Mia.
Minagaminaga, *a.* rotten, of wood, mats, &c.
Minagoru, one kind of yam.
Minibore, name of a shellfish.
Minimini, name of a shellfish.
Miri, *s.* small gravel.
Mirigini, *s.* north wind; north.
Miro, *s.* dirt.
Miro, *a.* dirty.
Misikona, *adv.* small, with *vara* to grow.

Misina, small, of men or animals, *Tau misina.*
Misikamisika, small.
Mo, *adv.* only (with *s.*), indeed (intensive with *v*).
Moa, a fish with long projecting lower jaw.
Moale, *v.* to rejoice.
Moale, *s.* delight, happiness.
Moemoe, *s.* reef, both barrier and detached.
Moia, to tread on.
Moiatao, *v.* to be trod upon.
Moiatao gauna, a reserved thing, not to be sold, or given away.
Moidedi, steps slipping.
Moitao, to keep back, hide.
Moda, *s.* a bag.
Mogea, *v.* to twist. Of speech, to pervert.
Mogea, *s.* to twist off, as a cocoanut from its stalk.
Mogo, the name of a tree.
Moko, *adv.* almost.
Mokona. See Makona.
Mokorereva, *s.* the name of a bird.
Momo, *s.* rubbish; *a. fig.*, plenty, many.
Mōmo, *s.* the placenta.
Momokani, *a.* true, faithful. Momokani etomamu, certain.
Momoruna, *s.* crums, &c.
Mone, *s.* cakes of sago, taro, &c. boiled.
Monea, *v.* to boil in a cloth.
Monege, *v.* to race, as canoes.
Moneke, *v.* to be pock-pitted.
Moni, *s.* money. *(Introduced.)*
Mora, *s.* the name of a small land crab.
Moru, *v.* to fall from a height.
Moru, *s.* the name of a fish.
Moruta, soft, of fish or flesh not fresh.
Motu, *b.* to break, as string.
Motu, *s.* the name of a race of natives living at Port Moresby and neighbourhood.
Motumotu, *s.* island; detached portion of the reef.
Motukamotuka, rotten, torn, of mats, nets, &c.
Motumotu dava lalona ai, an atoll.
Motumotu patatari, very low island.
Moukamouka, *v.* to be rotten, (of cloth),

Mu, *s.* a slab of a tree, hence a door made of such.
Mu, *v.* to coo as a dove; to be dumb.
Mudumu, white ant.
Mukia, *v.* to break up and crush leaves in the hand.
Muko, *s.* handkerchief.
Mukoro, *s.* the nose-stick; a beam.
Mukuroa, larvæ of hornet, &c.
Munu, *s.* turtle egg.
Munuta, *v.* to vomit.
Muramura, *s.* medicine.
Muramura tauna, doctor.
Muri, an intensive added to verbs of going, &c., as *Heau muri, Laka muri.*
Murimuri, *s.* outside; away from.
Murina, *s.* the back of anything. *Ruma murina.*
Murina hadikaia, to backbite.
Murina laka, to follow.
Murinai, *a.* next.
Muritai, *a.* younger. With *tau* or *hahine.*
Musia, *v.* to suck, as a bone, or a cocoanut through the eye, with smacking noise of the lips.
Mutu, *v.* to sink.
Mutu, *v.* to express by squeezing, as cocoanut oil.
Mututania, to sink away from.

N

N is pronounced as in English.
Na, particle for 1st pers. sing., and placed between pronoun and verb, as, *lau na diba-mu.*
Na, suffix for 1st pers. sing., his.
Nadanada, just beginning to smell, high.
Nadi, *s.* a stone; iron, metal.
Nadi gabuna, stony.
Nadi gini, a long stone standing up, a monumental stone.
Nadi larebaia, to build a stone wall.
Nadikuro, a rock in the sea, as coral, &c. (Not so high as *haga*).
Nadi motu, rock in sea away from reef.
Nadinadi, small stones; seed; the kidneys; shot.
Nadi kubolukubolu, pebble.
Nado, *interj.* of surprise. *Lau dahakai nado.*

Nadua, *v.* to cook by boiling.
Nahu, *v.* to swim.
Nahu hanai, to swim across as a river.
Nahu, spear of red wood, (used both in hunting and war).
Nahuana tohoa, to be watchful, to be careful.
Naidac, *s.* the name of a fish.
Naimenaime, *s.* a flying ornament of house or ship distinguishing the Vahoi family.
Naimuro, one kind of banana.
Nala, *v.* 1st pers. sing. past, from *lao,* to go.
Nama, *v.* 1st pers. sing. past, from *mai,* to come.
Name, *na* and *me.* 1st person sing. pro with euphonic *me.*
Namo, *a.* good.
Namonamo, carefully.
Namo herea, becoming, choice.
Namo, *s.* mosquito.
Namumaua, a fish.
Nanaia, *v.* to warm the hands over the fire; to shampoo a sick person with warmed hands; to toast.
Nanaia, *v.* to bespeak a thing; to give payment for praise—*Oi dahaka mamo? Oi qarume abia lau nanaia.* Payment by the one who sees the new moon first.
Nanadai, *v.* to question, to inquire.
Nanadu, *v.* to cook. (A general term.)
Nanadu tauna, a cook.
Nanamo, occasional plural of *namo,* good.
Naniko, *s.* a wasp.
Nao, *s.* white men, foreigners.
Napera, cigarette wrapper.
Nara, name of tree (similar to cedar but harder.)
Nāri, *v.* more commonly naria, to wait for, to expect; to take care of.
Nato, word postfixed to verb, 1st pers. sing. to indicate, was about to —, but, &c.
Natu dogoro, brother's son.
Natuadora, *s.* a child whose parents are living. The opposite of *ihareha,* an orphan.
Natu na, *s.* child; the young of animals.
Natuna karukaru, babe.
Natuna momo, prolific.
Natu rahai, *s.* nephew or niece.

Nāu, *s.* an earthenware dish or bowl.
Naua, *v.* to scrape, to polish, to plane.
Naua gauna, *s.* plane.
Nega, *s.* time.
Nega daudau, a long time.
Nega dika, a bad time, misfortune.
Nega hoho, often.
Nega idoinai, constantly.
Nega se vanaha, a short time.
Negana, season.
Negarinaegari, very clear water, of river, sea, &c.
Nege, *adv.* used in composition, signifying, "away from," *Kahuanege*, to let go.
Nege a, *v.* to throw away, to relinquish. *Negea daure*, intensive.
Negea dobi, to throw away from one and down.
Nēka, *a.* limpid, clear.
Nemai a, *v.* to name after some one.
Nese, *s.* ridge of mountain or hill.
Nese hanai, to cross a river on a fallen tree as a bridge.
Nesenese, of nose, thin (as Europeans).
Neseriki, crew of boat or ship. *Neseriki memero*.
Nevari a, *v.* to sprinkle.
Nihi, *v.* to dream.
Ninoa, *s.* mountain mist, fog, vapour.
Nita, papaw tree or fruit. Rarotongan name.
Niu, *s*, coconut tree and mature fruit.
Noga. Noka, *v.* to wake.
Nogo, *s.* the name of a crane. Also Noko.
Noho, *v.* to dwell.
Nohobou, to dwell together.
Noho dika, to be in misfortune.
Noho kava negana, leisure.
Nohorinohori, to delay, to stay a long time when sent to village, &c.
Noho taritari, to sojourn, to remain.
Nohu, *s.* the name of a stinging fish.
Noinoi, *v.* to beg; to entreat.
Noi hegame, to beg.
Noka. *See* Noga.
Nokarea, to talk in one's sleep.
Noko, *s.* a sea-bird, a crane. *See* Nogo.
Nonoa, *v.* to roast on sticks; broil.
Nononono, name of a shell-fish.
Nonu, name of a tree.
Noro, *s.* the name of a fruit. (Similar to *maita*.)
Nua, *s.* inner bark of a tree.
Nuai, to honor, to respect. Equal to *Qahia*.

Nua na, projection of stomach, used also of the eyeball, *mata nuana*.
Nuana bada, *a.* corpulent.
Nuanua, to grovel, as a pig.
Nubagana, *v.* to be unoccupied, waste. (Of land.)
Nudugara, *s.* the name of a shell-fish. (One kind of oyster.)
Nui a, *v.* to place a water or cooking pot on the ground. *Hodu nuia*.
Nuiakau. As Nuia.
Nuiakubou and Nuiabou, to put food dishes or bowls together in one place in preparation for eating.
Nulu, *s.* the fibrous substance which grows round the base of the coconut leaf, the *stipule;* coarse cloth; a sack.
Nurina, *s.* dregs.

O

O has always the round full sound of o in open.
O, yes, used much at Tubuseleia and Kapakapa.
Oboro, *s.* capsicum. (*Introduced*). *See* Urehegini.
Obu, term of respect addressed to a widow, as *Keua obu e* (a Kabadi word).
Obue, leaven. (*Introduced*.)
Oburo, *s.* a small cup-shaped pottery bason.
Odai a cvaeva, washed to and fro, as canoe without anchor, figuratively used of those who have no friends or relations.
Odo, small white shell worn by chief.
Odubora, *s.* a red parrot.
Oduga, *s.* the name of a lizard.
Ogoa, *s.* plumbago.
Ogoagoa, dark shining colour.
Ogoeogoe, a stranger.
Ogogami, *v.* to be orphaned, to be destitute.
Ogogami, *s.* a poor man, as opposed to *lohiabada*.
Ohe, side.
Ohuduka, *s.* a large scaly lizard.
Oi, *pron.* thou.
Oiamu, *pron.* for you, thine (of food and drink).
Oibe, *adv.* yes, just so.
Oiemu, *pron.* for you, thine.

Ola, v. went.
Ole, s. large mesh fishing net.
Omada, s. chestnut.
Ome, verb. partic. for pres. tense, second per. sing. or plur.
Ominuo (from the Greek), v. to swear, to take an oath.
Omoiomoi, to show disrespect by crowding up where a chief is sitting. *Lohiabada e omoiomoilaia.*
Ono, a fish.
Onogo, bastard palm.
Orai a v. to carry on the head, as a waterpot, or a burden.
Ore, v. to be finished, done.
Ore, s. a squall, storm (longer than guba).
Orea, a company, troop, class.
Ore na, s. a remnant, what is left.
Ori, s. clouds, light rolling clouds.
Ori, name of a tree.
Ori a, v. to grate cocoanut, to chew pandanus fruit.
Oro, s. rattan cane.
Oroa, one kind of banana.
Oroaoroa, name of a tree.
Orooro, s. a mountain.
Orooro beruta, mound. Orooro komoge, s. peak.
Orooro komuta, a hill, rising from plain.
Orooro mo, mountainous.
roma na, s. the fashion, style, order of a thing, as posts of a house, a tree for felling, armlet, &c.
romana kara, example, pattern.
rorobu, name of a fish.
Oroua, one kind of banana.
Ota, fruit of a palm, chewed as betel nut.
Oti, suffix of dual, and small numbers, as *ruaoti, tatoioti.*
Oto, word postfixed to verb, second pers., to signify, was about to— but.
Ouna, *adv.* yonder (near at hand).

P

P pronounced as in English, sometimes scarcely distinguishable from B.
Pāda, s. a disease resembling palsy.
Pāda, s. the space between earth and sky, air; the space between any two places; distance.

Padaia, v. to gather by breaking the stalk.
Padidi, a misfortune, fate. *Lau na padidi gaigai ese e korigu.*
Pāga, s. the shoulder.
Pāi, s. a shrimp.
Paia, v. to be bedazzled, as by looking at the sun.
Paila, s. pink earth, used for painting the face.
Pailapaila, a pink colour.
Pailipaili, v. to be taut.
Paitapaita, to blaze.
Pāko, a small chisel.
Pakoa. *See* Bagoa.
Pakosi, s. scissors. (*Introduced.*)
Palaheni. *See Balaheni.*
Palakapalaka, a. flat, as a board, &c.
Palaoa, flour, also bread. (*Introduced.*)
Palapala, s. hand, *ima palapala ; ae palapala,* foot.
Panaere, one kind of banana.
Panadagu, to stamp with foot.
Pani, a saucepan. (*Introduced.*)
Papa, v. to burst, to hatch (eggs); to open the eyes.
Pāpa bada, s. a flat rock.
Papalau, see *Babalau.*
Papapapa, s. flat rock.
Pāpu, v. to go in mourning. *Ia kakoa mate pāpuna.*
Parabole, a parable. (*Introduced.*)
Parapara, a frog.
Parapara, prone, prostrate on stomach, "spread-eagle."
Parara, v. to be split, opened, divided. *Lalo parara,* opened mind, enlightened.
Paravalo, s. a shelter, as a roof without walls.
Parikaparika, a. clammy, damp.
Paripari, v. to be wet.
Paroparo, a freshwater fish.
Pasi, a weeded space all round fence of garden.
Pasiahu, weeded space round coconut.
Pata, s. a shelf, a table.
Pata, rotten (as a dead body), corruption ; of food boiled to pieces.
Pata ia, v. to pat, to pound.
Patakapataka, v. to be overdone (of food), to be boiled to rags.
Patapata, v. (intens. of pataia), to continue to pat. *Ima patapata,* to clap hands.

Patatari, with *motumotu*, low island.
Pāu, *s* a cardboard-like covering for feather plumes, &c. *Mānupāu;* banana-leaf venetian flag.
Pauda, gunpowder. (*Introduced.*)
Paudae, *v.* to jump down into the sea from the beach.
Paudobi, *v.* to jump down into the sea from a canoe, &c.
Pavapavana, king, queen, always used with *hanua* or name of place.
Pēka, *s.* spathe of *kamokamo*, from which the ear bursts.
Pekara, despised, ignominious, lazy.
Pepa, paper. (*Introduced.*)
Pepe, *s.* banner.
Pere, to spread, increase, as melons, &c., used figuratively of people.
Perepere, *s.* young cocoanut when nearly ripe. *Karu perepere.*
Peri, band used for tying feet together to climb.
Perukaperuka, *a.* flexible, not stiff. The opposite of *tororo.*
Peta ia, *v.* to bale by jerking the water out.
Petapeta, to scatter, as by fowls scratching.
Petapetalaia, *v.* to splash over; to waste.
Peva, *s.* a bow.
Piu henia, *v.* to spread a report.
Piua, *hari puia*, to spread a report.
Piu a dae, *v.* to take a fly, &c., out of water with a stick.
Piu a isi, to lift up on a pole.
Pidi a, *v.* to fillip.
Pidipidi, *v.* to knock, to fillip; hence *pidia*, to shoot with a gun.
Pilateri, *s.* phylactery. (*Introduced from the Greek*).
Pipita ia, *v.* to clean out a pot or dish by wiping out with the forefinger.
Pisili, *s.* spray.
Pisipisina, *v.* to splash.
Pisi rohoroho, *u.* to shatter.
Pitopito, *s.* small insects, such as weevils, &c.; a button. (*Introduced*).
Piupiulai a, *v.* to squander, waste.
Pou, *v.* to burst, from fermentation, &c.; to be crushed, as a reed, &c.
Poudagu, *v.* to explode.
Pouka, *a.* rotten, of fruit.
Podi, *v.* to glance off, as a spear.

Pohu a tao, *v.* to beat into, as waves into a ship.
Poka, a canoe baler made of sago frond.
Popora, to be unfortunate in catching no fish, having no *kohu* when friends come.
Popora ia, *v.* of *guba*, to have no rain.
Popoto, *s.* a steep river-bank.
Poruporu, young *nara* tree before it becomes red.
Pose, cat. (*Introduced*).
Posekaposeka, shallow, as a plate or dish.
Posena, abbreviation of *posekaposeka.*
Posi, *s.* the bladder.
Posi a, to draw close to, to cuddle, as infant in canoe when rough, &c. *Ia e posia vareai.*
Poua, a feast for dead a day after death.
Puapua, two canoes lashed together, *vanagi puapuana.*
Pudipudi, preceded by *boka*; pain in bowels, followed by diarrhœa.
Puki, to slip off, or out of, hence to pass away, to be gone.
Pūla, *s.* a very high night tide.
Pulu, or Puhulu, large stick for fence-making.
Pune, *s.* the common Torres Strait pigeon.
Pune gobu, large blue pigeon.
Pupu na, something to distinguish place or thing, a memorial token.
Puri, stick with which marking done previous to tattooing, pencil or pen.
Pure, Rarotonga word for prayer, used in motu for public worship.
Puripuri regena, a rib joint of pork.
Puruki a, *v.*
Pururu a, *v.* } To spit out.
Puse, *s.* sack. (*Introduced*).
Puta, *s.* sponge.
Putaro, a lichen which grows on stones under water.

Q

Q, as in English in queen.
Qa, to speak. *See* Koau.
Qabira, a stone hatchet, rough and strong, for felling trees.

Qabu, to be left.
Qabuqabudia, the remaining few.
Qada, a fish.
Qada ia, *v.* to pierce with a spear; to wound; to run a splinter into the foot, to be cut with a stone, to stab.
Qadaqada ia, *v.* to shake, as water in a bottle.
Qadi, *s.* a locust; also stone used as anchor, or as sinker for fishing-line.
Qadi a, *v.* to strike as with a rope; to fan away flies, to paint.
Qadilai a, that against which a thing is qadia, as to take a dog by its legs and dash its head against a stone.
Qadiqadi, to wobble about, as head of person in faint being carried by arms and legs.
Qado a, *v.* to prick out holes, as in a sieve, &c.
Qadobe, *v.* to cork.
Qadogi, *a.* short, concise, low.
Qadu a, a knot, to tie a knot.
Qaebo, of wind, quiet, fine, fair.
Qagiloa, *v.* to go about together, to be inseparable.
Qagiqagi, *s.* toes or fingers, according as it is preceded by *ae* or *ima*.
Qagiqagi dodori, the fore-finger.
Qagu, *v.* to catch a falling thing; to dodge a spear. Used with *metau* or *gada*.
Qagugu, *v.* (preceded by *doru*) to be bent down with weakness or old age.
Qahi a, to respect, to honour.
Qaidu, *v.* to be broken, as stick, bone, &c.
Qalaha, *s.* shark.
Qalahu, *s.* smoke.
Qalimu, *v.* to conquer, to overcome, to succeed.
Qama, *s.* phlegm.
Qamala, to bless spears by sorcerer.
Qamala tauna, sorcerer whose office it was to make spears successful.
Qamo, a small fish so called.
Qanaki, to tie stone for anchor.
Qanau, *s.* a rope.
Qanua, *v.* to spear. When a spear is thrown, if it does not miss, it is *qanua*.
Qaqa, a lump, as of sago.

Qara, *s.* the head.
Qara utua, to behead.
Qara gauna, bonnet, hat.
Qara gegea gauna, a coronet or crown.
Qara koukou (shell of the head), skull.
Qara roko, violent headache, whole head.
Qara tupua, the crown.
Qara harana, brains.
Qara kopina, scalp.
Qara bada, *s.* the sword fish.
Qara haboua, *v.* to collect payment, as for murder ransom.
Qara qaitu, *s.* American axe.
Qarahu orooro, a volcano.
Qarana, payment for damage, or injury done. *Uma qarana*, &c.
Qare, *s.* sign of death or misfortune, as breaking *hodu*, &c. *Mate qarena*.
Qari, *s.* the bottom of the sea; a bog; slime.
Qarotoa, *v.* to take care of, to look well after. Syn. *Dōsia*.
Qaru, *v.* to bark.
Qarume, *s.* a fish. (The general name.)
Qasi, *s.* stalk. *Bigu qasina*, banana stalk.
Qatu a, *s.* knot.
Qatuaqatua, knotted.
Qauta, *a.* ten. Qauta ima, fifteen.
Quata ta, eleven.
Qinai a, to pillow.

R

R, as in English, but often very light, scarcely distinguishable from L.
Ra, prefix to *rua*, in counting persons, *tau rarua*.
Raba, *v.* to go on all fours (as a turtle).
Rabana, *v.* to hunt.
Rabia, *s.* sago; arrowroot.
Rabora, *s.* turmeric.
Raborarabora, *a.* yellow, cadaverous, sallow.
Rabu, particle of enumeration in things of length, ten, as *rabu rua*, 20.

Ragaia, v. to pull up, to transplant.
Ragaraga, s. side, just under the arm-pits.
Ragaraga, s. the name of a disease in head (erysipelas?).
Rahaia, to point sticks, as for fence.
Rahala, s. north-west monsoon. Also Lahala.
Rahea, s. fornication.
Raho bada, s. a term of respect.
Raho namo, a. good looking, handsome (of a man).
Rahna tano, of tide just turned from high.
Rahu a utu, to sever ; to go through breakers, as a ship.
Rahukau, heavy surf on beach.
Rahupou, to slap thigh in bravado. *Kunu rahupou.*
Rahurahu, s. ashes, fire-place.
Raiva, v. to move. With a negative, *se raiva*, to be unwilling ; can't be bothered.
Raivarniva, to move.
Raka, v. to step, to walk.
Rāki karaia, v. to cower.
Rakia, to draw a pipe.
Rako, a twig. *Au rakona.*
Rakorako, young small wood.
Raku a, v. to make up the fire.
Ralama, track in grass by treading it down.
Rama boha. (*See* Lama boha.)
Rama hehuhu. (*See* Lama hehuhu.)
Rama kepere. (*See* Lama kepere.)
Rama tutuna, region between crown of head and forehead. *Anterior fontanelle.*
Rami, s. petticoat, waistcloth.
Rami abia, of a girl who has had intercourse with a man (as in Hebrew, uncovered).
Rami hebou, s. a virgin.
Ramo, v. to chew the betel nut.
Ramu, s. root.
Rani, v. to be hemorninged, to be overtaken by the morning.
Ranu, s. water, juice, liquid.
Ranu buloa, to dilute.
Ranu seia, to bale out water.
Ranukaranuka, a. watery.
Rapu, drift wood. *Rapu audia.*
Rara, s. blood.
Rara, descendants. As *Veve* and *Gara.*
Rara arukubou, a bruise.

Raradikaedae, s. dropsy.
Raraga or Raraka, v. to stumble on one side, as from a slippery road, or by stepping on a loose stone ; to stagger, to totter.
Raraia, v. to sun, to dry ; to stare, to watch. Raraigu, &c.
Rarakararaka, bloody.
Raranadi, hunting spear of red wood.
Rari, see Lari.
Raria, s. fine sand. Laria.
Raro, clay (used in making pottery).
Raro duba, dark-coloured clay.
Raro kaka, red clay.
Raroa, s. a flood which covers the grass.
Raroraro, battens on roof at right angles to rafters. (Purlins.)
Rarua, a. two (persons).
Raruoti a. two (persons). Also used as dual with pronouns. *Umui raruoti.*
Rata, s. milk.
Rata matana, nipple.
Rata ia. *See* Lataia, v. to condemn an absent one to death.
Rau, s. leaf.
Rāu, v. to crawl, as a child, snake, &c. ; to move, as the moon, stars, &c., in the heavens.
Rāu tui, to crawl through a small low hole into a house or garden.
Rau a, v. to scrape, or gather together with two hands.
Raua ia, v. to warn of an intended attack ; to shield ; to save.
Raudae, to crawl up, as frogs into house.
Raurau, preceded by *gorere*, a continued illness.
Ravana, s. father-in-law ; son-in-law.
Ravana, hahine, mother-in-law ; daughter-in-law.
Rave, ravea, to raft logs.
Rea, adv. accidentally, as *qadaia rea.*
Rea ia, a. to forget, to lose.
Rei, s. grass.
Rege, s. a joint of meat.
Regena. Regeregena, s. noise, clatter. *A si regeregena*, Hush !
Reho, s. sore mouth.
Reke, s. fishing net.
Repati, large white lily.
Rore, to spread, as light at dawn.
Rere, here and there, from place to place.

Rerevarereva, many different things.
Resea, to split, of vegetables, &c.
Reva ia, v. to condemn to death when the victim is present.
Revareva, s. tattooing; anything striped or variegated; hence writing, printed matter. *Revareva hatua*.
Revareva, a war canoe.
Revo, a fish.
Rigi, s. branch.
Riki, v. a misfortune from having violated taboo of house.
Rimuna, s. fringe, edge.
Rio a, v. to gird.
Roē, asthma.
Roi, flax. *Vanea roina*.
Roboa, s. to adze smooth, as a canoe after *keilea*.
Roboa, s. first-born; first-fruits.
Robonarobona, sharp bows, of canoe.
Roda, one kind of mangrove.
Rodu, a fish.
Roga, s. the name of a sweet-smelling herb.
Roge, s. a store-house; store-room.
Roge a, v. to store in *roge*.
Rogea tauna, one who stores, an industrious man.
Rogoni, v. to cook for food for visitors, &c.
Rogorogo, v. to be pregnant, to conceive.
Roha, v. to look.
Rohadae, look up.
Roha maorona, length (of house):
Roha dobi, to look down.
Roharoha, to look about.
Roha lou, to look back.
Roha, s. fathom.
Roha, to measure, to fathom.
Rohe a, to string a bow.
Rohe ahu, v. to drum over the dead.
Roherohea, v. to dandle a baby; to shake one in order to awaken.
Roho, v. to fly, to leap, to skip.
Roho boio, to be lost, dead in bush, drowned, &c.
Rohodobi, to jump down.
Rohohanai, to leap over; to break through.
Roho hanaihanai, hisina, contagious or infectious disease.
Rohoīsi, to jump up.
Rohokau, to perch, to light on.

Roho a, v. to cancel; to rub or wash out, to raze.
Rohodaerohodae, v. to palpitate, as the heart.
Rohomauri, to escape, as from troops, &c.
Rohoroho, intensive; generally used with *dika*.
Rohouda, to leap into, as waves into a boat.
Rokohu, s. (*See* Lokohu.)
Roku, name of a shell-fish.
Romua, to pat pottery into shape.
Ropo, logs on which to launch canoe or boat.
Rore a, v. to spread, as branches on the ground, as stones spread out, not heaped up.
Roro, cracked.
Roroho, large stinging ray.
Rorokaroroka, stiff, rigid.
Roroma, v. to murder a visitor in a village, generally treacherously; also to murder a single person met on road, &c.
Rosi, s. fastenings of sail to yard, rohans.
Rosi a, v. to nurse a child; to throw the arms around, to hug, as a captive in war, to clasp in the arms, to embrace.
Rotona, narrow, as mat, cloth, &c.
Rovae, a bunch (of coconuts), *niu rovaena*.
Rovorovo, name of a bird.
Rua, v. two.
Rua ahui, twenty.
Ruaoti, a couple.
Rūā, v. to detain; to withhold.
Ruarua, v. to dig.
Rube a, v. to try a stick or spear by holding it in the middle and shaking it.
Rudu, side of chest.
Ruhai a, v. to untie, loosen.
Ruha ia nege, to cast off.
Ruhu a, to loose, as sail.
Rui, s. dugong.
Ruku, v. to grunt.
Ruma, s. a house.
Ruma gaudia, furniture.
Ruma karaia, to build a house.
Rurua, s. small rattan cane.
Ruruki, to slip down, or through, to strip off by drawing through fingers.

S

S in purely native words never occurs before *a*, *o*, or *u*.
Sabati, *s.* sabbath (*Introduced from the Hebrew.*)
Satauro, *s.* a cross. (*Introduced from the Greek.*)
Se, a negative, used in sing. only.
Seasea, *s.* the side of a house on the outside. With *dehe*, side verandah.
Seamata, ripe coconut. *Niu seamata.*
Sebaka, *s.* back of a house. *Ruma sebakana.*
Sebi na, as *Dekena*, by side of.
Sede, bamboo drum or tomtom.
Sedila. Don't know.
Sega, *v.* to clear the bush for a garden. *Sega taraia.*
Segea, *v.* to sharpen a knife or axe.
Sehanai, to hear indistinctly.
Sehe, slanting, *Haginia sehe.*
Sei, *s.* flea.
Seia, *v.* to pour.
Sela, for, *Asi ela.*
Selai a dobi, to rush down, as a waterfall.
Seliseli, or Seriseri, *s.* a rubbish heap.
Seme, *adv.* not. *As asi eme.*
Sene, *adv.* long, long ago.
Sene, great grandchild, great grand father or mother.
Senu. Senusenu, *s.* a collection of things, a heap.
Senukasenuka, heaped up.
Sepe, *s.* a small white shell, worn by chiefs.
Se qahiamu, to be disrespectful.
Seri na, *s.* a flock of animals or birds.
Seriseri. (*See* Seliseli.)
Serosero, *s.* the second row of calking in *lakatoi.*
Seseahu, *s.* curtain.
Sesedaeroha, *v.* to rise to the surface, as a diver, dugong, &c.
Seseha, *s.* the sea-coast just inland of the mangroves. *Seseha dala lao.*
Seseha, *a.* brackish, as water in *sescha.*
Sesera, *s.* elegy.
Seuseu, *v.* to look out, as from the masthead; to look at house or canoe to see if straight, to show how to do a thing as carpentering. *Scuseudia ia e hamaorolaia.*

Seuseu na, a pattern, model, example.
Severa. Severasevera, *a.* thin.
Siahu, *a.* hot. *Lalo siahu*, hot-tempered, angry. Siahusiahu, lukewarm.
Siahu, *s.* power, authority, supernatural power.
Siai a, *v.* to send. Siaia lao, to dismiss.
Siaro, *s.* a large red fish.
Siba ia. to be left to do work alone.
Sibirere, *s.* light wood, used by children for toy spears.
Sibogu, *pron.* I only.
Sibomu, *pron.* thou only.
Sibona, *pron.* he himself, very self, only, alone.
Sibona namo, to excel.
Siga, small bamboo.
Sigara tauna, leader of hunt.
Sihaurisihauri, *s.* pustule.
Sihi, *s.* a man's girdle; the paper mulberry from which the girdle is made; to abstain from sexual intercourse. See below.
Sibi lasi, naked.
Sihi daudau, *v.* to sleep apart from one's wife a long time.
Sihi kahikahi, *v.* to sleep apart from one's wife for a short time.
Sihi korikori, *v.* to sleep apart from one's wife, not to cohabit.
Sike, *v.* (preceded by ae) to limp, to stand, or walk, on tiptoe.
Siko, *s.* prolonged illness.
Siku, *v.* to be perturbed, anxious. (Used with *lalo.*)
Sili, *adv.* aside.
Silo, oyster.
Sina dogoro, mother's sister.
Sinaia, *s.* a wave.
Sinaiana, *s.* ocean swell, high waves which do not break.
Sinabada, *s.* thumb, big toe.
Sinahu, *a.* hundred.
Sinana, *s.* mother.
Sinana, *a.* mature (of animals).
Sinaruru, noise and tumult because of some evil report.
Sinavai, *s.* river.
Siniura, a prickly creeper.
Sinoleke, bower bird.
Sio, a fish.
Sioko, to squat with posterior near ground.
Siokomu, *s.* one kind of banana.
Sira, name of a tree.

Siri, v. to get out of the way, to move aside.
Siri, s. a verse. (*Introduced meaning.*)
Siri a, v. to chip ; to cut up firewood.
Siriana reaia, to break or spoil a thing from carelessness.
Siriana basio reaia, to charge to be careful.
Sirigogoha, a shell fish.
Siriho, s. a reed.
Sisia, s. a dog.
Sisibaia, v. to compose a song. *Ane sisibaia.*
Sisiba henia, v. to admonish, reprove, advise.
Sisiba tauna, s. one who reproves, an adviser.
Sisidara, s. feather head-dress.
Sisihu, oyster shells.
Sisimo, light shower.
Sisipo, s. the entire outrigger of a large canoe.
Sisisina, s. a very small piece.
Sisina, s. a small piece.
Sisiri a, to sprinkle.
Sisivana, adv. equal to, as far as.
Sitona, wheat. (*Introduced.*)
Siusiu, s. an indecent dance on *lakatoi* when they are ready for sea.
Sivaia, v. to turn, to reverse (end for end).
Sivarai, s. a report, an account, a story.
So, adv. not. As Asio.
Sopu, soap. (*Introduced.*)
Sugo, s. a yoke. (*From the Greek.*)
Suke, s. a fig tree. (*From the Greek.*)
Sunago, s. synagogue. (*From the Greek.*)

T

T is pronounced as in English, except before i or e, when it is pronounced as ts. As *mate*, pronounced matse, *raruoti* is raruotsi.
Ta, a contraction of tamona.
Ta, a prefix to toi, for people, as *tatoi.*
Tāba, to drivel.
Tābata, tabata, a lump, mass, as of clay.
Tabaiahu, v. to daub with mud, &c.

Tabero, s. a shallow bay.
Tabekau, v. to lean against.
Taboraia, with *daba*, to be quite daylight.
Taboro, s. yam harvest.
Tabu, one kind of feast.
Tabu (*See Dabu.*)
Tabubutabubu, s. to shake, as with the wind. *Ima tabubutabubu,* to shake, of the hand, so as not to take a steady aim. To knock together, as knees.
Tadaia, v. to beat out the bark of the paper mulberry, for making native cloth.
Tadi, s. sea-water.
Tadika, to be salt.
Tadikaka, s. cousins, family relations.
Tādikāka, s. brothers and sisters by the same parents.
Tadi rahai, s., younger cousin.
Tadina, s. younger brother, or sister, younger cousin.
Tadiva, s. the name of a fish, red mullet.
Tae, a tree, the bark of which is used for sewing biri, and for making thatch.
Tāga tauna, s. a rich man.
Tāge, s. excrement.
Taga a, v. to paint one's face all over.
Taguma, a fish.
Tagutagu tauna, hasty, impulsive, one who rushes off without waiting to hear whole story, one who answers when another's name is called.
Taha, used with āu, s. a splinter, a small piece of wood. *Au taha. Aegu āu tahana e qadaia.*
Taha, used with kudou, v. to be distressed, perturbed.
Tahairame, s. Syn. Ravana.
Tahi a, v. to dig out, to take earth out of a hole, to burrow.
Taho a, v. to throw a spear, to throw anything to, but not at any one.
Tahoakau, to throw.
Tahoa dobi, to dash (on the ground).
Tahodiho, s. the West.
Tahotaho, s. of children playing with light spears, *Tahotaho mo karaia.*
Tahu a, v. to seek, to examine.
Tahugumu, with suff. seek me.
Tahu taudia, hunting party.

I

Tahua rerevarereva, to seek many different things..
Tahula, *s.* a slight relapse after a severe illness. *Gorere tahula Lau gorere ma tahulaia.* A few remaining ill after a general epidemic.
Tahutāi, *v.* to seek with tears.
Tahuni, *v.* to cover in, as a body in the grave.
Tahure, a fish.
Tāi, *v.* to cry; to howl (of dogs). Taitai.
Tai gadigadi, death wail, deceased's deeds celebrated, also to yell out in quarrelling.
Tai heuduri, to cry after a father or mother, as a child does.
Tai lolololo, to cry out lustily.
Tāi momo, *a.* fretful.
Tāia, *v.* to coil in the hand.
Taia, *s.* ear.
Taia ibuku, *v.* to listen stupidly and not understand what is said.
Taia kisiri, discharging ear.
Taia kudima, deaf.
Taia manoka, *s.* willing obedience.
Taia, *s.* fin at gills.
Taigana dika, selfish, greedy, churlish.
Taigana namo, unselfish, generous, peaceable.
Taihu, *s.* a man's sister; a woman's brother.
Taihu rahai, a man's female cousin; a woman's male cousin. *Rahai* takes the suffix. *Taihu rahaigu.*
Taikotaiko, *v.* to shake the head.
Taina, *a.* some (things). Plural, *taidia.*
Taina, *s.* morsel. Taina ania, to partake of.
Taitai, *v.* to weep, to cry. As Tāi.
Taitu, sweet yam.
Tako, one kind of grass.
Takona, *s.* bunch (of fruit), cluster.
Talaia, *v.* to sting (of the hornet).
Talabili, *s.* bulwarks of *lakatoi.*
Talo, *s.* a vegetable (*arum esculentum*).
Tamalu, *s.* umbrella. (*Introduced.*)
Tama, *s.* father; uncle.
Tama dogoro, father's brother, *tamagu dogorona..*
Tama rahai, *s.* uncle.
Tamanu, *v.* to charge, to exhort.

Tame, *ta* and *me*, first pers. pl. inclusive, with *me* euphonic particle. *Ita tame moale*, we are pleased.
Tamona, *a.* one.
Tamoru, numb.
Tamotama, *v.* few, here and there one, rare; also Tamotamona.
Tanatana, cry of white lizard.
Tanitano, *s.* the name of an evil spirit, supposed to possess a man when in a fit.
Tano, *s.* earth, soil; country.
Tano ai, ashore.
Tano dubu, ant-hill.
Tano tauna, a countryman.
Tano bada, *s.* the earth, the land, as distinguished from sky and sea.
Tano gagaena, *s.* a desert.
Tao, to draw after one, *iena ai e taomu.*
Taoa, to track.
Tao a kunu, *v.* to press down.
Tao a tao, *v.* to hold down, to press down.
Tao a kohi, *v.* to break, as a coconut shell by crushing.
Taoatari, to show disrespect by boasting in presence of chief, or man to whom the credit is due. *Lohiabada e taoatari.*
Taoha, a scab.
Taola. (*See* Taora.)
Taona, followed by *torea*, *v.* to betray As *Taotore.*
Taora, *s.* level ground, a plain. Taoraia, to make level.
Taotao, *s.* necklace (of shells).
Taotore. *See* Taona.
Tapo a, *v.* to fan.
Tara, *s.* the name of a fish.
Tara, *v.* to shine.
Tarai, to adze, to chop, to cut wood.
Tarai hepatapata, *v.* to hack.
Taraki a, *v.* to be wounded by an arrow.
Tarava e atu, to make a law, takes suffix of those to whom it is given, *tarava e atuda*, law given to us.
Taravatu, *s.* covenant; hence commandment, law.
Tareko, *s.* hollow seeds used as a rattle on drums, &c.; also, name of tree to which they belong.
Tari, *s.* rudder, steer-oar.
Tariadae, to steer seawards when rowing.

Tariadiho, to steer landwards.
Tariatao, in steering, to go off the wind.
Tari karaia, v. to steer.
Tari tauna, steersman.
Tarikatarika, adv. of intensity, thoroughly, continuity.
Taritari, adv. continuity, permanence, &c.
Taroma, one kind of banana.
Taru, v. to cover, as with a sheet, to wrap oneself in.
Taruahu, to wrap completely.
Taruadiho, to put down loaded kiapa.
Taruha, v. to camp, to pitch tent.
Taruha hebou, s. a camp.
Taruha e ladaia, to strike camp.
Taruka, of feet, tender from long confinement to house, aegu e taruka.
Tataiautu, v. to transgress, to cut off, as speech, to pull through breakers.
Tataiakohi, to strike and break.
Tataia kerehai, to turn about.
Tatakunu, v. to strike and be fast on a rock or reef, as a canoe or ship.
Tatakau, to touch on rock without being fast.
Tatakau, s. a collision.
Tatatata, to run with short steps like child learning to walk.
Tau, s. the body.
Tau mate, a corpse.
Tau, s. a man. *Tau Elema.* Elema man.
Tau anikaanika, a strong, able, valiant man.
Tau harihari, intermittent fever.
Tau mauri, restless, fidgetty.
Tau a dae, v. to hang up.
Tauihuai, s. the sons between first and last born.
Taubadadia, s. elders.
Tauala, round, smooth, stone club.
Taubada, an elderly man.
Tauguna, s. the first-born son.
Tauhau, s. a youth.
Tauhalō, v. to cheer, to comfort.
Tau latana e dae, disrespectful to husband.
Tau manokamanoka, s. languor.
Taumauri, fidgetty, restless, troublesome.
Taumise, stunted, small.
Taumuritai, s. son subsequent to tauguna.

Tau na, s. a man. (*See* Tau.) Generally used with a noun of quality. *Koikoi tauna,* a liar.
Taunabinai, just so, all right.
Taunabunai, as Taunabinai.
Tauna eme lo, mature, full grown.
Tauna se raiva, unwilling, can't be bothered.
Taunimanima, s. man (generic, including male and female).
Taupetaupe, s. a low swing.
Taurahani, a. eight.
Taurahani ahui, a. eighty.
Taurahani ta, a. nine.
Tauratoi, a. six.
Tauratoi ahui, sixty.
Tauru, s. hades; unknown ocean space.
Taurubada, s. the covering party in an expedition for plunder, &c.
Tāutāu, name of small iguana.
Tau ta, s. somebody.
Tau varotavarota, a. lean, skinny.
Tavanana, v. to get food in anticipation of a feast.
Tavea, one kind of yam.
Titania, tares. (*Introduced.*)
Tō, stay of house, prop to fence.
To instead of so, negative 2nd pers. sing.
Toa, to be caught in net.
Toa, to blow, of the wind.
Toa, to land on beach.
Toadiho toadiho, to call at many places along coast in canoe journey.
Toana, s. a sign, a limit, a mark.
Tobo a, v. to suck. (*See* Topoa.)
Tobukatobuka. (*See Dobukadobuka.*)
Todena, s. gum. *Au todena.*
Toea, s. white shell armlet.
Togea, v. to spear, when the person speared is above, as Christ on the cross.
Togo, s. the fruit of one kind of mangrove (aniani), not edible.
Tohē, s. a large *uro* for putting raw sago in.
Toho a, v. to try, to mark for cutting, to rule lines.
Tohotoho, v. to mock. *Umui ia dahaka o tohotohoamu.*
Tohu, s. sugar-cane.
Tohua, a fish with long-pointed head, and small mouth.
Toi, a. three.
Toi ahui, thirty.
Toia, v. to shred, to insert.

Toia hedavari, v. to meet on the road.
Toiaroro, v. to stretch out, as the arm or leg.
Toia vareai, v. to insert, as the nose-stick.
Toibolo, to meet, as two currents.
Tomamu, to think, to purpose, to say. *Lalomu dahaka e tomamu,* what do you think? ·
Tolo, a fish, a herring.
Tolumu, s. *See* Tomulu.
Toma, *adv.* like, thus.
Tomadiho, v. to prostrate oneself, to worship.
Tome, instead of *asi ome,* negative, 2nd pers. sing.
Tomena, s. resin. Used as a charm for large dugong and turtle nets.
Tomulu, s. the goura pigeon. Also tolumu.
Topo a, v. to suck, as an infant, to suck without noise; to kiss, as Europeans.
Tora, a belt.
Toratora, s. shin.
Tore, to rise. *See* Helaitore.
Tore a, v. to cast the net.
Tore a, v. to mark the design on the body with lamp-black and water previous to tattooing; to write.
Torelai a, written about.
Torehai, added to *heni, abia,* &c., to signify repayment.
Toreisi, v. to raise from a sitting or lying posture.
Toreisina, s. a rising up, a resurrection.
Toretore, v. to try a *lakatoi* by sailing to and fro.
Tororo, a. stiff, strong, of a stick or spear.
Tororotororo, stiff, rigid, as the body in a fit.
Tororotororo, s. epilepsy.
Toto, name of a tree.
Toto, s. sore.
Toto, one kind of mangrove.
Totōdae, s. a north-east wind, a north-east gale.
Toto na, s. the object in coming or going to a place. Used with the suffix of the person to whom one goes. *Oi lau totogu dahaka?* Why have you come to me?
Toutou, s. a spot, a mole.
Toutou, v. to be spotted.

Tovili, s. the kernel, as of the pandanus fruit.
Toviri, s. the kernel of the pandanus; larvæ of the wild bee.
Tua, a piece (of wood, string, &c.)
Tua, hold, or "down below" of a ship.
Tūa, v. to slacken, to let go; to let friends go.
Tuadobi, v. to let down by a rope, &c.
Tuakatuaka, short piece.
Tuara, one kind of banana (eaten by chiefs only).
Tuari, s. troops, company of warriors.
Tuari hegegedae, to beseige.
Tuari lao, to go to war.
Tubu, v. to ferment, to swell.
Tubu, to shoot, to grow.
Tubu, to hit, of any missile; also to reach as in race, *name tubu gunaguna.*
Tubu rahai, great uncle.
Tubua, s. the crown of the head; top of anything upright. With *dina,* noon. Of a post, *au tubua,* upright.
Tubuahu, s. constipation of the bowels.
Tubu dia, s. posterity; ancestors.
Tubuka, s. feather head-dress for dancing.
Tubukau to ask permission. *Biaguna tubukau henia.*
Tubukohi, s. first appearance of menses. With suffix *tubugu.*
Tubu na, s. grandparent; ancestor; descendant.
Tubu rahai, s. great uncle or aunt.
Tubu tama, s. ancestors.
Tubu tama hereva, s. tradition.
Tudaga, to sulk, to refuse to be conciliated.
Tuha, name of a tree the leaves and root of which are used to stupefy fish.
Tuhutuhu, young shoot.
Tui, s. knee.
Tuihadāi, Tuihadaiatari, to kneel on both knees.
Tui hanai, to enter through a low door by stooping.
Tui kebere, s. knee-cap.
Tui boio, v. to lose the way, to be bushed.
Tui a, v. to quiet.
Tuidae, s. rafter.

Tumou, *s.* small pole in *lakatoi*, parallel with *ikoda* but above *ilava*.
Tumuru. *See* Turumu.
Tunu a, *v.* to bake pottery. Tunutunu.
Tupi na, *s.* the tail (of birds).
Tupua, *s.* crown of the head. *See* Tubua.
Tupua, *a.* upright.
Tupua ai hehuhu, bald on crown.
Tupuahu, *a.* costive.
Tura na, *s.* a friend. (Of the speaker's sex.)
Tura dosi, a real, permanent friend, or friendship.
Tura rahai, a temporary friend or friendship.
Turi a, *s.* a bone.
Turia niava, backbone.
Turia rudu, rib.
Turia, *v.* to plait an armlet, to sew.
Turiabada, *s.* the name of a fish.
Turia duhu, *s.* a child who grows slowly.
Turia kirara, *s.* a child who grows fast.
Turiariki, *v.* to discompose, to vex.
Turituri, *s.* native rosewood.
Turiaturia, *adv.*, energetically, vigorously.
Turoa, *v.* to hollow out (as a canoe or tub).
Turua, *v.* the name of a bird, the laughing jackass.
Turua duiduina, fires in a row along beach.
Turubu, *s.* cassowary feather headdress.
Turu hanai, *v.* to wade across a river.
Turumu, *s.* goura pigeon. *See* Tumuru.
Tutu a, *v.* to spear by holding the spear in the hand, to bayonet, to buffet.
Tutuhi a, *v.* to strike the foot against a stone.
Tutuhi a, to mash, as ripe bananas.
Tutukatutuka, *v.* to stand firm, as a house or post in a strong wind, to be steady.
Tutuqata hahine, real wife with whom a man has lived from youth.
Tutututu a, *v.* to beat gently with clenched fist, as a sick person to relieve pain.

U

U is always sounded as oo in English, as in fool.
Uainananegai, *adv.* three days hence.
Uala, *s.* crocodile.
Uamagi, to stand in awe of.
Uamagi tauna, one who inspires awe.
Ubama, *s.* a hornet.
Ubi, *s.* the name of a bird.
Ubu a, *v.* to feed, as a child, or a pet, to cherish.
Uda, *s.* thick bush, forest.
Uda ia, *v.* to place in a box, canoe, &c.
Udo, *s.* also Hudo, the navel.
Udu, *s.* mouth, nose, beak.
Udu a, to carry a child astraddle on the neck.
Udu baribara, hammer-headed shark (?).
Udu bibina, lip.
Udu gogona, snoring.
Udu gogona e daemu, to snore.
Udu honu, mouthful.
Udu maduna, nostril.
Udu mauri, a chatterer.
Udu kibi, of a water-pot with spout.
Udu koba, flat nose.
Udu lahalaha, wide nose.
Udu mauri henia, to be saucy to, to jaw.
Uduguilai, *v.* to curse.
Udulata, *s.* the name of a fish.
Udu makohi, *s.* bleeding from the nose.
Udu nesenese, thin nose (as Europeans).
Udu resenaresena, narrow, thin nose.
Udumotu, the name of a fish.
Uhau, plural of *tauhau*, young men.
Uhe, *s.* the end of the yam, which is kept for planting; any seed for planting.
Uhe a, *v.* to turn over.
Uheaela, to turn right side up, to right.
Uhe a hebubu, to spill by turning over, to overthrow.
Uheoho, piece of cliff falling, as from earthquake.
Uhika, *s.* a wild duck.
Uihala, *s.* the yard to which one side of the crab-claw sail is fastened, the foot of which is tied to the mast.

Ukava, a large bird of prey, eagle.
Ulaeo, a fish.
Ulato, plural of *haneulato*, young woman ; also *ulatodia*.
Ulo, one kind of yam.
Ulo, to fetch wood and water by betrothed for her future husband.
Uloulo, *s.* maggots.
Ulu a, *v.* to climb, as a cocoa-nut tree.
Uma, *s.* a garden, an enclosed cultivated plot.
Uma hadoa, *v.* to cultivate.
Umu a, *v.* to paint the face with a device.
Umui, *pron. pl.* you.
Umui emui, *pron. pl.* your. *Umui emui ruma*, your house.
Una, Unauna, *s.* fish scale.
Una, there.
Unahi a, *v.* to scale a fish. *Qarume unahia*.
Unai, *adv.* there ; (opposed to *inai* here) ; that.
Unai negana, *adv.* then.
Unama, *interj.* a lie, "gammon."
Unamo, compound of *una* there, and *mo*.
Unananega, *adv.* four days hence. The unananega of Sunday would be Thursday.
Unauna, one kind of banana.
Unia, a fish.
Unu, *s.* breadfruit.
Unu, *adv.* there.
Unubamona, *adv.* like that.
Unuheto, *adv.* thus. (Away from the speaker).
Unuká, *adv.* contraction for *unu kaha*, on the other or off side, further.
Unukaratoma, *v.* to do thus.
Unukoautoma, said thus.
Ununega, *adv.* an indefinite future time.
Unuseni, *adv.* yonder, in that place.
Upamaino, *s.* the name of a game of play.
Ura, *s.* crayfish.
Ura, *v.* to will, wish, desire.
Ura henia, to love, to desire.
Ura henia lalodika, to desire, or love greatly.
Ura henia turiariki, to desire greatly, angry if not obtain.
Urana ura, to desire.
Ura dika, *a.* self-willed, headstrong.

Ura qalimu, a free man, in contrast to a servant who has to do the will of another.
Urara, name of a tree.
Ure a, *v.* to turn over a thing.
Uregadi, one kind of banana.
Urehegini, *s.* capsicum.
Uria, *s.* the month of August.
Urita, *s.* cuttlefish, octopus.
Uriuri, a brown colour; colour of Motuans skin.
Uro, *s.* native earthenware pot ; grindstone.
Uro bada, cauldron.
Uru, *s.* deep groaning ; stertorous breathing, as when near death. *Varani ganagana karaia hari ia uru mo ;* a generation.
Uru a, *v.* to climb.
Uru a diho, to dip.
Usi, *s.* penis.
Usiusi, *s.* pimple, wart, stye on eye.
Uto, *s.* float of fishing-net.
Utu, *s.* flood.
Utu, *s.*, louse.
Utu a, *a.* to draw water ; to cut off.
Utuadae, to rise as a flood.
Utua nege, to sever.
Utugomu regena, rump joint of pork.
Utuha, *s.* a meeting-place, where two villages meet by appointment.
Utuha, *v.* to make an appointment to meet at the *utuha*.
Utubada, *s.* very high tide. *Ututu bada*, deluge.

V

V is sounded as in English.
Vabala, hunting spear of white wood.
Vabara, vine with fruit like black grapes.
Vaboha, *s.* a lizard.
Vaboha, *v.* to be lowering and gloomy, of the sky. *Tano e vabohaia*.
Vabu, *s.* a widow, a widower, especially during the time of mourning.
Vabura, *s.* dusk, dark.
Vaburema, name of a shell-fish.
Vada, sign of present and past time.
Vadaeni, the end of, the finish ; that's all.
Vadaeni, *interj.* Enough ! *Adv.* quite.

Vadivadi, *s.* guests,. visitors.
Vadivadi, to visit. *E vadivadidiamu.*
Vādo, *v.* to live unmarried,. as a widow or widower. *Ia vado noho,* to be barren, of trees, &c.
Vado koriko, to remain unmarried, an abusive term.
Vādovādo, *s.* tall cocoanut tree.
Vadu, a chisel.
Vadumo, stick to which canoe is made fast.
Vae, hunting spear of white wood.
Vāga, *s.* catkin of the betel pepper.
Vāga (a little shorter than the above), to fast. *See Anivaga.*
Vaga, a temporary hut with ridge.
Vagaia, *v.* to shell, to take off the shell.
Vagege, *s.* jealousy, envy.
Vagilovagilo, to grow slowly, as a child.
Vagivagi, *s.* finger ring.
Vago, to feed, as children, or destitute.
Vagoai a, to hide, to suppress, as a crime or fault.
Vagoro, *s.* the bush after the grass has been burnt.
Vagoro, *v.* to clear the grass for a garden. *Vagoro karaia.*
Vagulai, preceded by *laka,* to turn away indignantly, contemptuously.
Vaha, *s.* the cheek; the opening at gills of fish.
Vahabada, a swollen cheek.
Vahaleleva, a fish.
Vahorita, *v.* to rob. (A term of reproach.)
Vahu, *s.* uncultivated land, bush.
Vahudagu, *v.* to startle by shouting.
Vahuvahu, *s.* Chinese rose.
Vai a, *v.* to take out of a pot, box, &c.; to discharge cargo. *Lakatoi anina vaia.*
Vaia, vavaia, prefixed to nouns or pronouns signifies, constantly, habitually. *I aia emu kara.*
Vaina, *s.* a small bag, a pocket.
Vainananega, *s.* three days hence. The vainananega of Sunday is Wednesday.
Vaira, *s.* the face, the front.
Vaira hamue, to scowl.
Vaira hūa, *v.* to frown.
Vaira huaia, melancholy, angry.
Vaira lao, *v.* to go to meet some one.
Vairana, of *lakatoi,* bows.
Vairanai, *prep.* before.

Vaisiri, *s.* the name of a fish. Also Vasiri.
Vaitani, *adv.* fin shed, ended. Used with a verb, as *Daroa vaitani,* also intensive, as *lasi vaitani.*
Vaivai, wild mango.
Vakera, large native rat.
Vakoda, *s.* a cane.
Vala, as *dina,* sun.
Vala dika, cloudy, overcast.
Vala namo, clear, bright.
Valahuvalahu, *adv.* with itaia, to see dimly, not to be able to distinguish persons.
Valakavalaka, *s.* mildew.
Valāu, *v.* to run a race.
Valavala, *s.* cobweb.
Valavala, midriff.
Vale a, to slap thigh, or buttock.
Vamu, *s.* animals fit for food.
Vanaga, *s.* the name of a small black fish.
Vanagalau, *s.* the name of a fish.
Vanagi, *s.* a small canoe.
Vanaba, a measure of time, generally used with negative, *se vanaha,* a short time.
Vanea, *s.* the name of a tree.
Vanea, *s.* flax from the bark of the vanea, from which the strongest dugong nets are made.
Vanega, *s.* (usually followed by ai) the day after to-morrow; the day before yesterday; hence, past time, not very long ago.
Vanota, one kind of black wallaby.
Vanovano, to be late, of a ship expected, or of a journey.
Vaoha, sea urchin.
Vapavapa, a fish.
Vapu, *s.* a widow (in mourning).
Vara, *v.* to grow; to be born.
Vara bada, luxuriant.
Vara, *s.* birth.
Vara bamona, cousins.
Varaguna, *s.* the first-born child; the elder of two persons spoken of.
Varahu, *s.* steam; perspiration.
Varaia, door fastened by cord, also box, *kohu,* &c.
Varani, *s.* yesterday.
Varani hanuaboi, last night.
Varavara, *s.* relations; dependents.
Vareai, to enter. To go inland to the plantations. *Ia e vareai.*
Vareai e lasilasi dinana, time about 2 o'clock.

Vari, name of a tree (the silk cotton).
Varia, dance before going on a voyage to get accustomed to keep awake.
Variri variri, v. to blink.
Varivari, s. looking-glass; glass window.
Varo, s. fishing-line; large net (for dugong).
Varo, sewing cotton.
Varo tauna, the owner of dugong net.
Varo, v. to line, as a basket.
Varo ta, a. ten full-grown cocoanuts. Niu varo ta.
Varotavarota. See Tau varotavarota.
Varovaro, s. veins; arteries; tendon.
Varubi, one kind of banana.
Varure, landslip. See Havarure.
Vaseha, v. to joke.
Vasi, v. to go to some one or to a place near, also of voice and sound, &c.
Vasiahu, s. hot water.
Vasika, s. a flint used as a knife; knife (superseded by kaia).
Vasilai a, v. to take a thing to one near, or to some definite place spoken of.
Vasiri. See Vaisiri.
Vasivasi, s. a sign of a coming event, as sneezing, muscular quivering, &c. Lauegu vasivasi.
Vata, s. the name of a banana stem from which inferior nets are made.
Vata, short ladder used for bananas.
Vata, Vatavata, s. ghosts; an unknown spirit supposed to have the power of killing whom he will.
Vatari tauna, or hahinena, a sorcerer or sorceress.
Vatavata, s. a ladder; a ghost.
Vauto, s. wild orange.
Vaura, s. cuscus.

Vava, to cover, as box with tin, cloth, &c.
Vava, a man's sister's children, a man's wife's brother's children.
Vavae, s. wick. (Introduced.)
Vave, to send for (persons).
Vavevave, to go to fetch, ia vavevave ela.
Vea, a. calm (in the day).
Vea, v. to be becalmed (in the day).
Vedaia, v. to pour water in a chatty or any water-vessel.
Vehadi, s. the name of a month (June).
Vehadi hirihiri, July.
Vehadi, name of tree.
Veo, s. brass or copper. (Introduced word.)
Verara, one kind of banana.
Veri a, v. to pull, to draw out, extract, to subtract.
Veriahu, to close in, as with fence, wall, &c.
Veri a isi, to pull up.
Veri a dae, to draw up.
Veri a tao, v. to steer towards land, to the left in coming into harbour.
Veri na, s. a company, as of people drawn or attracted by shoal of fish, &c., incorrectly used for class, company, &c.
Vero, v. to crawl, as a snake.
Vesi, s. semen maris.
Vesi gohugohu, region of bladder.
Veto, s. an abscess.
Vēvē, v. to run as water; to dissolve, to trickle.
Veve, descendants; a tribe named from an ancestor.
Veve hanaihanai, a. pavement.
Vidigara, skinny, bony.
Vilipopo, s. a sling.
Vine, s. vine. (Introduced.)
Viropo, blossom bud just bursting.
Viroro, fresh-water tortoise.

SENTENCES AND PHRASES.

What is thy name? Oi ladamu daika?
Where is thy house? Oiemu ruma edeseni ai?
Where is the Chief? Hanua lohia edeseni ai?
What have you come for? Oi dahaka totona oma?
When did you (*plu.*) come? Edananega umui oma?
When will you (*plu.*) go? Edananega umui baola?
I am hungry. Lau name hitolo.
I am thirsty. Lau ranu mate.
I want to sleep. Lau mahuta na koaulaia.
Bring some fire. Lahi a mailaia.
Bring some water. Ranu gurita a mailaia.
Bring some young coconuts. Karu haida ba mailaia.
Bring some bananas to sell. Bigu haida ba mailaia baia hoihoi.
What is the price of this? Inai dahaka davana?
What do you want for the fish? Qarume dahaka davana?
I don't want to buy. Lau asina hoihoi.
Go away (*sing.*) and return to-morrow. Oi lao, kerukeru ba lou mai.
I go the day after to-morrow. Lau vanegai bainala.
Put it in the house. Ruma lalonai ava atoa.
Bring in the food. Malamala mailaia.
Be quick. Kara haraga.
Come quickly. Aoma haragaharaga.
Sweep the house. Ruma daroa.
Cook the food. Aniani; or, malamala, nadua.
Is the food ready (cooked)? Aniani vada maeda hani?
Open the door. Iduara a kehoa.
Shut the door. Iduara ba kouahu.
Bring me some water that I may bathe. Ranu ba mailaia lau baina digu.
Where is the road? Dala edeseni?

Wash all the clothes. Dabua idoinai ba huria.

Wash the clothes to-day; we sail to-morrow. Dabua hari harihari ba huria; ai kerukeru baia heau.

How many canoes have gone? Vanagi auhida vada heau?

All the village has gone fishing. Hanua idoinai haoda lao.

Get the boat ready and we will go. Umui boti hagoevaia ita baita heau.

Lower the sail and put out the oars. Lara ava atoa diho, bara karaia.

The oar is broken. Bara vada qaidu.

Let us keep in-shore because the sea is rough. Ita badibadina lao hurehure garina.

Are you ill? Oi gorere hani?

Where is the pain? Hisi gabuna edeseni ai?

When did your illness begin? Edananegai oi gorere e vara?

Are you costive? Bokamu hetubuahu hani?

My child is very ill? Lau natugu e gorere bada.

Where have you come from? Oi ede amo mai?

Where are you going? Oi ede lao; or, Oi ede bo laomu?

Take it carefully or it will break. Abia namonamo makohi garina.

The sea is very rough? Davara vada e hurehure bada.

Wait until the wind drops, and then go. Umui noho lāi naria haine mate ba heau.

Come to-morrow and help me. Oi kerukeru baoma lau ba kahagu.

Come (*plu.*) every morning to work. Daba idoinai baoma gau ba karaia.

I will pay you when you have finished. Oi ba karaia vaitani, lau davana baina henimu.

I did not say so. Lau unu asina koautoma.

I did not send them. Lau idia asina siaidia.

I gave you plenty of food. Aniani momo lau umui na henimuiva.

Who will go with you? Daika oi ida lao.

I want to go fishing. Lau haoda lao urana na uramu.

Which hatchet do you desire? Edana ira oi o ura henia?

I will teach you every evening if you will come. Oi baoma lau adorahi idoinai baina hadibamu.

Why does he forbid them? Ia dahaka gau idia e koaudiatao?

SENTENCES AND PHRASES.

We are afraid of the sun. Ai dina garina a garimu.
The village boys are afraid of the foreigners. Hanua memero nao taudia garidia e garimu.
What are they doing? Idia dahaka o karamu?
The sun has turned. Dina vada eme gelo.
The sun has gone down. Dina vada dogu dobi vaitani.
The tide is rising. Davara vada hagaru.
It is high tide. Davara vada bada.
The tide is falling. Davara gomata e guimu.
It is low tide. Gomata vada e gui davara maragimaragi.
The sun is hot. Dina vada e garagara.
Let us seek a shade until evening. Ita kerukeru gabuna baita tahua, ela bona adorabi.
You go before and we will follow. Oi ba laka guna, ai oi murimu aia laka.
Call your companions and let us go. Umui bamomui a boilidia ita baitala.
I told you to wait here for me. Lau na koau umui iniseni noho lau ba narigu.
Tell them to go and sleep in the village. Idia ba koau henidia dia hanua lao bae mahuta.
Good-night all. Umui iboumui ba mahuta.

APPENDIX.

NAMES OF DIFFERENT KINDS OF BANANAS.

Akarua	Garokoni	Kusita
Oroa	Gudu	Meuraba
Oroua	Hagavara	Naimuru
Uregadi	Hola	Panaere
Unauna	Huitabu	Siogomu
Babaka	Kaiakiri	Taroma
Banaere	Kamea	Varubi
Dau	Kameamoa	Verara
Deure	Kokome	

NAMES OF FISH.

Abae	Bĕki	Dumu sisia
Ademela	Borebore	Duribaroko
Adia	Boboda	Gaburu
Ahakara	Budia	Gani
Ahuiahuia	Buna	Ganiahuota
Anama	Dae	Garava
Ariaoda	Dabutu	Huinaimi
Ialata	Dahudahu	Huhula
Ituari	Dahulu	Kavaitoro
Ono	Dalaia	Kila
Ororobu	Daladala	Kururu
Udulata	Daqula	Laumaere
Ulaeo	Daraki	Ladi
Unia	Derekaka	Lagai
Balala	Dinaha	Lagere
Barubaru	Dono	Lahalaha
Bebe	Duadua	Laheta
Bedo	Dumu	Lui

APPENDIX. 141

Maimera	Namumana	Taguma
Mabui	Qada	Tahure
Makoa	Qalabada	Tāla
Māmi	Qalaha	Tolo
Manariha	Ramuta	Vahaleleva
Maraua	Revo	Vanaga
Matakaka	Robu	Vanagalau
Matavabu	Rodu	Vapavapa
Meinchute	Siaro	Vasiri
Mida	Sio	
Naidae	Tadiva	

SHELL FISH.

Batata	Gumaulu	Laketo
Bedebede	Kaiva	Laro
Bisisi	Keadi	Maimai
Bobo	Kekerema	Mamalāu
Bokabada	Kevekeva	Mataatu
Bokani	Kevakulo	Minibore
Bokani bisisi	Kiribogairigaio	Mininuni
Bomaboma	Kirigaibogaibo ⁾	Nononono
Budugara	Kuadi	Nudugara
Butubutu	Kunukunu	Qamenau
Dala	Kururu	Roku
Dihudihu	Laia	Sirigogoha
Dudu	Laina	Siro
Gaiagaia	Lagalaga	Vaburema
Gili		

NAMES OF TREES.

Aniani	Budoa	Kavera
Araara	Gava	Keakone
Ori	Gea	Keavaro
Oroaoroa	Gilaki	Kerolo
Urara	Higo	Kilima
Besere	Hodava	Kohe
Borokó	Hotamu	Koukou
Budabuda	Kakabeda	Kuluha

Lataba
Maita
Magi
Mogo
Mudoru

Nala
Niu
Nonu
Sira

Turituri
Totō
Vaivai
Vari

NAMES OF YAMS.

Agavaita
Alo
Ulo
Badukalo
Bagara
Batu
Bubui
Divoi
Gata

Gete
Heiga
Kabukabu
Kahugo
Kemaiore
Kohi
Kokorogu
Korua
Lovai

Madina
Makota
Maloa
Manonoha
Minagoru
Papakadebu
Taitu
Tavea

NAMES OF BIRDS.

Odubora
Ogororo
Uage
Baimumu
Bisini
Bogibada
Digudigu
Duna
Gahuga namo
Galo
Gobu

Haba
Kaekae
Kalai
Kanage
Keboga
Kema
Kibi
Kiloki
Kisikisi
Kitogala
Kivivi

Koisere
Kouaga
Kunumaga
Lokohu
Manubarara
Nogo
Pune
Pune gobu
Turua
Turumu

COMPARATIVE VOCABULARY OF SEVEN NEW GUINEA DIALECTS.

THE first column in the following vocabulary represents the language spoken by the Motu tribe (see page 1 in Grammar). The second column is the dialect of Keapara or Hood Bay. The people of Bulaha, or Hood Point, speak the same language with slight variations. The inland villages, and also the large village of Kalo, speak almost the same dialect.

The third column is the language spoken in the large district of Galoma, a few miles east of Hood Bay.

The fourth column is that of South Cape. This dialect is spoken with some variations by the tribes scattered from Orangerie Bay to Milne Bay. The languages spoken at Heath Island and at East Cape are as different as those of Hood Bay and Galoma. Want of space has prevented these being included in the vocabulary.

The next column is from the west of Port Moresby, and presents the districts inland of Redscar Bay. Between Kabadi and Hall Sound are the villages of Naara; and these speak a language with more of the Maiva or Lolo element in it.

The sixth column represents the language spoken by the people of Maiva, Kivori, &c., west of Hall Sound. Closely allied to this is the Lolo dialect, spoken by the tribes in that large and populous district.

The last column, Toaripi, is a specimen of the languages spoken by the tribes in the Gulf of Papua. It is in many particulars essentially different, both in grammar and vocabulary, to the others, and is spoken by people darker in colour, and different in habits to those in the Eastern peninsula.

The words have been collected as follows:—In our college at Port Moresby we have youths from almost all the places above-mentioned. These have been there long enough to have a thorough knowledge of the Motuan. I printed the list of words and gave them out, a slip at a time, to be filled in by the most intelligent of the students. In this way several of them were completed by natives only, while in other cases the original lists were filled in by Rarotongan or Samoan teachers employed in our Mission. With the exception of Kabadi and Toaripi the whole of the words have been carefully read over with the natives of the several districts, and are as accurate as they can be made without a personal knowledge of the languages. In the case of Toaripi, the murder of Tauraki, the mission teacher, has deprived me of the opportunity of correcting the slips from there. The teacher was one of our most intelligent men, and by far the best linguist we had. Philology has sustained a loss in his untimely death. Some of the words collected by him were revised by Mr. E. G. Edelfelt, a gentleman who resided for some time at Motumotu. He objected to many of the words spelt with *d*, and thought *r* should be substituted, such as *siare* for *siade*, *da* for *ra*, &c., but as I have had no opportunity up to the time of going to press of deciding, I have left the words as the deceased teacher wrote them, merely pointing out the probability that in some cases *r* might be substituted for *d* and *vice versa*.

W. G. LAWES.

NOTE TO THIRD EDITION.

Keapara and Galoma have been revised by Rev. A. Pearse, South Cape by Rev. C. W. Abel, and Toaripi by Rev. J. H. Holmes, and Maiva by Rev. H. M. Dauncey.

W. G. LAWES.

15 June, 1896.

COMPARATIVE TABLE OF NEW GUINEA DIALECTS.

English	Motu	Keapara	Galoma	South Cape	Kabadi	Malva	Toaripi
above	atai	ahai	lai	ova	aruna	uvi	arari
afterwards	gabo	kabi	gapi	muriai	avoa	muri	aito
all	ibounai	maparara	mapararia	gamagari	bounana	ikoinai	foromai
anchor	dogo	rogo	rogo	ro	itoo	too	fave
and	mai	e	e	ma	mai	manu	eata
angry	badu	paru	paru	siaiau	iduava	opuere	kitouroi
arm	ima	gima	ima	nima	ima	ima	mai
arrow	diba	riba	ripa		dibaua	paki	farisa
ascend	daekau	raeeau	rarage	uavasee	kaekao	karaau	patai
ashamed	lemarai	opi ma	mara	taumacamaea	emaridiva	haumaea	memariti
ask	nanadai	renagi	lenagi	luesio	rauaina	vaknivakai	avaroi
awaken	haoa	vahoa	baoa	anhanoi	vanoa	vaona	sukaputapai
back	doru	kini	ou	dagira	pulipuli	kape	avasa
bad	dika	laava	laba	baoa	kaka	kia	malolo
bag (small)	vaina	goroa	pora	tana, topo	kana	mahoa	oroa
bamboo pipe	baubau	baubau	baubau	bauban	kemona	ireire	kika
banana fruit	bigu	hani	gabua	asai	lamana	uarupi	meae
banana-tree	dui	pukare	pagave	asailiena	koroi	akaea	arikaka
basket	bosea	balaa	poea	bosa	kakana	pohea	posea
bat	mariboi	maopa	maopa	mariboi		apoapo	kararouka
bathe	digu	rigu	rikn	dui aedui	kuru	uele	masukui
beach	kone	one	one	kerekore	kepaana	poe	miri
beeh-de-mer	korema	korema	awa	ieduba	kupe	korema	korema
beg	noinoi	nogi	nogi	avanori	nonina	noinoi	mealoki
bird	manu	manu	manu	manu	manu	rovorovo	ori
bite	koria	olia	olia	ieretai	arasiava	urina	putavai
black	koremakorema	ruparupa	ruparupa	dubaduba	kupakupa	uapulauapula	meuru
blind	matakepulu	ma abu haru	ma apuapu	mata kibukibu	makaerere	maha iau	ofaesosoro
blood	rara	lala	lala	osisina	rara	aruaru	ovo
board	leilei	bua	bua	morumoru	papaóna	lailai	susu
body	tau	auuipara	kapa gauna	tau	kau	hau	maoa

146 COMPARATIVE VIEW.

English.	Motu.	Keapara.	Galoma.	South Cape.	Kabadi.	Maiva.	Toaripi.
boil, v.	nadua	nanu	nalu	ilauriga	nakuna	tatuna	epai
bone	turia	iliga	iliga	siata	kuriana	uria	uti
bottle	kavabu	ma	ima	ile	kavapu	kavapu	kavapu
bow, s.	peva	pewa	pewa	siri	dipa	hunu	apo
boy	nero	melo	melo	nerumeru	urame	miori	siare
branch	rigi	raha	laga	lagana	reena	rena	rakai
breadfruit	unu	gunu	unu	unuri	aarupu	oki	seo
break (string)	motu	rui	rui	iemotu	okova	nohu	sarapai
break (stick)	qaidu	oru	oru	itagodu	para	healaurina	topukavai
break (skull)	kokoauru	paiurri	pairuru	oirapai	karauru	ahururuna	sukai
bring	mailaia	veahamaiagia	veamaiagia	ureama	maiaina	omaiaina	autiria
bring forth	mara	wala	kapi	ihaisu	paiau	mauri	miauai
broken	makohi	maa	ropa	taesi	pâpava	paa	toharai
brother (younger) or sister	tadina	arina	arina	auataumurita	kadina	hatina	marehari
brother (elder)	kakana	arinagune	ana	tuahana	kadina	aana	paua
butterfly	kanbebe	pepe	pepe	bebo	poióo	peropero	kaokao
buy (or sell)	hoihoi	boiboi	boiboi	uneune	inaina	kauakaua	itaialoi
came	oma	vehamai	veamai	ilaoma	kemaiva	omai	tiripe
cassowary	kokokoko	kirapu	kilabu	guinabou	viona	vio	uiva
centipede	aiha	haiva	gaiva	alihei	coraka	raaraa	cope
chest	geme	opa	komakoma	kapakapa	pasipasina	haharana	haipasa
chief	lohia	vele	bele	kuiau	ovin	ovia	pukaii
chief (high)	lohiabada	veleon	belegana	vasavasa	oviapaka	oviapaka	pukarirovaea
chin	hade	hare	gari	gaeagaea	vakeana	ate	uale
clothes	dabua	lapuga	labua	ruru	kupuna	havuni	puta
cloud (light)	ori	iloha	lauba	eaada	ori	authau	mea
club (stone)	gahi	gabi	paira	putupntu	sapiá	amaria	maholo
club (wood)	kaleva	lepe	goa	crepa	okuna	puraa	poti
cocoanut (tree)	niu	aima	palobo	nin	nin	tona	la
cocoanut (young fruit)	karu	lao	rao	aru	mauka	vei tona	lafaure
cocoanut (mature fruit)	niu	niu	niu	niu	niu	kilokilo	latororo
cold	keru	nagule		vaoo	vioua	ama	mekoko

NEW GUINEA DIALECTS.

English	Motu	Kerapara	South Cape	Kabadi	Maiva	Toaripi
come!	aoma	vehamai	laoma	omanai	mai	koatiria
come "	mai	vehamai	laoma	mai	mai	koatiria
conduct	kara	'ala	lanlau	vavai	vavai	mai
conquer	qalimu	walinnu	adidiri	oaka	aivala	ivara
cook, v.	nanadu	nann	lanriga	nakunaku	tatutatu	epui
cooked (done)	maela	hala	imaisa	cara	anati	sauai
cooking pot	uro	gulo	gureva	urona	uro	eraera
crayfish	ura	ki	vagima	o'una	aihi	makoko
crocodile	uala	lugaha	varagohe	uī	puaea	sapen
crowbar (planting stick)	isiva	gari	gori	si'o	ihiua	sima
cry	tai	agi	don	diareva	hai	fi auai
cup	kepere	peli	bia	ini'an	ouon	kakumoisa
cut	ivaia	boroa	nigoi	ivaia	inana	eraraia
dance	mavaru	pala	saga	varia	cuī	choi
dark	dibura	muna	masigiri	vapune kaiva	uabura	murumuru
day (to)	harihari	coma	vanta	iavaruna	bariu	iso
day (after to-morrow)	vanegai	waoma	asibena	maranina	elani	a
deceive	koia	wapa	bora	erepaniava	oina	rohorai
descend	diho	rigo	pesa	naeolo	riri	faukai
desire	ura	liliwaonagi	henna	uranada eurava	arina	hahea roi
dew	hnnu	amo	benben	ameru	pen	seo
die	mate	wareha	mate	ekeo	ari	opai
dirty (earthenware)	miro	milo	lii	mirona	opu	sirisiri
dish (earthenware)	nau	nagu	gaoba	kavia	ororo	saisa
displeased	lalodika	ao alava	nua banea	aokaka	aoma ekia	hai arara
distant	dandan	laulau	rohuroha	paana	homaa	savori
do	karaia	'ala	ginauri	vavaia	vavaina	pisosi, &c.
dog	sisia	waeha	vanuhe	oveka	naeha	ave
don't know	sedila	pana	ibai	inanō	iamotaina	aoaro
doorway	iduara	vanagi	dobila	akena	pihia	utape
dream	nihi	nivi	cnoeuai	inivi	nivi	hivahitatai
drink	inua	niua	nom	inura	moinu	laria

147

COMPARATIVE VIEW.

English.	Motu	Keapara.	Galoma.	South Cape.	Kabadi.	Maiva.	Toaripi.
drive (away)	luluα	iu	giu	aiduei	o'oma	uunu	larivatai
drum	gaba	kapa	kaba	boiatu	apa	imaravu	opa
dry	kaukau	auau	auau	pitapitari	akarona	ororo	halara
dwell	noho	alu	alu	min	miava	miaho	pavai
ear	tain	cha	ega	bea	kaina	hain	avauth
earth	tano	wano	arima	tano	kanona	ano	tetere
east	meiriveina	lahai ragena	lai ragena	earuabu	kaeaona	tototaina	kanritupe
eat	ania	hani	ganigani	ai	eaniva	moana	laria
eight	taurahaui	auravaivai	auravaivai	harigigi haiona	karavani	avavani	
elbow	din	gαnα wauwauna	ima laina	nimasiu	otuotu	ova	maikiri
enclose	koua	kanahabu	kanagabu	gudui	avina	kori kaiarona	sasaakai
evening	adorahi	lavilavi	labilabi	maimailahi	raviravi	lavilavi	mefautu
excrement	tago	age	age	koe	kae	hae	epai
eye	mata	ma	mi	mata	maku	maha	ohe
face	vaira	waira	birana	ao	ioinana	uairu	arofave
fall	keto	eo	eo kali	guri	kedi	cho	pitoi
fall (from height)	moru	corigo	peovali	beu	vairausi	cho	putoi
fat	digara	riga	ua	momona	mera	oho	tapare
father	tamana	amana	amana	tamana	auanana	hamana	oa
fear	gari	kali	kali	matausi	mekauva	marik	toro
feast	aria	lewa	lewa	soi	naku	tatu	sosoka
fierce	dagedage	alahala	galagala	mauamanabara	vaioo	lipulipu	otite
find	davaria	rawalia	rawalia	lobai	kavaria	tavauahauia	cavai
finished	ore	aiki	gabuwagi	ohi	eveova	eore	roroka roi
fire	lahi	alova	alova	oeagi	auaraara	iravu	lahari
first	guna	gune	reparepa	baguna	avai	uai	omopa
fish	(arume	mahani	magani	cama	veana	maia	ekaka
fish, v.	haoda	veabu	peabu	taueama	burua	vaeha	tapora
fish-hook	kimai	kau	kau	auri	kapona	naku	forama
five	ima	imaima	imaima	harigigi	ima	ima	mea farakeka
fly, s.	lao	nagama	nagama	urouro	aokama	aomehn	ropea
fly, v.	robo	robo	lobo	loi	rova	rovo	soeai
food	malamala	hauhauhaui		aiei	kepana	pohama	lariatao

NEW GUINEA DIALECTS.

English.	Motu.	Kerepunu.		South Cape.	Kabadi.	Maiva.	Toaripi.
foolish	kavakava	awaawa	awaawa	iauiaure	poopoo	poopoo	meakakare
foot	ae palapala	hage gunapa	gage	ae laulau	aena panavana	aepanava	morakou
forbid	kouualu	ilawai	ilawai	ribagudu	seiakao	hinavuna	savuteai
forehead	bagu	bagu	paku	deba	paunana	pau	harihari
forget	reaia	ugumagi lewa-lewa	palabu lewa-lewa	nualui	reanavu	reana	haisafai
four	hani	vaivai	baibai	hasi	vani	vani	rauka rauka
fowl	kokorogu	polo	bolo	kamkam	kokoroo	kokoro'u	kokoro
fowl (jungle)	keboka	walio	walio	kolauto	kepo	kepoko	hahauka
friend	turana	hana	gana	heriam	enakauna	enahau	moraitai
fruit	luahua	bua	buana	uaua	vekopi	vuana	fali
full	honu	bonu	bonu	monau	eakava	vonu	soauai
garden	uma	araha	laraga	oea	ropa	uma	oru
girl	rioa	ligo	ligo	urio	evara	veraiua	aravai
girdle (men)	sihi	ivi	ibi	sihi	sivi	ihavuri	si
girl	kekeni	iso	iao	siu	vaisi	uahoualio	more
go!	aola	hao	lao	lau	ouakana	mono	tereia
God	lao	hao	lao	lau	kana	ao	terai
good	dirava	palagu	palau	eaubada	dirava	tirama	karisu
good-night	namo	nama	nama	loro	nonoa	namo	lareva
grand parents	hamahuta	io ala	aloraioalu	aioni	kamenō	haparua	iavaia
grass	tubuna	ubuna	ubuna	tabuna	kupuna	kupuna	papa
grow	rei	mu	mu	rei	reina	tuvu	kavuru
hair	vara	ka'a	kala	tubu	kupu	lama	asai
have, take, get	hui	bui	bui	uru	iduna	vui	tui
hatchet	ira	giro	gilo	ilana	ira	uapila	nao ita
he	abin	habia	gabia	abi	kavarava	iiuu	avai
head	ia	i.	ia	ia	iana	ia	areo
head (back of)	qara	lepa	repa	nagara	roona	ara	aro
heart	gedu	keru	keru	gedu	ekuua	eku	measuta
heavy	kudou	komana	malaha	tutueveu	nuana	aoukoi	hai
heel	metaut	meau	meau	mou, poroho	sinaa	puma	pason
	ae gedu	hage gaguna	qalili	ae keduri	ekucku	neacna	morakiri

150   COMPARATIVE VIEW.

English.	Motu.	Kerepunu.	Galoma.	South Cape.	Kabadi.	Maiva.	Toaripi.
here (opposed to there)	inai	eraa	enai	inai	iinana	eineia	mehe
here (in this place)	iniseni	enai	enaio	inai	iinanai	eineia	reho
his, hers	ena	gena	gena	enana	ena	ena	areve
his (food)	iana	hana	gana	ana	nomaena	iana	areve
his	iena	ia gena	ia gena	ena	ena	iena	areve
house	ruma	numa	numa	numa	ruma	itu	uvi
house (sacred or plat-form).	dubu	lubu	rubu	dubu	ro'e	marea	cravo
how	ede heto	laa e alaiwa	laa e alaiwa	edoha	adiveka	aehoma	leafeare
hundred	sinahu	inabuna	inabuna	tataoharigigi simate.	ponpou	hinavu	....
hungry	hitolo	vio	laka	guriam	orana	mare'a	erosoanai
hunt	labana	apana	labana	bebedura	apana	apana	tapora
I	lau	au	lau	eau	nana	au	arao
ill	gorere	vi	vi	asiebo	epaova	inaoa	ekaloi
inside	lalo	aona	laona	alo	aona	aona	hai iri
jaw	auki	waivana	gare	gadigadi	nainainana	ate	uale
jealous	vagege	mlua	vemaeu	aiaromagigiri	vaiora	vaki'a	hai alala
kill	alaia	vagi	vagi	uruui	akunia	ahuna	paeaia
kiss	aheralu	verabu	rabule	alagoi	kevaipauva	pauna	meresisi
knee	tui	wauwau	ui	turi	aena	ovaova	arihau
knot	qadua	waua	bawau	hesio	podina	pova	fasai
know	diba	ripa	ripa	ata	isanava	iovina	ore
lamp-black	guma	milo	milo	dumu	uma	umu	alo
large	bada	kamu	kamu	lailai	babaka	apauana	rovaea
lash (a large canoe)	laia	ligoa	ligoa	seoliu	vaia	virina	fasai
laugh	kiri	mamai	mamai	maruhi	vaimai	iriri	area uai
lead	hakaua	vai	vevai	voeai	omakanaina	vakapa	lariovi
leaf	rau	lau	lau	luguna	meka	rau	tolo
leave alone	mia	mia	mia	otava	miava	menoho	areaca
left hand	lauri	auri	auli	seuseuri	carina	aoari	maiava
leg	ae	hage	gago	ae	ae	ae	mora
lie, s. and v.	koikoi	wapa		borabora	reparepa.	vaiohi	apeva

NEW GUINEA DIALECTS.

English.	Motu.	Keapara.	Galoma.	South Cape.	Kabadi.	Maiva.	Toaripi.
lie down	hekure	maoali	maoali	eno	enodo	enoti	iavai
life	mauri	maguli	mauri	mauri	mauri	mauri	makuri
light	diari	maea	malagani	marana	rani	ea	ovava
lightning	kevaru	laua	laua	namanamari	iamana	eimare	kevaru
lips	bibina	bibina	pipina	sopa	bibinana	pinana	taipi
listen	kamonai	amonagi	amonagi	gataiei	onova	ona	mapai
liver	ate	lau	nuanua	ate	nuana	aho	hai
loins	koekoe	voee	warimo	gasapaapaa	oeoena	hoana	kararapa
look	itaia	gia	ia	ilalau	isanava	ihana	ofaeavai
louse	utu	gu	u	tuna	nmuni	uhu	ape
lungs	baraki	ae	gae	ateburoburo	apaapa	iua	....
male	maruane	manuwaro	maruane	tamoana	kauna	koa	kaisava
man	taunimanima	auuilimalima	anuilimalima	tan	kauda	maearima	karu
man (as opposed to woman).	tau	au	au	tau	kau	hau	vita
many	hutuma	guma	uma	moutuana	ko'uaua	mako	rauapo
marry	headava	vearawa	begarawa	tavasora	vevavine	haoainivo	raeai
mat	geda	gepa	gepa	leiaha	eka	ire	kite
milk (and breast)	rata	la qarana	la qarwna	susu	rakana	rata, tutu	ko
mine	egu	gegu	geku	enagu	euna	o'n	arave
mine (/food)	lanegu	augegu	au geku	enagu	euna	aueu	arave
mine (/food)	lauagu	auagu	auagu	agu	duna	aua'u	arave
noon	hua	bue	bue	navalai	uena	naoa	paparo
morning	daba	lapa	lapa	maraitomtom	kabaerere	lani	miori
morrow (to)	kerukeru	lapalnga	pogipogi	maraitom	marana	mara	vevere
mother	sinana	inana	inana	sinana	aidana	hinana	lou
mother (or father) in-law.	ravana	ahama	agama	bosiana	ravana	rauana	ova
mountain	orooro	holo	golo	oeatupi	aapu	oeo	raepa
mouth	udu	muru	muru	ava	ake	pina	ape
name	ladana	arana	arana	esa	akanaua	ataua	rare
navel	udo	bulo	bulo	usona	puko	botoa	raravo
neck	aio	liaigo	gaigo	gado	kemona	aio	kavarehan

English.	Motu.	Keapara.	Galoma.	South Cape.	Kabadi.	Maiva.	Toaripi.
net (*fishing*)	reke	lee	lō	hiaua	roena	lee	rehe
new	matamata	valigu	walibu	harihariu	makamaka	mahamaha	are
night	hanuaboi	pogi	bogi	maiona	vapukana	lavi	faita
no	lasi	aikina	noaia	niṟee	veʼo	ahai	kao
nose	udu	ihu	iru	isu	itu	itu	overa
offspring	natuna	nauna	nauna	natuna	nakuna	nahuna	atute more
olden time	sene	lauvoha	lauvagi	manuga	avainana	uaivaha	evera
one	tamona	obuna	abinna	esega	kapoa	hamomona	farakeka
only	siboma	gerehaua	gereana	iaboin	sipona	kipona	harin
ours (*exclusive*)	ai emai	aigema	aigemai	aiemamai	naida emai	aiemai	elavo
paddle v.	kalo	leva	leba	ninnaoi	aona	vote	teisaria
paddle s.	hode	leva	leba	vose	odo	vote	teisa
pain	hisihisi	vi	bibi	amamana	nunnunva	haiara	hehea
palm (*of hand*)	ima lalona	gima aona	labaloea	nima alona	pauava	ima aoaa	morakou
paradisea raggiana	lokohu	tiake	tiake	sini	oou	inehi	ho
peace	maino	maino	maino	roni	maino	vaivua	tairu
pearlshell	mairi	alo	lalo	giuiuba	mairi	mairo	isave
penis	usi	waea	waea	duga	usina	ani	fe
pettieoat	rami	rami	awai	nogi	divana	kiva	mate
piece	taina	ina	iala	begana	ka	hana	taheka
piece (*small*)	sisina	kirikiri	lipilipi	begana	wakn'a	papana	taheka
pig	boroma	pae	pac]	sarai	boroma	aiporo	ita
pigeon	pune	buno	pune	gabmbu	raurdea	reuria	sna
place n.	gabuna	kabuna	abu	asa	apuna	ekana	oti
place v.	atoa	ao	ole	tore	koreado	horotina	vinvai
play	kadara	ulaula	ulaula	aihea	enopoo	papuru	avaroi
pleased	lalo namo	ao uama	hao nama	nua iroro	aononoa	aona cnamo	hailareva
porpoise	kidului	ihu	ihu	uriuriabobo	uriaua	kaipu	maurisa
pour	seia	popoa	wagi	ini	poura	heina	hiveia
power (*generally supernatural.*)	siahu	iabu	iabu	gigibori	sian	hiavu	aihchea
pregnant	rogorogo	uvia	inu	boga	memeroa	puna	ereovai
pull	veria	kero	golia	momosi	verina	verina	aruvaia

NEW GUINEA DIALECTS.

English.	Motu.	Keapara.	Galoma.	South Cape.	Kabadi.	Maiva.	Toaripi.
rain	medu	gupa	kupa	uabu	upa	avara	lai
rainbow	kevau	ewau	lalaupu	vari	evau	opa	levai
rat	bita	uluve	ulube	ibou	kaua	kaua	aili
refuse (reject)	kakakaka	vilalavilala	lalalala	buiabuia	pairapaira	viro	mohari
rejoice	koauedeede	ilaperehopo	ila velavelave	tauotaota	paoava	uvo	kaeavauai
relations	moale	verere	berele	kode	raauva	aonamo	hailarevaroi
return	varavara	walawala	walawala	ehana'eao	koaena	hatiaana	paumarehari
riches	lou	waiule	labure	uio	erō	mue	forerai
right (hand)	kohu	linala	laula	gogo	diaada	kepu	etau
ripe	idiba	riba	riba	tutuna	idibana	itipa	toare
river	nnage	ola	ili	buina	mairoo	aiva	mea
road	sinavai	wai	wai	saga	akena	ate	inai
rope	dara	laopara	lara	eda	kere'a	taeara	otiharo
run	qanau	wanau	aiai	tari	onan	anan	horou
sacred	heau	laka	rabu	aitautau	veau	veau	soea
sago	helaga	veaha	begaha	tabuna	rove	rove	ovariave
sail, s.	rabia	rapia	lapia	rapia	rapia	pareo	poi
salt	lara	la	lula	vorivori	idinua	raea	auvia
sandbank	dameua	lama	rama)	arita	dina	tamena	makaikara
satisfied	boe	nukunuku	iluilu	daudau	toro	pau	uiri
scatter	loka kunu	guramae	iabu	boka sese	amoulcuva	aniari	erefefese
seold	karoho	lobolobo	lobolobo	taaaorigori	kapanana	otaraina	tovouseai
sea	koaukoau	veila	ilaila	diraha ariri	ekduva	aviavi	seravui
sea (deep)	davara	lama	rama	gabogabo	kavara	aku	makaikara
sea (rough)	gadobada	lawapara	rawapara	gabotum	kavarapakaua	akupaka	matorie
seek	hurehure	au	lapoa	vovori	rōia	roio	mataiva
send	talua	abu	abu	iooi	kaura	tavuna	eli
seven	hitu	ugu	unagi	hetaunari	uraina	uhuna	itapai
		uabere aura-	auraoi wabuna	harigigi rabui	karakoi kapea	avaihau hamo-	
		vaivai				mo	
shark	qalaha	paewa	paowa	baeva	oava	etoeto	itari
shelf (table)	pata	kolekole	balabala	hata	varana	itara	posa
shield, s.	kesi	gei	mali	opea	oroau	keti	laua

COMPARATIVE VIEW.

English	Motu	Keapara	Galoma	South Cape	Kabadi	Maiva	Touripl
ship	lakatoi	lakaoi	lakaoi	vaka	aunakoi	aunohi	vavaca
short	qadogi	upa	upa	kuukun	'ope'ope	koona	haruna
shoulder	paga	alo	alo	dabaearona	aropakuna	aro	soru
shout	lolo	oho	gogogogo	vovo	oova	cio	isei
side (by the)	dekena	lahana	elema	haserina	apanana	horena	haekao
sign	toana	rahailia	bairia	hciheinoi	koana	hoana	pupusukai
sink	muta	magu	palupulu	sariri	inukeo	euhu	toitapai
sister	taihuna	arina	arina	rouna	a'opana	haivuna	uaroa
sit	helai	aluali	aluali	hava	miado	miati	anavai
six	tauratoi	auraooi	anlaoi	harigigi esega	karikoi	avaihan	....
skin	kopi	opi	opi	opi	vaerana	parua	ruru
sky	guba	guba	bueuluku	gareva	kaakaana	kupa	kauri
sleep	mahuta	maun	man	eno	onova	parua	ivutu
small	maragi	kiri	kirikrí	gagiri	mara'i	papana	soieka
smell, v.	bona	eno	bona mocna	panena	makaana	timi	muia
smoke	qalahu	kobu	mugo	asu	siauna	hiavu	aikoela
snake	gaigai	gelema	ma	nota	paipai	elau	ikaroa
song (hymn)	ane	mari	mari	vana	rari	hui	fara
south	diho	labainaina	gaburigo	eavana	asiaona	ahidaina	seipi
speak	koau	ila	ila	ribai	esiava	avi	omoi
spear	io	olova	olova	alahia	uka	auarai	hara
speech	ere	kalo	rorirori	arina	maora	maiana	uri
speech (language)	gado	kalo	kalo	arina	maora	maiana	uri
spirit	fauna	palagu	laupa	carucarun	launa	anva	ove
spit, v.	kaundi	auinu	auiulu	gariso	ainuku	atoti	pca
stand up	toreisi	gulaai	kululai	toro	koore	mikiri	itoia
star	hisiu	gibu	biu	ipora	visiu	vihiu	koru
steal	henao	lema	lema	andhari	vainao	vainao	torea
stomach	boka	inage	uliina	boka	sinae	nua	erehoron
stone	nadi	vāu	ban	veu	vakuna	pihara	fave
stone, v.	hodoa	vau	laqa	tarai	viunava	ahuna	toaia
store house	roge	linaha numaua	laula numaua	samala	roke	itukoikoina	uvi seicka
straight	maoro	rori rori	lagoa	dudurai	neoro	vero	haura

NEW GUINEA DIALECTS.

English.	Motu.	Keapara.	Galoma.	South Cape.	Kabadi.	Mulva.	Toaripl.
strike (downwards)	botaia	waria	waria	tarai	upinava	ovina	toaia
string	varo	waro	waro	maina	poan i	uaro	ela
strong	goada	iliga	iliga	adidiri	iran	tavuru	rofo
substance (flesh)	anina	viroho	gania	aniona	unina	anina	maca
sugar-cane	tohu	omu	obu	garu	ake	oraova	ase
sun	dina	haro	garo	mahaua	akonu	veraura	sare
sweet potato	kaemadahu	mokela	mokela	kauua	iniven	taakaema	kauari
swim	nahu	nabu	nabu	tuba	na'ava	na'u	harivein
tail (quadruped's)	inua	iguna	giuna	delena	inna	aarena	aru
take	laohaia	luagia	faoagia	laei	ekanaina	aonina	aveterin
taro (plant)	talo	ale	ken	udo	rire	hovoo	soera
teach	hadibaia	gaharana	vebariba	hcata	vaisavaisa	ovaiovina	sabiriaraia
ten	qanta	geria	kapanana	saudondoi	ouka	haranhaen	......
theirs	edia	haria	geria	euadi	eda	ekia	creve
theirs (food)	adia	warna	garia	adi	ada	akia	creve
there	unai	wanai	wa	tenei	aarupu	uaa	rcha
there	unuseni	ila	wanal	nei	nananai	uaa	laisiei
they	ilia	vahapara	ila)	isi	iada	in	ereo
thigh	mamu	magivi	paga	gasa	di'udi'una	ape	maute
thin	severa	gemu	magipi	caroearo	kevekeve	nivinivi	sesera
thine (food)	emu	hamu	gemu	enau	emuna	emu	ave
thine	amu	oigemu	gamu	an	amu	amu	ave
thine (food)	oiemu	hau	goigemu	oaenam	emu	oiemu	ave
thing	gau	ugamagi	gau	ginaari	kanuna	nanu	etau
think	laloa	oi	uamagi	muatui	risavu	laonanu	haikaeai
thon	oi	oioi	goi	oa	onina	oi	ao
three	toi	orolo	oi	haiona	koi	aihau	oroisoria
throat	gado	pia	ronorono	gado	akonana	ako	kavare
throw away	tahoa	piahoa	laqa	tu	viuna	kapona	toapaia
thus	negea	veiana	laqaoa	gabaei	viuna	neena	putapai
tide (falling)	bamona	manara ehauna	beaina	doha	boinana	avana	mafeare
time	komadagui	lahani	lina	magu iesiva	eomaka	para eahi	maovai
	nega		lagani	huiana	enona	lani	mea

COMPARATIVE VIEW.

English.	Motu.	Keapara.	Galoma.	South Cape.	Kabadi.	Maiva.	Toaripi.
tobacco	kuku	kuku	kuku	kuku	kuku	kuku	kuku
toe	ae qagiqagi	hage ririna	gage lirina	ae gigi	'ola'olana	ae uanuan	mora keka
tongue	mala	mae	mala	memena	mala	maea	uri
tooth	iso	rua	rua	mo'a	nise	nihe	tao
tree	au	hau uba	gaubu	ocagi	au	matiu	tola
true	momokani	aunauna	aunauna	mamoltoi	monooi	tohanu	kofa
turtle	matabudi	haohao	gaogao	vonu	a'en'ena	vonu	akeake
two	rua	lualua	lualua	rabui	rua	rua	oragoria
two days hence	uainananegai	waomana	warerepogoni	imaisina	maraniaona	uelani	iso
two days hence (more than)	unananegai	wawaomana	waunliraga	galilina	tapaverere	uaelani	poaru
two (men)	rorua	luara	lalugoi	rabui	kandaruda	terarua	ereuka
untie	ruhaia	luga	ruva	cairi	riasa	ruvuna	felaukei
village	hanua	vanuga	banua	eanua	vanua	aiara	karikara
visitor	vadivadi	wariwari	variva	taunana	kodina	vaki	sariva
vomit	munuta	mumua	mumua	nuarive	urava	aiora	musiavai
voyage (to go)	hiri	viri	vili	adaadansi	lio	viri	salima
walk	laka	laa	lou	tautausi	kana	kaa	tereia
walk (about)	lou	laabolaabo	laivalaiva	hareharensi	epoepo	kaoao	moraveita
wallaby	magani	wagi	wagi	vavauri	vaiaru	itavala	pisoru
war	alala	veali	beali	iala	akunku	ou	maula
warriors	tuari	au veali	au mala	iala	akuaku kauda	huari	semese
wash v.	huria	puligi	puligi	denri	ru'ana	utunaina	masukai
water	ranu	nanu	nalu	goila	veina	vei	ma
we (exclusive)	ai	ai	ai	ai	naida	ai	lao
we (inclusive)	ita	ia	ia	ita	isada	aika	ereita
weak	manokanaoka	moila	lepei	beruberu	manomanova	aveave	pataita
went	ela	lao	leo	lano	kekuna	eao	sisisi
west	tahodiho	lahai rigona	haro riboribona	ealasi	variana	tivotaina	avaru
					knivapai		
wet	paripari	nupa	nupa	buta	eveïvra	veivei	surusuru
what?	dahaka?	rahau?	ragau	saha	kava	tava	larerekaru
where	edeseni?	arigia	ariai	aidobu	aenaiva	acae	lemoa

NEW GUINEA DIALECTS.

English	Motu	Keapara	Galoma	South Cape	Kabadi	Maiva	Toaripi
which?	edana?	hauarigia	ariai	aitea	aenava	aeena	lehara
white	kurokuro	uloulo	urouro	posiposi	raran	rauaraua	measea
who?	daika?	laii	liai	eai	kāi	tai	leisa
widow	vabu	wapu	wabu	vabu	opu	uapu	ualelese
wind	lai	agi	agi	mana	avivina	lani	mea
wind (north)	mirigini	walaka	gabuano	heubeu	marairaun	maraira	malulu
wind (south-east)	laulabada	wau	wāiau	horiborimai	vareaua	vaura	mauta
wind (north-west)	rahara	avala	avala	ealasi	revona	varuru	avara
woman	hahine	ravine	babine	sine	vavine	vavine	ua
wound (*by spear*)	qodaia	kinia	kinia	aidilhai	oona	komona	sukai
yam	maho	mala wapa	gani	apoi	pure	taa	maho
yes	oi be	ina	namu	e. aboiesaha	ea	ain	a
yesterday	varani	warahani	waragani	lahi	ravina	uarani	area
you	umui	omi	mui	omi	uiida	uai	co
young man	tauhau	au varigu	koloa	hevari	oreore	hivitoi	milafu
your's (*food*)	amui	hami	gami	ami	amui	ami	eve

Sydney: Charles Potter, Government Printer.—189

www.ingramcontent.com/pod-product-compliance
Lightning Source LLC
Chambersburg PA
CBHW020306170426
43202CB00008B/513